MANCHESTER
Secret & Strange Places to Visit

Paul Chrystal

- for Rachael, Rebecca, Michael, Simon & Sara

DestinWorld
publishing

"Wisdom is the main thing; therefore get wisdom, and when you've got it you'll get understanding. Engage with wisdom and she'll lift you up; she will bring you distinction when you embrace her."

- Proverbs 4:7, **Manchester Central Library motto**

First Edition 2025

ISBN: 978-1-7398194-5-3

Front cover image ©Haydon Waldek; Maps by Simonetta Giori

© 2025 Paul Chrystal

British Library Cataloguing-in-Publication Data

A catalogue record for this book is available from the British Library.

Published by Destinworld Publishing Ltd.

www.destinworld.com

Printed in China

FSC
MIX
Paper
FSC® C145202

Acknowledgements

Thanks to Heather Roberts, Archivist and Museum Manager at Royal Northern College of Music for permission to use the images of Alice Pitfield's locks of hair as owned by the Pitfield Trust – and to Manchester Digital Music Archive for their assistance in facilitating this. Thank you to John Mee for permission to use his stunning photos of Afflecks as at *www.johnmeephotography.com*

The Communications Department at Manchester City Council kindly allowed me to photograph and use the giant bee which is on display in Manchester Central Library - *communications@manchester.gov.uk* - and on our back cover.

Thanks to Emma McBeath, Heritage Manager, The Pankhurst Centre for permission to use the photograph showing one of the group of women hired as apprentices in construction skills to help in the rebuilding of 60–62 Nelson Street, now the Pankhurst Centre.

Max Wieland, of the Communications Team at Stockport Council was kind enough to allow me to use the wonderful close-up of Old Father Time on Winter's Clockhouse in Little Underbank in Stockport, so my thanks to him.

Aidan O' Rourke gave permission for use of the evocative and disturbingly contemporary statue 'Adrift.' Gemma Parker of the Modernist Society and Magazine has allowed me to use the image of their shopfront. The photo of The Lowry comes courtesy of "Marketing Manchester/Rich J Jones".

The images of Joy Division's Ian Curtis and James's album cover, *La Petite Mort*, come courtesy of Simon James Crossley; *www.simonjamescrossley.com*. As do his photos of the sumptuous and fantastical Richmond Tea Rooms and the Gita Bhavan Hindu Temple.

Olive Youmbi of Valé et Oli - a joint venture between Valery Touchet & Olive Youmbi - has kindly given permission to use two of her beautiful, colourful handmade fabrics, based on the cultural references of African wax print. She then creates scarves, accessories and homewares, taking apart her fabrics and, using patchwork and quilting techniques, building them back together into practical, beautiful items for everyday use. This comes via Anneka Woods, Marketing & Digital Officer for Manchester Craft and Design Centre.

Margaret Lawless, photographer of the beautifully bizarre *White Nancy* at Bollington, has given permission for me to use her image via the Copyright and Licensing Team at Art UK. The image of the palatial John Rylands Library comes courtesy of "Marketing Manchester/Rich J Jones".

About the Author

I went to the universities of Hull and Southampton, where I studied classics (BA Hons and MPhil), and Sorbonne University, Paris; then for the next 35 years I worked in medical publishing.

More recently I have been history advisor to various Yorkshire visitor attractions, writing features for national newspapers, and broadcasting on talkRADIO, History Hack, BBC local radio all over the place, on Radio 4's 'PM' programme and on the BBC World Service.

I am a contributor to a number of history and archaeology magazines, and TV and radio programmes, and the author of over 160 books published on a wide range of subjects including classical history, social and industrial history, women's studies, the BAOR, the 'Troubles', pandemics (including COVID-19) and epidemics, biowarfare and many local histories.

I am past editor of York History, journal of the York Archaeological & York Architectural Society and of Yorkshire Archaeological Journal. I am contributor to and a regular reviewer for 'Classics for All', an editorial advisor to Yale University Press and a contributor to the classics section of OUP's 'Bibliographies Online'. My books have been translated into Chinese and Japanese.

By the Same Author

Bramhall Through Time

Old Fallowfield

Old Didsbury

The Pubs of Manchester (in press)

A History of Britain in 100 Objects

The Book in the Ancient World: How the Wisdom of the Ages was Preserved

A History of the World in 100 Pandemics, Plagues & Epidemics

World-Changing Women: 150 Women who Rewrote the Histories of Ancient Egypt, Israel, Greece and Rome

Women at Work in World Wars I and II: Factories, Farms and the Military and Civil Services

'The Reading Girl' by Giovanni Ciniselli (1832–1883). She was brought from Italy by Daniel Adamson, the first chairman of the Manchester Ship Canal Company and then gifted to the Manchester Central Library by his family in 1938.

But what is she reading we all ask? The Library reveals that, originally, it was a poem called The Angel's Story, which was printed on paper and pasted into her marble book. Yet, by the time she reached the library, this had disappeared. It is probably the poem by Adelaide Anne Procter published in 1843 by J.M. Dent in 'Legends & Lyrics & Other Poems by Adelaide Anne Procter'.

Contents

Once in a century restoration and redevelopment of the town hall and albert square continues apace with a completion date in 2026

AREAS OF MANCHESTER

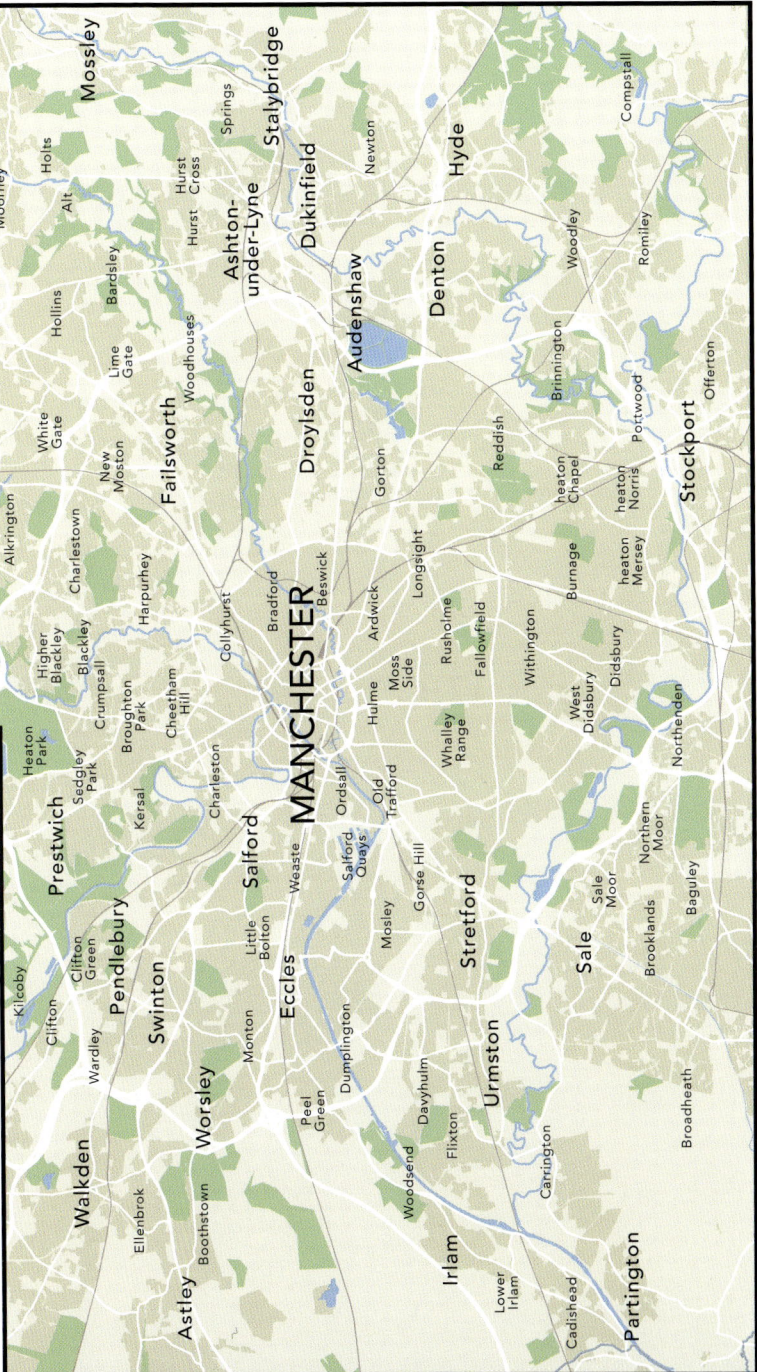

CENTRAL MANCHESTER

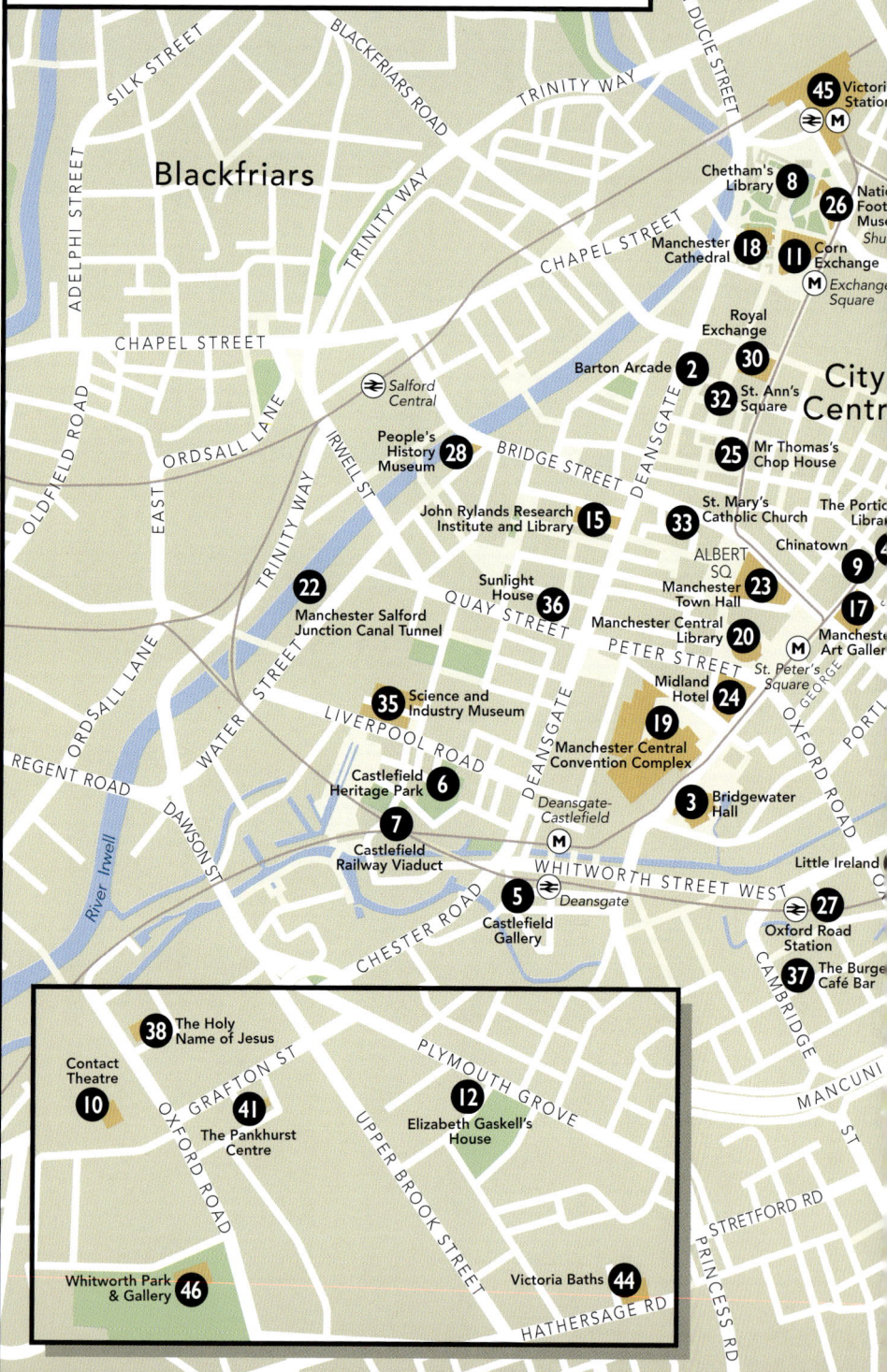

Blackfriars

City Centr

- 45 Victori Statior
- 8 Chetham's Library
- 26 Natic Foot Muse *Shu*
- 18 Manchester Cathedral
- 11 Corn Exchange
- *Exchange Square*
- 30 Royal Exchange
- 2 Barton Arcade
- 32 St. Ann's Square
- 25 Mr Thomas's Chop House
- The Portic Libra
- 28 People's History Museum
- 15 John Rylands Research Institute and Library
- 33 St. Mary's Catholic Church
- 9 Chinatown
- 23 ALBERT SQ. Manchester Town Hall
- 17 Mancheste Art Galler
- 22 Manchester Salford Junction Canal Tunnel
- 36 Sunlight House
- 20 Manchester Central Library
- 24 Midland Hotel
- *St. Peter's Square*
- 35 Science and Industry Museum
- 19 Manchester Central Convention Complex
- 6 Castlefield Heritage Park
- 7 Castlefield Railway Viaduct
- 3 Bridgewater Hall
- 5 Castlefield Gallery
- *Deansgate-Castlefield*
- *Deansgate*
- Little Ireland
- 27 Oxford Road Station
- 37 The Burge Café Bar

Salford Central

River Irwell

- 38 The Holy Name of Jesus
- 10 Contact Theatre
- 41 The Pankhurst Centre
- 12 Elizabeth Gaskell's House
- 46 Whitworth Park & Gallery
- 44 Victoria Baths

Street labels: SILK STREET, BLACKFRIARS ROAD, TRINITY WAY, GREAT DUCIE STREET, ADELPHI STREET, CHAPEL STREET, ORDSALL LANE, EAST, IRWELL ST, TRINITY WAY, OLDFIELD ROAD, CHAPEL STREET, BRIDGE STREET, DEANSGATE, QUAY STREET, PETER STREET, GEORGE, OXFORD ROAD, PORTL, WATER STREET, LIVERPOOL ROAD, DEANSGATE, ORDSALL LANE, DAWSON ST, REGENT ROAD, CHESTER ROAD, WHITWORTH STREET WEST, CAMBRIDGE, MANCUNI, OXFORD ROAD, GRAFTON ST, PLYMOUTH GROVE, UPPER BROOK STREET, ST, STRETFORD RD, PRINCESS RD, HATHERSAGE RD

▼ Map continues to left ▼

OUTER MANCHESTER

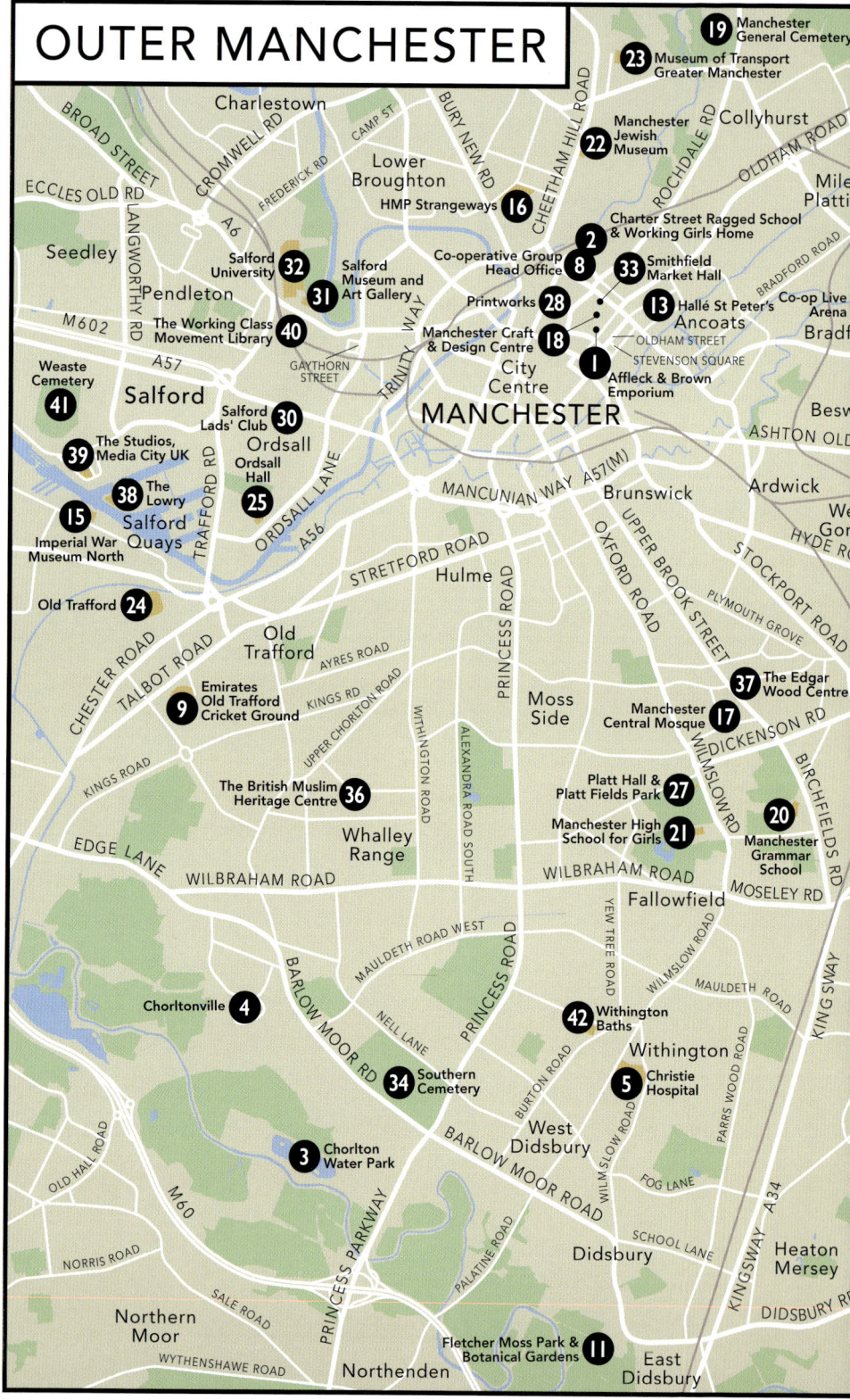

Manchester
General Cemetery **19**

Museum of Transport
Greater Manchester **23**

Charlestown

CAMP ST

CROMWELL RD

FREDERICK RD

BROAD STREET

ECCLES OLD RD

LANGWORTHY RD

A6

Seedley

Pendleton

M602

A57

Lower
Broughton

BURY NEW RD

CHEETHAM HILL ROAD

Manchester
Jewish **22**
Museum

Collyhurst

ROCHDALE RD

OLDHAM ROAD

Mile
Platti

HMP Strangeways **16**

Salford
University **32**

Salford Museum
and Art Gallery **31**

The Working Class **40**
Movement Library

GAYTHORN
STREET

TRINITY WAY

Charter Street Ragged School
& Working Girls Home

Co-operative Group **8**
Head Office **2**

Printworks **28**

Manchester Craft **18**
& Design Centre

City Centre **1**

MANCHESTER

33 Smithfield
Market Hall

13 Hallé St Peter's

Ancoats

OLDHAM STREET

STEVENSON SQUARE

Affleck & Brown
Emporium

BRADFORD ROAD

Co-op Live
Arena

Brad

Besw

ASHTON OLD

Weaste **41**
Cemetery

Salford

The Studios, **39**
Media City UK

The Lowry **38**

Salford
Lads' Club **30**

Ordsall

Ordsall **25**
Hall

ORDSALL LANE

A56

MANCUNIAN WAY A57(M)

Brunswick

Ardwick

UPPER BROOK STREET

We
Gor
HYDE RO

STOCKPORT ROAD

15 Salford
Quays

Imperial War
Museum North

TRAFFORD RD

Old Trafford **24**

CHESTER ROAD

TALBOT ROAD

Old
Trafford

AYRES ROAD

KINGS RD

UPPER CHORLTON ROAD

STRETFORD ROAD

Hulme

PRINCESS ROAD

Moss
Side

OXFORD ROAD

PLYMOUTH GROVE

37 The Edgar
Wood Centre

Emirates **9**
Old Trafford
Cricket Ground

KINGS ROAD

The British Muslim **36**
Heritage Centre

Whalley
Range

WITHINGTON ROAD

ALEXANDRA ROAD SOUTH

Manchester **17**
Central Mosque

DICKENSON RD

Platt Hall & **27**
Platt Fields Park

Manchester High **21**
School for Girls

WILMSLOW RD

BIRCHFIELDS RD

20 Manchester
Grammar
School

MOSELEY RD

EDGE LANE

WILBRAHAM ROAD

MAULDETH ROAD WEST

NELL LANE

PRINCESS ROAD

WILBRAHAM ROAD

Fallowfield

YEW TREE ROAD

WILMSLOW ROAD

MAULDETH ROAD

KINGSWAY

Chorltonville **4**

BARLOW MOOR RD

42 Withington
Baths

Withington

PARRS WOOD ROAD

Chorlton **3**
Water Park

Southern **34**
Cemetery

BURTON ROAD

West
Didsbury

BARLOW MOOR ROAD

WILM SLOW ROAD

5 Christie
Hospital

FOG LANE

SCHOOL LANE

A34

OLD HALL ROAD

M60

NORRIS ROAD

SALE ROAD

PRINCESS PARKWAY

WYTHENSHAWE ROAD

Northern
Moor

Northenden

PALATINE ROAD

Fletcher Moss Park & **11**
Botanical Gardens

Didsbury

Heaton
Mersey

DIDSBURY RD

East
Didsbury

Map labels:
OLDHAM ROAD
Newton Heath
DROYLSDEN RD
LORD LANE
BRISCOE LANE
Phillips Park Cemetery
Clayton
NORTH RD
BANK ST
TURING WAY
6 Clayton Hall Living History Museum
ASHTON NEW RD
A662
Openshaw
Fairfield Moravian Settlement
10
ASHTON OLD ROAD
CHAPMAN STREET
Gorton Monastery 12
A57
STANLEY GROVE
Gorton
HYDE ROAD
MOUNT ROAD
GORTON ROAD
MATTHEWS LANE
Levenshulme
North Reddish
STOCKPORT ROAD
Reddish
REDDISH ROAD
Heaton Moor
South Reddish
MOORSIDE RD
HEATON MOOR RD
WELLINGTON ROAD NORTH
MANCHESTER ROAD
Heaton Norris
M60
DIDSBURY RD
MERSEY SQUARE
Stockport Viaduct 35
Hat Works 14
Robinsons Brewery Visitors Centre 29
Stockport

1	Affleck & Brown Emporium
2	Charter Street Ragged School & Working Girls Home
3	Chorlton Water Park
4	Chorltonville
5	Christie Hospital, Wilmslow Road
6	Clayton Hall Living History Museum
7	Co-op Live Arena
8	Co-operative Group Head Office
9	Emirates Old Trafford Cricket Ground
10	Fairfield Moravian Settlement
11	Fletcher Moss Park & Botanical Gardens
12	Gorton Monastery
13	Hallé St Peter's
14	Hat Works
15	Imperial War Museum North
16	HMP Strangeways
17	Manchester Central Mosque
18	Manchester Craft & Design Centre
19	Manchester General Cemetery
20	Manchester Grammar School
21	Manchester High School for Girls
22	Manchester Jewish Museum
23	Museum of Transport Greater Manchester
24	Old Trafford
25	Ordsall Hall
26	Phillips Park Cemetery
27	Platt Hall & Platt Fields Park
28	Printworks
29	Robinsons Brewery Visitors Centre
30	Salford Lads' Club
31	Salford Museum and Art Gallery
32	Salford University
33	Smithfield Market Hall
34	Southern Cemetery
35	Stockport Viaduct
36	The British Muslim Heritage Centre
37	The Edgar Wood Centre
38	The Lowry
39	The Studios, Media City UK
40	The Working Class Movement Library
41	Weaste Cemetery
42	Withington Baths

Preface

Manchester: Secret & Strange Places to Visit is really two books in one: it is first a travel book focussed on the lesser known and intriguing places you can explore and enjoy in Manchester and its immediate environs, suggesting places of interest and significance that you may want to go to either as a curious local resident or as a dynamic get up and go visitor. Information on what to look out for when you get there is given.

Its second function is to illuminate places and people of historical significance which have defined and characterise the city and the region, but the places may not always be places you can visit; they merit inclusion because their contribution to Manchester's history and current life is so important that to omit them would give an incomplete and lop-sided picture of Manchester's legacy and its character. Examples of these essentials include the artist Valette, the Haçienda, the Christie Hospital, Strangeways prison and Manchester's marvellous music and literary heritages.

The book also has a chapter on Stockport – how could it not? And, of course, we include Stockport in the chapters on literature and music.

Introduction
Rain City? Colonialism, Cottonopolis, Slavery & Radicalism

What is it that is unmistakeably indicative and emblematic of Manchester and its heritage? Many things and many people, of course. Here are five suggestions.

Rain City?

We start with somewhere that isn't anywhere in particular in Manchester: it's often all over the place, because rain can be everywhere in Manchester and its surrounding conurbations and hills. Manchester has a reputation as the archetypal Rain City: rain is one of the emblems of the city. It is as much a civic badge as the ubiquitous bee; for many people - residents and those who have never been to the city - think Manchester and think rain, drizzle, mist, a *haar*, a sea-less sea fret.

But that's not such a bad thing – Manchester's abundant rain and its glowering clouds lend it a character which most shrug off as damply inevitable and get on with their lives – stoical lives which, come rain or shine, are

What is now the Kimpton Clocktower Hotel in Oxford Street, in the rain. Formerly The Palace, and before that Refuge Assurance

amply enriched by the wonderful architecture old and very new, the heritage left by the still resonating world-changing industrial revolution, the revivified galleries, museums, libraries and universities, the life-affirming and significantly real influencers who persist in role-modelling for subsequent generations – Engels, Pankhurst, Gaskell, Rutherford, Lowry and Turing. Then there are all those wonderfully calming parks and inspirational public spaces, and a football heritage to die for. 'And, in the end', there's always the evergreen memories left by Manchester music on repeat: from the Hollies and Herman's Hermits to Oasis via the Smiths and the Stone Roses, Factory Records and the Haçienda…

So, who really cares about the rain? It's become a bit of a tired cliché and a metaphor for the city when in reality it's just as much a positive as it is a plus, it's Mancunian character-forming and it has helped to spawn and shape all of those wonderful, unique treasures you can now read about which no other city can shake an umbrella at[1]. If anything in Manchester popular culture sums all this up, this does:

Take me back to Manchester

Take me back to Manchester when it's raining
I want to wet my feet in Albert Square
I'm all agog for a good thick fog
I do not like the sun, I like it raining cats and dogs
I want to smell the odours of the Irwell
I want to feel the soot get in me hair
I don't want to roam I want to get back home
To rainy Manchester[2]

Cottonopolis

They christened Middlesbrough 'Ironopolis' when it suddenly came of age and transitioned, seemingly overnight, from a few farm cottages to a seething steel city exhaling fire and choking smoke and shoe-horning its workers into ranks of barely habitable houses with sanitation to die for[3]. Manchester witnessed a similarly shocking baptism by fire and smoke and a rude awakening when cotton became the largest single import into the country and Manchester wasted no time at all transforming it into cotton goods which became the largest single export out of the country accelerated by enlightened foreigner - friendly companies based in the port of Manchester – all this at

Ancoats

a time when Britain accounted for eighty per cent of global cotton yarn and fabric production. Manchester was pivotal in both the export and the import textile trades, and a select few reaped the financial rewards on a prodigious scale. Manchester alone saw the number of cotton mills rise from two in 1790 to 66 in 1821; the number of cotton mills in Manchester reached its zenith at 108 in 1853. By 1870 Manchester was Cottonopolis.

Yet another outcome was, as with Middlesbrough, that lamentable housing, living and working conditions was inflicted on the workers and imposed on the women and children in particular who, when the mills and factories came, were obliged to leave the homes and fields which had long been their traditional workplace, and take up work in those dreadful mills – long hours, dangerous, often toxic conditions, monotony, bullying, sexual abuse and miserly pay were the usual low points of a day's work – all before they headed homeward to their other (unpaid) job: keeping home and family together. A double shift, then: the one poorly paid, dangerous, undignified, filthy and tiring, the other unpaid, sometimes humiliating, similarly abusive at times and even more exhausting. Records show the average age at death at times to be 17 in the working classes. No wonder, then, the demonstrations like Peterloo and the strikes - and the forming of a place hungry for reform and a hotbed of latent sedition and overt radicalism.

Manchester and its environs provided the perfect conditions for a cotton industry, and yes, rain was never far away. Successful cotton yarn spinning relies on high humidity, a damp and temperate climate which also made Manchester the go-to place for the trade in fustians, woollens and 'Manchester velvet' – an early corduroy. That perennial dampness reduces the chances of the material breaking up in the process of making it into textiles. The fast-flowing Pennine rivers were the mighty engines - this relentless power supply which supplied the factories with constant energy ably assisted by local coal. The proximity of the entrepot of Liverpool, the Mersey and the canals all facilitated and expedited this trade.

How did it all begin? Over the German Ocean the Flemish weavers saw the potential and laid the foundations of an emerging centre for textiles around 1360, as captured by Ford Madox Brown in one of his murals.

After this, immigration generally boomed – Armenians, Irish, Jewish, people from Pakistan, India, East Africa, Iran, Poland and Spain – all contributed to Manchester as a burgeoning cosmopolitan European city.

Weaving of cotton in Lancashire did not really begin until the 1600's, using raw cotton imported by the East India Company, although at this stage pure cotton fabric could not be woven in this country because domestic spinning methods were too crude to spin cotton of the right quality and strength to be used for the warp yarn (because the warp has to be stretched taut on a loom for weaving).

In the mid-18th century Manchester was still a relatively small market town where the population numbered between 4,000 to 6,000 people, though it was during this period when handloom weaving exploded and mechanised spinning

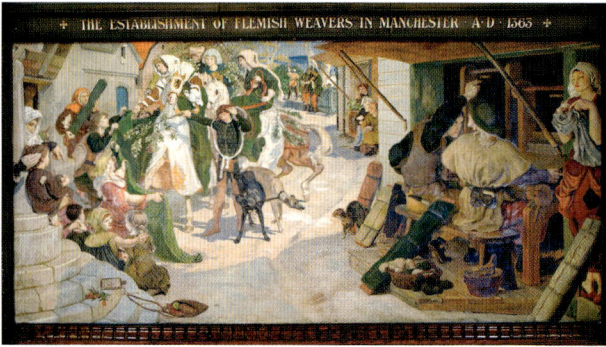

Ford Maddox Ford – The Establishment of Flemish Weavers in Manchester. AD 1363. Manchester Art Gallery (1882). See https://victorianweb.org/painting/fmb/paintings/8.html

Queen Philippa of Hainault rides into Manchester in the spring sunshine and is greeted by some of the Flemish Weavers who were invited to England under Edward III's act of 1337.

inventions in the 1760's allowed abundant and cheaper yarn which helped cater for increased demand. This complemented the invention of the John Kay's fly shuttle in 1733, which allowed handweavers to weave much faster and so produce more cloth and to weave wider cloth more easily.

Due to continued persecution in Belgium there was a second wave of Flemish weavers who came to the city, impelled this time by a sense of existentialist urgency as they were fleeing persecution back home. This time the material they produced was fustian – a heavyweight coarse cotton fabric often used for menswear, notably later in the 19th century when political radicals sported fustian jackets as a symbol of working-class solidarity - particularly Chartists in the 1840s. The result was that cotton-based products were firmly established in Manchester. This is really where the story of Manchester as a city begins because the wealth and growth of Manchester is predicated on the growth of cotton.

The Industrial Revolution was just beginning: Manchester and its environs lay at the centre of it all; the town started to change rapidly while England went from being an agricultural society to a mass production society where factories and mills superseded the home as the place of work and manufacture. In this case with cotton produced and traded on a scale never seen before.

In 1816 Joseph Aston regaled us with some impressive statistics:

'The whole of the factories in Manchester spins threads, in one year, which, tied together, would measure the almost incredible length of 313,385,384, miles!! A length of threads sufficient to wrap round the earth nearly twelve thousand times'[4].

African American anti-slavery campaigner Sarah Parker Remond, who visited Manchester in 1859 to campaign for the abolition of slavery. "When the true history of the antislavery cause shall be written, women will occupy a large space in its pages; for the cause of the slave has been peculiarly woman's cause."

African American abolitionist leader Frederick Douglass, 1845.

See https://globalthreadsmcr.org/sarah-parker-remond/

However Aston calculated this fantastic figure we will never know, but we must concede that 'the extraordinary image… summons up a powerful picture of world dominance – of a single city exerting a far from benign global influence'[5]. This, of course, resonates within global economics and the power generated by monopolisation of the trade in one single commodity; it also echoes the involvement in the odious corollary that is slavery and, in terms of export markets, 19th century colonialism.

Colonialism

Colonialism rears its head when Jonathan Silver invites us to marvel at the wonderful Egyptian collection in the Manchester Museum - but he brings us up short when he asks, hypothetically, what would happen if '18,000 undiscovered historical artefacts relating to Manchester had been illegally taken out of the country and installed in a museum in North Africa. We can only speculate on what the response in the city would be in such circumstances'[6]. Silver goes on to speculate that political leaders would demand the return of the stolen goods, public protests would break out and commentators would decry such an act as 'barbaric, immoral and a cultural crime'.

Slavery

Sadly, another consequence of Manchester's cotton trade and its subsequent wealth was to implicate the city in another form of trade: the noisome trafficking of millions of humans to work, and die, on cotton, tobacco, and sugar plantations. Manchester's transformation was heavily reliant on the transatlantic slave trade, and on the exploitation of millions of enslaved African people who were forced to grow the cotton which supplied Manchester's mills.

EMPIRE MARKETING

Colonialism in action: 'trade follows the flag' - Empire Marketing Board flag showing British trade 1926–1933 by Hugh Williams, in Manchester Art Gallery. These are the years when Britain 'aggressively controlled' about 70 countries around the globe.

In many of these 70 nations 'Sustainable systems were destroyed and appropriated, tens of millions died and livelihoods were made precarious. All of this was justified by the British sense of racial superiority'.

There are those who believe that we should return the booty that now forms Manchester's wonderful Egyptian Collection as well as millions of other artefacts which grace our galleries and museums the length and breadth of the country. Odious as colonial looting, slavery and First Nation depredation are, we cannot rewrite history. What we can do, though, is very simple: and that is sympathetically but rigorously redraft the signage, labels and literature, online stuff and film that describes and depicts these ghosts of colonialism and slavery to ensure that it always pays due and historically accurate regard to the full role both played in our cultural and political history – in other words break the often insincere and disingenuous silence and offer up a complete and honest picture as to how and why these artefacts happen to be here.

Running a global empire did not give us an entitlement to treat the indigenous peoples of that empire like animals, nor did it make it acceptable to plunder and export the existentialist cultural treasures of the countries involved. The least we can do is acknowledge the egregious sins of our often arrogant and supremacist past and redraft the nightmares into a proper historical record with context that is mindful of all the associated ramifications and is taught properly and honestly in our schools, colleges and universities.

Radicalism

The history of Manchester is awash with radicalism, Manchester is defined by its radicalism: it has nurtured and attracted more than its fair share of radical people and it has a good number of places that echo and chime with radicalism, radicalism that usually aims for the common good and the eradication of exclusivity, opacity and any number of dubious institutional isms. Manchester's radicalism persists to this day with the sterling work carried out by places such as the Pankhurst Centre, the Working Class Movement Library, the wonderful People's Museum, and the Salford Lads Club to name just four. Indeed, as this book was going to press in late May 2024, a March for Palestine – good humoured, well organised and respectfully policed - headed along Oxford Road and made its point, not taking things lying down…

---

1. *Wet, real and culturally influential as it is, Manchester rain is a phenomenon bordering on the urban mythical. Manchester languishes about 15th in the league table of UK wet cities, clouded over by such damp places as Cardiff, Preston, Glasgow and Leeds. Indeed, if you were to calculate the number of days when it actually rained in a given year, Manchester fails to achieve a podium finish at joint 5th with Leeds and Bradford, and around 150 wet days.*

2. *A traditional north country balled featured in Mike Leigh's Naked (1993). The rainy reputation had even percolated to the distant northern city of Hull where Beautiful South composed 'Manchester' in 2004: it reached #41 in the UK charts. The song also appeared on their album Superbi:*

   From Northenden to Partington, it's rain
   From Altrincham to Chadderton, it's rain
   From Moss Side to Swinton, hardly Spain
   It's a picture postcard of 'Wish they never came'…
   From Cheetham Hill to Wythenshawe, it's rain
   Gorton, Salford, Sale, pretty much the same
   As I'm caught up without my jacket once again
   The raindrops on my face play a sweet refrain…
   What makes Britain great
   Makes Manchester yet greater

3. *In 1851 Middlesbrough's population was 7,431 living in 1,262 houses; this rose in 1861 to 19,416 living in 3,203 houses In 1862 Prime Minister Gladstone was moved to say: "This remarkable place, the youngest child of England's enterprise, is an infant, but if an infant, an infant Hercules". Middlesbrough was now widely, and descriptively, known as Ironopolis. By 1873 the iron field around the town was turning out 5 ½ million tons of ore and 2 million tons of pig iron.*

4. *Joseph Aston, A Picture of Manchester, 1816*

5. *As Paul Dobraszczyk, Manchester: Something Rich and Strange p. 81, Manchester 2020*

6. *Jonathan Silver, 'Museum', in Paul Dobraszczyk, Manchester: Something Rich and Strange pp. 59–63*

Central Manchester

Richmond Tea Rooms; courtesy of Simon James Crossley,
www.simonjamescrossley.com

'Image of Genesis', 1929-31 (marble) by Epstein, Jacob (1880-1959). Jacob Epstein's 'Genesis' shows a heavily pregnant woman with a face based on an African mask. It is carved out of marble, weighing 3 tons and was first exhibited at Bluecoat in 1931 when nearly 50,000 visitors paid sixpence to see what was considered Britain's most shocking sculpture. When shown as part of Epstein's February 1930 exhibition at the Leicester Galleries, the response to Genesis was vicious, not just from the popular press but from more serious journals. It is now resplendent at the Whitworth.

Whitworth Gallery, Oxford Road

60,000 artworks and installations in this astonishing and inspirational collection have been delighting visitors since 1908.

As well as artworks the gallery offers The Natural and Cultural Health Service (NCHS), a programme of outdoor activities that promote good physical and mental wellbeing ranging from Meditating in Nature to Gardening for Good Health (GROW) to Sow & Grow: Wildflower Meadow Sowing. In addition Friends of the Whitworth present a series of free Sunday afternoon concerts that are open to all when students from the Royal Northern College of Music perform in the South Gallery, overlooking Whitworth Park. Past concerts have ranged from classical flamenco guitar to contemporary flute.

The Whitworth boasts notable collections of watercolours, sculptures, wallpapers and textiles, with a special focus on modern and contemporary artists including works by Gainsborough, Degas, van Gogh, Gauguin, Pissarro, Picasso, Moholy-Nagy, Paul Klee, Walter Sickert, Henry Moore, Barbara Hepworth, Ford Madox Brown, Eduardo Paolozzi, Francis Bacon, William Blake, David Hockney, L. S. Lowry, and a superb collection of works by Turner.

The Snowman, Whitworth Park

Whitworth was the inventor of the Whitworth rifled musket, the world's first successful sniper rifle.

The park comes courtesy of a legacy from Sir Joseph Whitworth and was laid out on Potter's Field on the edge of Moss Side on the corner of Moss Lane East and Oxford Road which was then owned by the uncle of **Beatrice Potter**. Moss Side and weapons would appear to be inextricably linked because engineer Whitworth was the inventor, among other things, of the Whitworth rifled musket, widely regarded as the world's first successful sniper rifle.

Nate Lowman created the fascinating sculpture here in 2014. Composed of three spheres of decreasing sizes stacked on top each other. A carrot nose and button eyes complete the bronze effigy: the iconic figure of winter. But it really looks nothing like a snowman with its dark bronze material, and there lies its significance.

This disparity is emphasised further by the sign on the lower sphere that reads: "I will be dead soon". Lowman wished to bring attention to the dark effect of climate change, using a familiar but impermanent symbol of our childhood and past to highlight our lasting effect on the future.

The university halls of residence over the road are called 'The Toblerones' because they look like buildings in an Alpine skyscape. One of them (Aberdeen House) is where Number 6 Thorncliffe Grove was; **Engels** was a lodger here, as is shown by his blue plaque.

The Contact Theatre, Oxford Road

'We like to put young people centre stage'

On the outside it looks like a Lego building gone wrong... symbolic, no doubt, of the originality and otherness of what goes on inside.

The website reveals that the fact that 35 per cent of attenders come from black, Asian or minority cultural backgrounds, and more than 70 per cent are under 35, explains why Contact won the first ever UK Theatre Award for the promotion of diversity in 2013. Founded as the Manchester Young People's Theatre in the 1970s, what makes Contact really distinctive is that local young people, aged 13 and upwards, sit at the heart of everything they do, playing a central decision-making role not only in what's shown on stage, but in every aspect of their activity.

The carbon footprint is vanishingly low making it one of the top 1 per cent of environmentally friendly public buildings in the north west while sophisticated monitoring and control systems minimise heat loss in winter and provide night cooling in summer. The kill switch ensures that all lights are switched off by the last person to leave the building. And that's all before the innovative and unique schedule of performances.

The Pankhurst Centre, Nelson Street

'The Pankhurst Trust brings together Manchester Women's Aid and the Pankhurst Centre'.

Emmeline Pankhurst (*née* Goulden; 1858–1928) was born at 8 Alpha Terrace on the site of what is now the Whalley Range Methodist Church on Sedgeborough Road. Sadly, there is nothing there to commemorate this. Moss Side, of course, had a reputation in the 1990s and 2000s as the Wild West of Gunchester: for example, between 1996–1998 there were 170 serious gang related incidents in which 90 people were injured and 12 died.

The Pankhurst family lived here between 1898 and 1907 and the first meeting of the Women's Social and Political Union (WSPU), later known as the Suffragettes, took place at 72 Nelson Street, in what is now known as the Pankhurst Centre. In the 60s this and neighbouring elegant and historically significant houses were allowed to fall into dereliction. It defies credibility that in 1978 this shrine to the natural order of things and the ultimate icon of resistance to the bastion of all male bastions was under threat of destruction as the wrecking ball that is the MRI advanced inexorably, gobbling up everything in its way. Everything? Even the site of one of the most significant events in all of British history? Well, women's history, that is, which explains a lot. It is interesting to know that through Community Programme Schemes the subsequent restoration was carried out entirely by women labourers, thus ensuring the fall of another male bastion. To ensure that the building was never requisitioned by the (un) developers an efficient and ultimately successful cohort of squatters occupied 72 Nelson Street 24/7 until the danger was over.

'The Pankhurst Trust brings together Manchester Women's Aid and the Pankhurst Centre. We work together to ensure the powerful story of the women who won the vote continues to inspire us all to challenge gender inequality, and to ensure that those suffering from domestic violence and abuse get the confidential help they need'.

The Pankhurst Centre was opened by Helen Pankhurst – Emmeline Pankhurst's great-granddaughter and Sylvia Pankhurst's granddaughter – and Barbara Castle on October 11th 1987, which coincided with the anniversary of the first meeting of the Suffragettes in 1903.

Sarah Hartley wrote in The Guardian 13 July 2011:

'In 2010 [artist Charlotte] Newson… created Women Like You, a photomosaic portrait made up of 10,000 individual images of inspiring women - celebrities, mothers, wives, daughters, politicians, scientists – all sent in by members of the public from all corners of the globe.

The original and intricate artwork took two years to complete and stands 3 metres high and 2.5 metres wide.

Thanks to Emma McBeath, Heritage Manager, The Pankhurst Museum for permission to use this photograph showing one of the group of women hired as apprentices in construction skills to help in the rebuilding of 60-62 Nelson Street.

For this project the artwork has been turned into a virtual birthday card for women to either sign or post their image onto, creating a personal and very public birthday message to the woman whose legacy transformed the lives of women in this country'.

This breathtaking photomosaic is built up from thousands of images put forward by members of the public who wanted to celebrate women who had inspired them – be they famous or otherwise – including mothers, (great) grandmothers, sisters and friends...

Elizabeth Gaskell's House, 84 Plymouth Grove

"I must try and make the house give as much pleasure to others as I can."

– Letter (69) to Eliza 'Tottie' Fox, 1850 –

"A man," as one of them observed to me once, "is so in the way in the house!"

Elizabeth Gaskell (1810–1865) and William, her husband, lived here from 1850 to 1913. William was an active Unitarian Minister at Cross Street Chapel and long-standing Chair of the Portico Library.

The website informs that a visit to the neo-classical house offers a chance to sit at Elizabeth Gaskell's 'desk' in the dining room, where her writing day was constantly interrupted with questions about the children or how long to boil the beef for tea. You can also see the window where Charlotte Brontë hid behind the curtains, too shy to join the company (rather like the opening scene in her Jane Eyre).

Here it was that Elizabeth wrote most of her major works including Mary Barton, Cranford, Wives and Daughters and North and South. She and William received celebrated personalities at the house, including **Charles Dickens, Charlotte Brontë, John Ruskin** and **Sir Charles Hallé**. The John Rylands Library holds the world's most important collection of literary manuscripts by Elizabeth Gaskell, including the only complete manuscript of *Wives and Daughters* and her celebrated biography of her friend Charlotte Brontë, our first modern biography.

As well as four daughters, Elizabeth had a son, William, who died in infancy of scarlet fever. As a distraction from her grief, her husband suggested that she write a novel. It was out of this sorrow that her first novel *Mary Barton* came to fruition. Published anonymously in 1848 it became very popular and was widely reviewed and discussed.

The Study, Morning Room, Drawing Room, Dining Room and Elizabeth's bedroom have been restored to how they would have looked in around 1857, using Elizabeth's letters, auction records and other primary research. Items originally from the house are displayed throughout, including paintings, furniture, Elizabeth's wedding veil, Paisley shawls, books and miniatures. The house comprises 20 rooms on two floors over a concealed basement with a front porch containing four columns carved with a lotus leaf shape. It also has a rotating exhibition space and an award-winning garden.

Gaskell was well-schooled in the reality of squalor and poverty through the research she did for her social novel, *Mary Barton* (1848) investigating in great detail the plight of the Manchester poor between 1839 and 1842. Although

she was born in the leafy comfort of middle-class Cheyne Walk (number 93) in Chelsea she was well qualified to expatiate on the disparities between north and south living by the time she reached Manchester via Warwickshire and Knutsford. When, in 1850, the Gaskells moved to Manchester, first to middle class Dover Street off Oxford Road, and then Plymouth Grove, Elizabeth, staying rooted, brought her cow with her and would gladly walk up to three miles to help another person in distress. A lottery grant was used to help restore the house's garden, where the Gaskells once kept pigs, poultry and the cow.

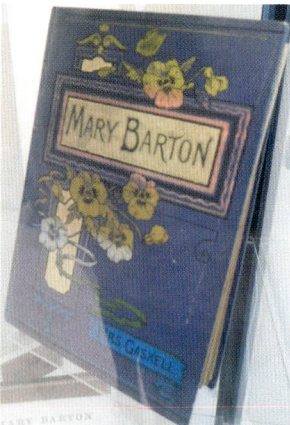

In Manchester, Elizabeth wrote her remaining literary works largely in the industrial genre, while William held welfare committees and tutored the poor in his study. Indeed, Elizabeth felt some guilt living in their well-appointed villa while many others close by subsisted in insanitary hovels. Nevertheless, the Gaskells were never what you might call frugal, what with their £150 yearly rent, 20 rooms and a cook, several maids, an odd-job man for outdoor work, as well as a washerwoman and a seamstress.

Manchester City Council have created an award in Gaskell's name, given to recognize women's involvement in charitable work and improvement of women's lives.

Victoria Baths, Hathersage Road

> *"a water palace of which every citizen of Manchester can be proud."*

When it opened in 1906, Victoria Baths was described as the 'most splendid municipal bathing institution in the country'. When it closed in 1993, everything from the ornate Edwardian tiles, mosaic floors and stained glass to the retro poolside changing rooms were perfectly preserved.

Now, it hosts some of the most exciting events in the city, the empty pools filled with craft, antiques fairs and food festivals. And then there is the Independent Manchester Beer Convention.

Post-pandemic 2022 saw the Baths reopen with a splash including many nightlife events including Red Bull Unlocked (when the city's finest DJs, musicians, mixologists, clubs, bars and culinary creatives came together to offer unique collaborations), cinema screenings, theatre performances, the return of the annual swim 'Big Splash', numerous weddings and a lot more.

The invaluable and unique Archive is catalogued and updated by the History Group, documenting the rich history of Victoria Baths, plus the Baths & Washhouses of Manchester and the history of swimming and Turkish Baths

in general. The unique Archive is available for private research by individuals or groups.

Victoria Baths opens from March/April to October/November each year for weekly guided tours, public open days and special events. For events visit https://victoriabaths.org.uk/

The University of Manchester

William Arthur Lewis (1915–1991), became the UK's first black professor in 1948. He was a prominent Saint Lucian economist.

The University of Manchester holds a special place in history. Its origins as England's first civic university are closely linked to Manchester's development as the world's first industrial city. The Victoria University of Manchester was founded in 1851, as Owens College which graduated to become a world class, cutting edge university complete with a first class medical and dental school. The university owns and operates major cultural assets such as the Manchester Museum, The Whitworth Art Gallery, the John Rylands Library, the Tabley House Collection near Knutsford and the Jodrell Bank Observatory – a UNESCO World Heritage Site.

The current University of Manchester was formed in 2004 following the merger of the University of Manchester Institute of Science and Technology (UMIST) and the Victoria University of Manchester after 100 years or so of close participation. UMIST grew out of the Mechanics' Institute, founded in 1824 which is also the date of foundation of the Royal School of Medicine and Surgery.

A tour will show you key sites where world-changing discoveries took place over time - including the first 'splitting of the atom' by Ernest Rutherford and the development of the world's first stored-program computer. The university is associated with 25 Nobel prize winners either as former students or staff, or as current members of various faculties. One winner of particular significance (1979) is William

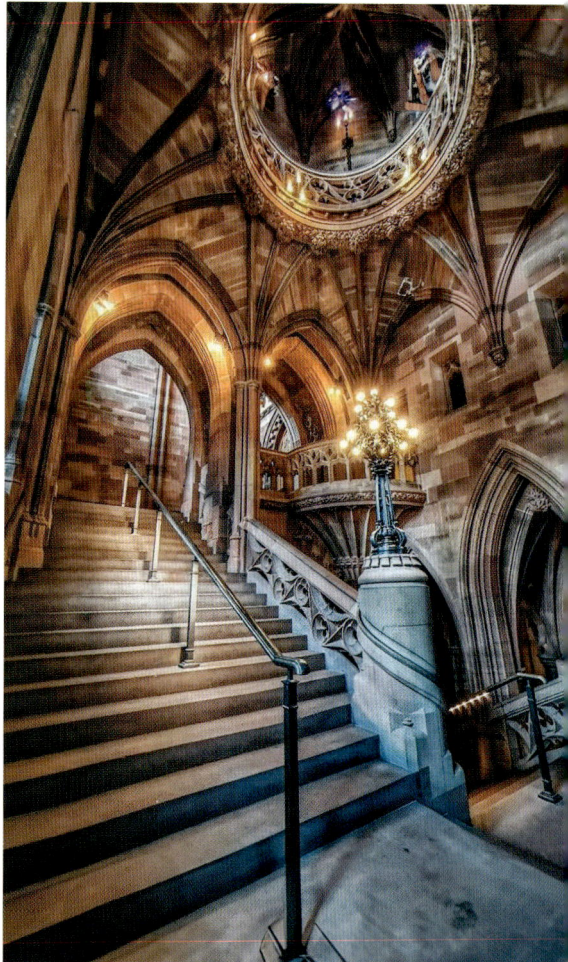

Arthur Lewis (1915 –1991), who was also the UK's first black professor in 1948. He was a prominent Saint Lucian economist.

The University of Manchester is top in the UK and Europe and third in the world for sustainability, indeed it is unique in British higher education 'in having social responsibility as one of our three core strategic goals, sitting equally alongside our commitments to research and discovery and teaching and learning in our vision and strategic plan'.

By the way…
The Ice Age Andecite Boulder

A huge lump of lava stands on a lawn in the University of Manchester's Old Quadrangle in front of the Beyer Building. It weighs over 20 tons and measures up eight feet by nine feet by five feet. It got here from Borrowdale in the Lake District during the last Ice Age, around 20,000 years ago.

The boulder remained hidden 28 feet below the surface for centuries. That is, until February 1888, when workers found the rock under Oxford Road during excavations for new sewers.

The Holy Name of Jesus, Oxford Road

"…a design of the very highest quality and of an originality nowhere demonstrative;..Hansom never again did so marvellous a church".

- Sir Nikolaus Pevsner

The Church of the Holy Name of Jesus on Oxford Road, Manchester, England was designed by Joseph Aloysius Hansom of York and built between 1869 and 1871. The tower, designed by Adrian Gilbert Scott, was erected in 1928. In 1860, William Turner, the first bishop of Salford, invited the Jesuits to make a home in Chorlton-on-Medlock, at the time a middle-class suburb, so Jesuits from St Helens came to settle. Holy Name was made a parish church and the building re-enforced the power of the Jesuit order. It is the largest church in Manchester: the church's dimensions and proportions are on the scale of a 14th-century cathedral.

The Smiths referred to the Holy Name church in one of the lyrics in Vicar in a Tutu, "I was minding my business lifting some lead off the roof of The Holy Name church".

Hansom suffered from severe depression and shot himself in his office on 27th May 1900. The pub in York's Market Street once named after him was a substantial rebuild in 1975 in the style of the cabs invented by Hansom; Victorian style paneling, glass (including skylight feature) and lighting lend the pub character. Architecturally, Hansom's best known work is probably the majestic

neoclassical Birmingham Town Hall. The Hansom Cab became so common a sight that Disraeli called it 'the gondola of London'.

Sir Nikolaus Pevsner described The Holy Name as "...a design of the very highest quality and of an originality nowhere demonstrative; ...Hansom never again did so marvellous a church".

The Royal Northern College of Music and Alice Pitfield

Alice Pitfield, a Russian émigré came to Manchester just before the October Revolution in 1917 and married Thomas,
Bolton-born composer, poet and artist, strict vegetarian and pacifist

You would be forgiven for expecting this entry to feature strongly on the college's pre-eminence as a cutting-edge conservatoire in classical music and its status as a centre of excellence in music education. Consider that a given and let's focus on Alice Pitfield, a Russian émigré who came to Manchester just before the October Revolution in 1917. Her story is narrated by Jenna C. Ashton in her chapter entitled 'Thread'[1] as a kind of metaphor for Cottonopolis. In Ashton's chapter Louise Bourgeois sets the scene for the all-important examination of two items from the Alice Pitfield archive at the Royal Northern College of Music:

The archivist brings out two wrapped artefacts, one soft, the other with a hard edge. Two textile pieces produced by Alice – a smaller embroidery sampler in a thin wooden frame and a larger linen piece, the latter likely created to be hung on a wall, the former a hobbyist creation. Both so different, and no information attached to either. These are like orphaned objects, and I must speculate to make sense of their presence and relevance here in the archive. Cottonopolis makes itself known once again: Alice's family owned cotton mills in Russia; Alice's husband, Thomas, grew up in the shadow of the cotton-spinning mills of Bolton; Thomas's own mother was a dressmaker. Cotton – thread – is an ever-present material for Alice and Thomas.

Ashton continues, telling us that

'Industry, revolution, movement, displacement; we find hints in Alice's writings, but perhaps best visualised in these two pieces. Her thread replaces words. The two textile pieces encapsulate the complexities of a Manchester that it is both domestic and public, international and local, traditional and modern'.

An earlier chapter in the same book ('Hair', p.156ff) also by Ashton is far more personal and poignant; it describes the locks of hair cut by Alice's mother and deposited by Alice:

A brown packet, *Mother's hair & mine*. The contents are soft, and well blanketed; I pull out two more packages of crumpled but untorn tissue paper. The first smaller package reads My Alice's hair, 5yrs old; the faded lead scrawl still visible. The second package has no inscription, but I know this to be Alice's mother's hair. *Mother's hair & mine*. A golden curl, an auburn plait. Daughter and mother, at once both present, yet so obviously absent.

---

1 *In Manchester: Something rich and strange, Edited by Paul Dobraszczyk and Sarah Butler, p.223ff*

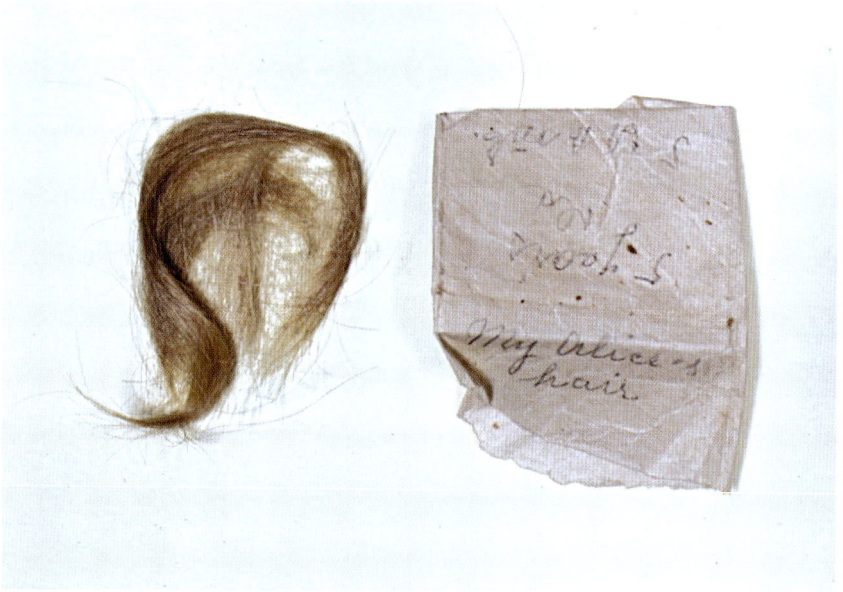

Thanks to Heather Roberts, Archivist and Museum Manager at Royal Northern College of Music for permission to use the images of Alice Pitfield's locks of hair as owned by the Pitfield Trust – and to Manchester Digital Music Archive for their assistance in facilitating this.

Ashton goes on to explain why such 'evocative' and moving artefacts are to be found in a cold and otherwise characterless collection: 'a packet of hair is tucked away among the artefacts of Alice Pitfield (née Astbury; 1903–2000), which exists to accompany her husband 's archive, Bolton-born composer, poet and artist, and strict vegetarian and pacifist, Thomas Pitfield (1903–99). In the archive, Thomas rubs shoulders with the great and the good of the music world, but his own creativity was (is) often negated. His influences of craft, folk customs, nature, speech and dialect have fallen foul of the curse of regionality'. Why are the locks there and what is their significance to Manchester? Perhaps it is quite simply insurance that if mother and daughter were ever parted they would remain together in a safe place, free from revolution and in her husband's musical alma mater.

Manchester Museum, Oxford Road

A multitude of fascinating and revelatory things to see, and hear: including Stan the T.rex, the Vivarium, and newly bred Harlequin frogs. Then there's the soundscape exhibition *Wild Chorus*, recorded and composed in summer 2020 by sound artist Harry Ovington. The artwork reflects a unique moment of global quiet and acts as an audio time capsule of the first lockdown, blending field recordings of nature with sonified weather pattern datasets.

'Manchester Museum has been working with artists and communities to make a rickshaw to display in the South Asia Gallery. Rickshaws are a major form of transport in many countries in Asia, and are often brightly decorated like this. Rickshaws, like bicycles, do not need petrol to run, as they are pedal-powered and a green source of transportation.

Inspiration for the decoration on this [made in Dhaka] was drawn from many movies from across South Asia, such as White Sun from Nepal, Paradesi from Sri Lanka, and Lunana from Bhutan'.

The museum is home to around four and a half million objects from all aspects of natural sciences and human cultures. It is not only a place for wonderment and fascination but it also has always been a hub for research and learning for public visitors and researchers alike. Restitution is an increasingly important factor in policy making: 'We are rethinking restitution and building new relationships with communities across the world and with those most intimately connected to our collections'

A research-led approach is evident from the displays; for example the fascinating and unique 'Lee Kai Hung Chinese Culture Gallery profiles some ground-breaking research collaborations; including Professor Henry Yi Li's work in Manchester and Hong Kong on smart textiles and Professor Shulan Tang's research and practice of Traditional Chinese Medicine. The new dinosaur gallery has been created to share "how to think like a palaeontologist"' The recent wonderful 'Golden Mummies of Egypt Exhibition' delighted more than a million visitors and showcased mummies and mummification, gold and an obsessive belief in the afterlife. So far so good but the exhibition uniquely revealed how important they were to the Egyptians themselves, and how long they survived after the last of the Pharaohs. The focus was on eschatology during the relatively little-known 'Graeco-Roman' Period of Egyptian history (300 BCE–300 CE). The Museum looks after 18,000 objects from Egypt and Sudan, mostly excavated at a time of British rule of Egypt in the 1880s–1910s when the treasures of these countries were seen as fair game by western archaeologists and shipped home, often denuding these and other countries of their cultural and historical heritage.

A detail from the Hulme Mural

Raking through the rubble, after St Augustine's Church blitz

Hulme Mural, Clopton Walk

Capturing the constant battle for decent homes, immigration following World War Two and the tumultuous periods of regeneration, the mural is a reminder of the transformation of Hulme across the ages.

- Radical Manchester

The 84-foot-long ceramic mural was created between 2000 and 2002 by the "Hulme Urban Potters" a group composed of students and tutors from the Hulme Adult Education Centre. It is an invaluable chronicle of the history of the community from Roman times to the present day and will reveal much to social historians and residents as it, hopefully, continues to be viewed and 'consulted' down the ages.

St Augustine's Church Blitz Montage, Lower Ormond Street/ Grosvenor Square

The collage is made from the mangled and fused chalices and other sacred vessels crushed in the destruction and rescued.

The second St Augustine's was built on York Street where the Mancunian Way and the National Computer Centre now cross York Street. This church was completed in 1908 but lasted a mere 32 years as it was destroyed in the Manchester Blitz of Christmas 1940, and in which Fr. George Street was killed. Lowry painted the scene of the

GRANBY ROW   YORK STREET

THIS MONTAGE
WAS ERECTED ON THE OCCASION OF
THE CONSECRATION OF THIS CHURCH ON
OCTOBER 20TH 1970
TO COMMEMORATE THE TWO PRECEDING
PARISH CHURCHES OF ST. AUGUSTINE.
IT IS MADE UP FROM
THE SACRED VESSELS RESCUED FROM THE
SAFE CRUSHED IN THE BLITZ OF
DECEMBER 22ND 1940
THE ARTIST, ROBERT BRUMBY HAS USED
SOME OF THESE VESSELS EXACTLY AS
THEY WERE FOUND.
THE REST, MAKE UP THE GENERAL METAL
WORK OF THE WHOLE PLAQUE.
THE EARLIEST OF THESE VESSELS CAME
FROM ROOK ST. CHAPEL BEFORE 1800.

destroyed church in 1945. In 1966 a new Church of St Augustine of Canterbury was built here with money from the War Damage Commission. The collage in one of the side chapels of the current church is made from the mangled chalices and other sacred vessels crushed in the destruction and rescued.

Little Ireland

In the area known as Little Ireland, the Parish of St Mary, Mulberry Street was unable to cope with the huge influx of Irish fleeing the Potato Famine (1845–1852); in twenty years, thirteen priests had succumbed to typhus while working amongst the city's poor. It became Manchester's oldest, smallest and most short-lived Irish slum. In his *The Condition of the Working Class in England* in 1844 Engels described it as a 'horrid little slum'.

Cellars, built to store wood, coal and non-perishable foods, were later rented out as cheaper accommodation leading to perpetual humidity and damp in which infectious diseases could thrive.

The main entrance.

Oxford Road Station

Unusually, the station sits on a Grade II listed viaduct, which was built in 1839 as part of the Manchester, South Junction and Altrincham Railway. To reduce load on this viaduct, the station uniquely makes use of laminated wood structures instead of masonry, concrete, iron or steel. English Heritage describes it as a "building of outstanding architectural quality and technological interest; one of the most dramatic stations in England". Nikolaus Pevsner described the station as "one of the most remarkable and unusual stations in the country".

Oxford Road street art

Kimpton Clocktower Hotel (formerly the Palace Hotel)

> *A towering example of an exemplary and sympathetic repurposing of a commercial space into an exceptionally sumptuous hotel*

A truly historic hotel at the corner of Oxford Street and Whitworth Street it was originally built bit by bit from 1891 to 1932 as the Refuge Assurance Building, famous for its opulence: cream and brown Burmantofts faience, vivid stained glass, decorated wrought iron and glazed brick which was intended to mitigate against the city soot and smog. The company was established in 1858 as a friendly society aiding the poor in the eastern suburb of Duckenfield; it was the Refuge Friend in Deed Life Assurance and Sick Fund with a complement of 1,900 clerks.

What is now the hotel's ballroom was originally the dining hall for Refuge employees, surely one of the UK's grandest staff refectories - the 2,000 males and females were required to sit separately. Women had to reapply for jobs if they married as was the norm, some areas of the building were for exclusively for men. The basement ballroom, the largest in the north of England, was used as a dance hall for workers in their lunch hour. Statuettes of Industry and Thrift emphasise the mission statement of the Refuge and the foundation on which the wealth of Manchester was built.

Taking centre stage in the magnificently ceilinged lobby with its stained glass cupola is the 200lb bronze horse sculpted by Sophie Dickens, great

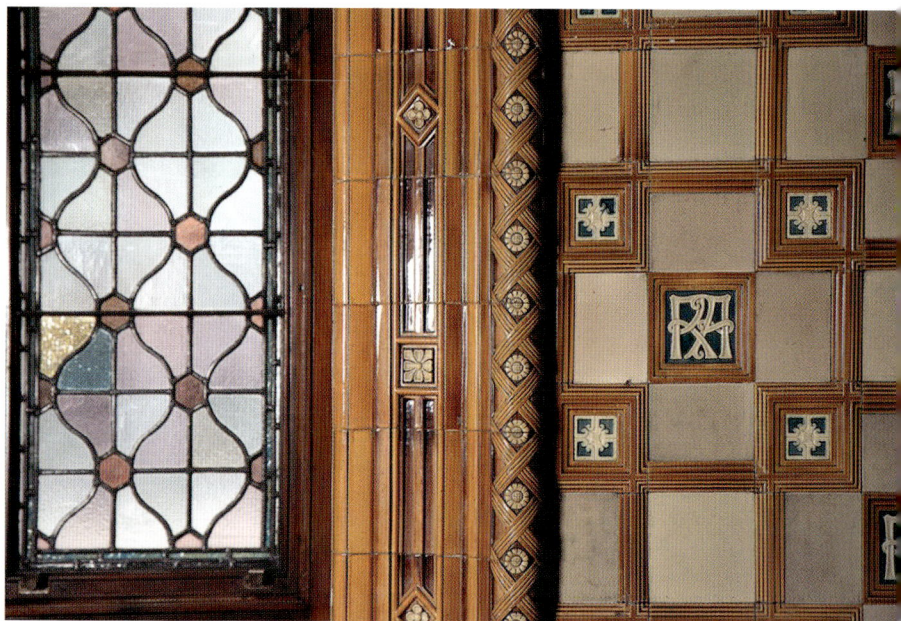

Exquisite tiling and glasswork at the Kimpton Clocktower Hotel.

THE GLAMOUR OF MANCHESTER

granddaughter of Charles. you can still see the outline of the turning circle used by horse-drawn coaches to bring mail in and then be turned round to head back out. The expansive 10,000 square foot dining room and bar, the Refuge, is enhanced by a glass roofed Winter Garden and a metal caged bar.

The Ritz, Whitworth Street West

Notable not just for its sprung dancefloor accommodating the 1,500 plus audiences and the impressive array of acts to perform there over the years, and as a set of A Taste of Honey, but also as the place where John Cooper Clarke met Salome Maloney:

I was walking down oxford road
Dressed in what they call the mode
I could hear them spinning all their smash hits
At the mecca of the modern dance, the Ritz…

In lurex and terylene, she hypnotised me
I asked her name, she said it's...
"Salome Maloney, queen of the Ritz"

Lacquered in a beehive
Her barnet didn't budge
Wet-look lips, she smiled as sweet as fudge
She had a number on her back
And sequins on her tits
The sartorial requirements
For females in the Ritz

Doing the Ritz

Central Manchester

The Anthony Burgess Café Bar, Cambridge Street

> *Burgess also composed over 250 musical works; he considered himself as much a composer as an author.*

The fully licensed Burgess Bar is set in the Georgian industrial splendour of Chorlton Mill on Cambridge Street, close to Oxford Road station. There is a range of Anthony Burgess books to browse or buy, and an ongoing Burgess exhibition illuminating the life of one of Manchester's greatest 20th century authors. The daytime café is currently closed, but event hire is available for any time of day, or in the evening.

John Anthony Burgess Wilson, FRSL (1917–1993), who published under the name Anthony Burgess, was a British writer and composer and although principally a comic writer, his dystopian satire *A Clockwork Orange* (1962) remains his best-known novel with its controversial film adaptation directed by Stanley Kubrick. He was born at 91 Carisbrook Street in Harpurhey, Manchester. After the death of his mother and sister, Burgess was raised by his maternal aunt, Ann Bromley, in Crumpsall with her two daughters; Burgess went to St. Edmund's Elementary School before moving on to Bishop Bilsborrow Memorial Elementary School, both Catholic schools, in Moss Side. He later reflected "When I went to school I was able to read. At the Manchester elementary school I attended, most of the children could not read, so I was... a little apart, rather different from the rest." Good grades ensured a place at Xaverian College from 1928–37.

Burgess published numerous other novels, including the Enderby quartet, and *Earthly Powers*. He wrote librettos and screenplays, including the 1977 television mini-series *Jesus of Nazareth*. He wrote as a literary critic for a number of publications, including *The Observer* and *The Guardian*, and wrote studies of classic writers, notably James Joyce. A versatile linguist, Burgess lectured in phonetics, and translated *Cyrano de Bergerac, Oedipus Rex* from the ancient Greek), *Miser! Miser!* – a translation of Molière's *The Miser*, and the opera *Carmen*, among others. Burgess was nominated and shortlisted for the Nobel Prize in Literature in 1973.

Less well known is the fact that Burgess also composed over 250 musical works; he considered himself as much a composer as an author. The epitaph on Burgess's marble memorial stone, reads: "Abba Abba", which means "Father, father" in Aramaic, Arabic, Hebrew, and other Semitic languages and is pronounced by Christ during his agony in Gethsemane (Mark 14:36) as he prays God to spare him. It is also the title of Burgess's 22nd novel, concerning the death of John Keats.

The largest archive of Anthony Burgess's belongings is housed at the International Anthony Burgess Foundation in Manchester. The University of

Anthony Burgess street art, Manchester
cc-by-sa/2.0 – © Matt Harrop

Manchester unveiled a plaque in 2012 that reads: "The University of Manchester commemorates Anthony Burgess, 1917–1993, Writer and Composer, Graduate, BA English 1940". It was the first monument to Burgess in the United Kingdom.

Burgess was taught history at Manchester University by A.J.P. Taylor, one of whose put-downs was 'Bright ideas insufficient to conceal lack of knowledge'. In Latin Burgess was tasked with rendering into Latin the Fred Astaire line 'you say potatoes and I say potahtoes'. This is what he served up:

Dico ego 'pomum', dicis tu phomum'.

Canal Street, Gay Village

A beacon of celebration in the city, the Gay Village is a must for any visitor to Manchester.

- Visit Manchester

A pedestrianised street that runs along the Rochdale Canal. It is the home of the original "Queer as Folk" and is recognized as the largest LGBT centre in the UK outside London.

Visit Manchester continues: 'Located just south of Chinatown, along and around Canal Street, the Village is both party central and a living piece of social history - proof that Manchester is one of the world's leading gay-friendly cities'.

Canal Street's development started when the Rochdale Canal was built in 1804, and pubs and other businesses sprang up to service the users of the canal, especially the people stopping at the lock nearby. By the 1950s the area had become a red light district with the decline of canal traffic and the collapse of the textile industry over the years.

In the 1980s, James Anderton, Chief Constable of Greater Manchester, accused gays of "swirling in a cesspit of their own making" and, according to Beatrix Campbell, author of Village People, "encouraged his officers to stalk its dank alleys and expose anyone caught in a clinch, while police motorboats with spotlights cruised for gay men around the canal's locks and bridges". Anderton, when questioned about the policing of the Canal Street area, denied that he was motivated by anti-gay prejudice and was merely enforcing the law on sexual activity in public toilets.

By the 90s things had begun to improve immeasurably: first there was the opening of 'Manto' which 'was seen as a queer visual statement of "we're here, we're queer – get used to it". Another catalyst for the expansion around Canal Street was its official recognition by Manchester City Council: following the passing of a number of non-discrimination policies on the grounds of sexuality in the late 1980s, the council was pioneering work in the advancement of lesbian and gay rights with a HIV/AIDS unit, sympathetic press and marketing officers, an Equality Group which appointed lesbians and gay men as officers to key departments like Libraries, Children's Services and Housing with much official emphasis placed on strengthening the community element of the Village. This included major support for the Mardi Gras, purchase of the Sackville Street Gardens in 1990, and becoming the first UK council to support civil partnerships.

The Mechanics' Institute, Princess Street

To provide basic education for the working class; to offer night school education to those who wanted to expand their meagre learning and better themselves after a hard day's work at the mill or down the mine.

The aims and scope of Mechanics' Institutes up and down the country were simply to provide basic education for the working class in the nineteenth century; to offer night school education to those who wanted to expand their meagre learning and better themselves after a hard day's work at the mill or down the mine.

The Manchester Mechanics' Institute is, however, notable as the organisation in which three hugely significant British institutions were founded: the Trades Union Congress (TUC), the Co-operative Insurance Society (CIS) and the University of Manchester Institute of Science and Technology (UMIST). In the 1960s the building was occupied by the Manchester College of Commerce.

The Manchester Institute was established on 7 April 1824 at the Bridgewater Arms hotel. The worker hungry for knowledge would have read this from the prospectus:

The Manchester Mechanics' Institution is formed for the purpose of enabling Mechanics and Artisans, of whatever trade they may be, to become acquainted with such branches of science as are of practical application in the exercise of that trade; that they may possess a more thorough knowledge of their business, acquire a greater degree of skill in the practice of it, and be qualified to make improvements and even new inventions in the Arts which they respectively profess.

Later changes included reading groups, a newspaper reading room, a change in the type of lectures, which became less rigidly based on scientific topics, as also did the library stock; edifying concerts, exhibitions and excursions played a more important role. Facilities for educating women and children were also introduced but a request to initiate classes in history was rejected because of fears that it would lead to debates about politics. In 1868 the first TUC Congress was held there.

Stained glass windows from 1988 depict, for example, the Fire Brigade Union and the Union of Construction, Allied Trades and Technicians are stunning.

By the mid-19th century, there were over 700 institutes in towns and cities across the UK and overseas, some of which became the early roots of other colleges and universities. If Manchester led to the creation of UMIST, then Edinburgh led to Heriot-Watt and London Mechanics' Institute became Birkbeck College at the University of London.

One of the women who attended the Institute was Mary Louise Armitt who founded the Armitt Museum and Library, an independent museum and library, founded in Ambleside in 1909.

Godlee Observatory, Aytoun Street

when papier-mâché meets 4,000 hear old meteorite

I often say, when walking through a town or city with a rich heritage, be sure to look up as well as down because there is often more up there than there is down here. Manchester's Aytoun Street and its Sackville Building is a case in point.

And where in the world can you visit a working Manchester Astronomical Society observatory made of papier-mâché which survived the 1940 blitz, and then hold in your hand a meteorite that crash-landed in Brazil over 4,000 years ago? Answer to both questions is the 1902 wonderful Godlee Observatory on Floor G atop university buildings in Aytoun Street.

Godlee Observatory is home to two original telescopes made by Grubb of Dublin: a Newtonian telescope that uses a concave primary mirror and a flat diagonal secondary mirror, and a refracting telescope that uses a lens as its objective to form an image.

If astronomy, wrought iron circular staircases and a trapdoor are for you, then Godlee is the place for you too.

Alan Turing Memorial, Sackville Park

a visionary thinker leaving a legacy that has influenced most of our modern inventions

Alan Turing was a man of many talents. From mathematics to cryptography to computer science, Turing was a visionary thinker in each field leaving a legacy that has influenced most of our modern inventions, and thanks to a bronze monument in Sackville Park you can sit and have a spot of lunch and a chat with him.

The 2001 Alan Turing Memorial, in Sackville Park, is a sculpture in memory of Alan Turing, a pioneer of modern computing whose work at Bletchley Park saved thousands of lives when it contributed to the curtailment of World War II by many months. Sadly, we repaid this momentous and patriotic achievement in the most disgraceful and shabby way.

Isaac Newton isn't the only Manchester celebrity who achieved fame with the help of an apple; tragically, Turing too is depicted holding an apple, but one he had injected with cyanide which he had elected to eat in preference to the indignity of the chemical castration he was offered. Sometimes the world moves on far too slowly despite, or because of the hypocrisy often endemic in those who defend bastions of, for example, homophobia, racism and misogyny.

See also
https://www.manturing.net/manufacturing-blog/2019/4/20/milk-bars

Richmond Tea Rooms, Sackville Street

'Go ask Alice when she's ten feet tall'[1]

Alice in Wonderland meets Salvador Dali. The place to go for an award winning 'Alice in Wonderland' themed dining experience. The restaurant is the brainchild of Nick Curtis and Andrew Underwood who say:

'From our enchanted forest area where you can dine under the twinkling lights in a woodland themed room, to the orangery which is the most warming garden even on the rainiest of Manchester days. We decided to think out the box and create a different and unique space that still kept a heavy influence from Lewis Carroll's 'Alice in Wonderland.''

Specialties include the Gay Pride Rainbow Cake.

1. *Lyric from White Rabbit, by Jefferson Airplane*

St Augustine's Burial Ground, Granby Row

> *Notorious for two things: the noisome stench and the 'black unctuous matter' that oozed from the foundations*

Where is it? The burial ground has long since been demolished and the site now forms part of the University of Manchester campus. But if you walk down Sackville Street and then turn left on to Granby Row, the burial ground was situated on the left-hand side.

Notorious for two things: the noisome stench and the 'black unctuous matter' that oozed from the foundations during the construction of an extension to the school on Coburg Street in 1854 – all emanating from the eighteen layers of coffins stacked on top of each other; and the nocturnal, clandestine work of Manchester's body snatchers anxious to keep the city's burgeoning anatomy departments well stocked with fresh and viable cadavers. You could get £10.00 for a pre-loved corpse with one careful (in some cases no doubt careless?) owner. That's about £1,150 in today's money.

William Johnson and William Harrison were the two hapless Resurrectionists in question, caught red-handed when a curious neighbour mistook them for thieves. Identification was problematic: Constable Lavender and his trusty beagles came upon several bodies that had been stuffed into cases, awaiting shipment to schools in Manchester and London. Lavender took out an advertisement in the local newspaper stating that the bodies would be on public display the following day, and, such was the anticipated demand, that viewing was by ticket. After a while all the bodies were claimed and re-interred. Johnson and Harrison were later found guilty and sentenced to fifteen months at Lancaster Castle.

The Vimto Monument, Granby Row

> *Vimto is an anagram of 'vomit' – proof indeed that branding was in its infancy in 1908*

Vimto (originally Vim Tonic) has its own large monument on the place where it was first created in 1908 in a factory by herbalist John Noel Nichols, who was looking to gain a foothold in the soft drinks market, capitalising on the Temperance Movement. The drink was made from a blend of fruits (grapes, blackcurrants, raspberries), spices and herbs that gave it a distinctly medicinal tang. Installed in 1992 the monument is a giant Vimto bottle surrounded at its base by outsized versions of some of the fruits and herbs used in the drink's production, all carved out of sustainable wood by environment artist Kerry Morrison. The observant reader will have noticed that Vimto is an anagram of 'vomit' – proof indeed that branding was in its infancy in 1908.

Vimto was concocted in Ayres Road in Salford and became a big hit, not just in Britain, but also in the Middle East where sales peak during Ramadan and in the Solomon Islands where it outsells Coca-Cola.

Victory over Blindness Statue, Piccadilly Station

The blind leading the blind then, but fixedly looking us in the eye at the same time

A very moving and thought-provoking bronze sculpture by Johanna Domke-Guyot is outside the main entrance of Manchester Piccadilly station commissioned by Blind Veterans UK to commemorate the centenary of the First World War. It was unveiled on October 16, 2018, and depicts seven blinded First World War soldiers leading one another away from the battlefield with their hand on the shoulder of the man in front; it is the only permanent memorial to the injured of that conflict. Dramatically, their likeness is based upon real veterans who all suffered blindness as a result of action on the frontline. Unusually a plinth is not used and the figures are situated at eye level to engage passers-by. The blind leading the blind then, fixedly but looking us in the eye at the same time.

Significantly it is not that far from the site of the convalescent camp at Heaton Park which treated and rehabilitated thousands of wounded First World War soldiers and sailors, including many with sight loss.

The Coroner's Court in London Road Fire Station.

London Road Fire Station (1906)

Facilities included a laundry, gym, billiards room and children's play-areas. The complex contained stables for the horses that pulled the fire appliances, and a blacksmith's workshop.

Not just your normal fire station: in addition to being a fire station, the building housed a police station, an ambulance station, a branch of Williams Deacon's Bank (later Bank of Scotland), a coroner's court, and a gas-meter testing station. This fire station was nothing short of ingenious in terms of design and practicalities: it operated for 80 years, housing 32 firemen and their families and six single firemen. Robert Bonner (1986)[1] tells us that

Facilities included a laundry, gym, billiards room and children's play-areas. The complex contained stables for the horses that pulled the fire appliances, and a blacksmith's workshop. There were electric bells and lights to alert firemen to an alarm, poles to expedite the firemen's response, suspended harnesses to allow the horses to be harnessed quickly, and electric doors. The fire station was also designed with foresight; the appliance bays were made wide enough to take motorised fire appliances. The station's first motorised fire appliance arrived in 1911, five years after it opened.

Bonner adds that the building has a ventilation system designed by Musgrave and Company to prevent the smells from the horses' stalls entering the firemen's living quarters. How? Fresh air was drawn in through the top of the fire station's tower, purified and circulated around the building. When the air reached the end of the circuit, in the stalls, it was extracted from the building. The system meant that the air in the building was replaced every 10 minutes. Ingenious.

After the war it became a training centre and in 1952 became the first centre equipped to record emergency calls. The building was the headquarters of the Manchester Fire Brigade until the brigade was replaced by the Greater Manchester Fire Service in 1974. The fire station closed in 1986, since when it has been largely unused despite several redevelopment proposals.

---

1. Bonner, Robert (1986), *The finest fire station in this round world: a history of the Coroner's Court in London Road Fire Station, Manchester*, Manchester: GMC Public Relations Unit pp. 3,9, 16; idem, (1988), *Manchester Fire Brigade*, Manchester: Archive Publications, p.56

Charles Street Pissotière

This essential piece of street furniture was to be found next to the Lass O'Gowrie pub on Charles Street with its outlet pouring directly into, and adding to the pollution of, the river Medlock; it saw its last splash in 1896. Manchester claims three other pissotières, including one on Great Ancoats Street. They only lasted until the 1890s and by the 1930s were replaced by 145 public conveniences – what happened in the intervening forty years I wonder. Only 31 of these were for women (21.37 per cent), on the grounds that women shouldn't be out on the streets anyway(!) It would appear that today the public convenience for both sexes is once again becoming an endangered species.

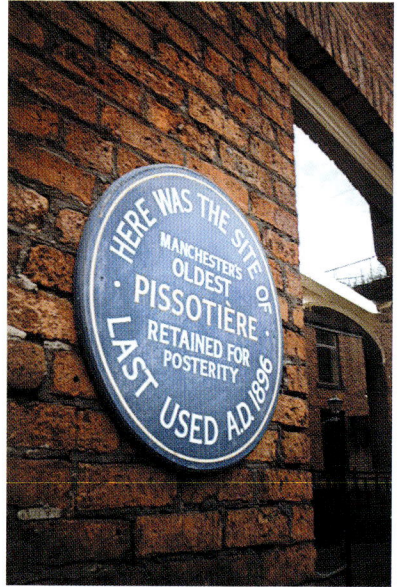

Retained for Posteriors

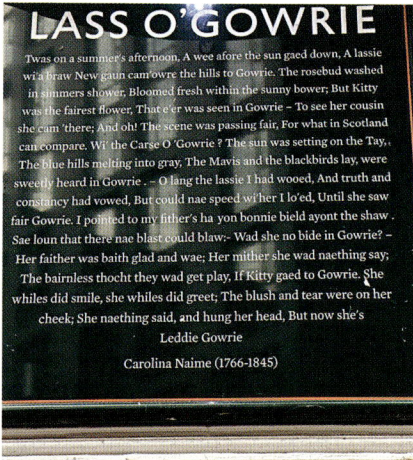

Plaque on The Lass O' Gowrie pub on Charles Street.

By the way…

The Toilets of Manchester Tour

- the city's 'most convenient tour', this guided walk explores the history of Manchester's provision and use of toilets, from the Industrial Revolution onwards.

See www.manchesterguidedtours.com

Bridgewater Hall

The main auditorium sits on a foundation of earthquake-proof isolation bearings that insulate it from noise and vibration from the adjacent road and Metrolink line.

A major Manchester concert venue covering the whole gamut of musical entertainment from jazz to classical by way of rock, pop and folk in 280 or so concerts every year. It is home to the 165-year-old Hallé Orchestra as well as to the Hallé

Choir, Hallé Youth Orchestra and Manchester Boys Choir, and it serves as the main concert venue for the BBC Philharmonic.

Acoustics? The building sits on a bed of 280 springs intended to insulate it from external sound. Sound proofing? The main auditorium sits on a foundation of earthquake-proof isolation bearings that insulate it from noise and vibration from the adjacent road and Metrolink line. It seats audiences of up to 2,341 people over four tiers in the auditorium: the stalls, choir circle, circle, and gallery.

The Archimedes Sculpture

'Εύρηκα'

Archimedes, or this version of him, sits under the railway arches on Altringham Street and depicts a larger than life-size Archimedes, springing out from his bath during that famous 'Eureka!' moment; he is captured in stone by Thompson Dagnall and was unveiled in 1990. 'Eureka!' derives from the Greek 'Εύρηκα' - meaning 'I've got it'. Archimedes of Syracuse (c. 287 BCE – c. 212 BCE) is one of the greatest mathematicians, physicists, engineers, inventors, and astronomers of all time. Plutarch gives us this description of just how obsessed Archimedes was with, and how passionate he was about, his work:

'being perpetually charmed by his familiar Siren, that is, by his geometry, he neglected to eat and drink and took no care of his person; that he was often carried by force to the baths, and when there he would trace geometrical figures in the ashes of the fire, and with his finger draws lines upon his body when it was anointed with oil, being in a state of great ecstasy and divinely possessed by his science'.

Dagnall captures this aura of the unkempt very well.

The killing of Archimedes at the end of the siege of Syracuse (213–211 BCE) is one of history's most notorious cases of mistaken identity. But Syracuse, the most beautiful of Greek colonial cities, had been well prepared for the siege: King Hiero II of Syracuse (r. 270 to 215 BCE) had installed catapults which outranged the Roman artillery, and a formidable array of anti-siege machinery. This was all the war work of Archimedes, a Syracusan citizen and the personification of a secret weapon, on a sabbatical from less bellicose research, now focusing on inventing military machinery. Eventually Marcellus took the city and allowed his troops to sack and plunder: one of the victims was Archimedes, run through by a legionary despite specific orders to spare him. When he burst in, the soldier demanded to know of Archimedes who he was as he poured over his plans and diagrams - but Archimedes was in no mood to be disturbed. Patience was in short supply, and Archimedes' instruments looked like good booty: the Roman slew him. Archimedes' last words were: "Do not disturb my circles", μή μου τοὺς κύκλους τάραττε, or, in Latin: *Noli turbare circulos meos*. Nothing in this riddle could have suggested to the soldier that he was confronting the protected Archimedes.

By the way...

Newton's Apple Tree

On the green outside the Pariser Building in Sackville Street there are six apple trees. They are said to be scions of the tree in Grantham under which Isaac Newton was apparently sitting when he conceived his theory of gravity. Manchester University is one of a number of specially selected science centres and museums across the UK including Jodrell Bank Discovery Centre.

The Midland Hotel, Peter Street

> *Hitler allegedly had his eye on the Midland as a potential Nazi headquarters in a conquered Britain*

This is the nearest most of us will get to the inside of a Rolls Royce. The Midland was where Charles Rolls met Henry Royce leading to the formation of Rolls-Royce Limited in 1904. The Beatles were famously refused access to the French Restaurant for being "inappropriately dressed". Hitler allegedly had his eye on the Midland as a potential Nazi headquarters for a conquered Britain. American intelligence speculated that the area of Manchester around the Town Hall was spared from bombing during the Second World War so as not to damage the Midland Hotel. Unlikely, since bomb aiming accuracy in those days was rarely that good.

The Midland opened in 1903, built by the Midland Railway to serve Manchester Central railway station, its northern terminus for its rail services to London St Pancras. The Railway News gushed that the hotel had over 70,000 guests in its first year and described it as a "twentieth century palace". The hotel had a 1,000-seat purpose-built theatre where opera, drama and early Annie Horniman performances were staged, and a roof terrace where a string quartet performed. Arriving guests were sheltered from the inclement Manchester weather by a covered walkway.

Manchester Central Convention Complex
Manchester Central or GMEX (Greater Manchester Exhibition Centre)

Originally it was for 89 years Manchester Central railway station until 1969; with its distinctive arched roof boasting a span of 210 ft – it was the second-largest railway station roof span in the United Kingdom. At its height, in the 1930s, more than 400 trains passed through the station every day. It closed to passengers in 1969 and was renovated as an exhibition centre. Originally called the G-Mex Centre, from 1982 it was Manchester's primary music concert venue until the construction of the Manchester Arena. After renovation the venue reverted to its former name Manchester Central in 2007.

30. The Theatre Royal, Peter Street

'one of the finest examples of theatre architecture to have survived in Britain from the first half of the nineteenth century'

- The Theatre Trust

The Theatre Royal opened in 1845. Situated next to the Free Trade Hall, it is the oldest surviving theatre in Manchester operating as a theatre from 1845 until 1921, when it closed in the face of growing competition from the Palace Theatre and Opera House. The building has since been converted numerous times for use as a cinema, bingo hall and nightclub. It has been unoccupied since 2009. Notwithstanding, the Theatre Trust says 'its monumental façade considered one of the finest examples of theatre architecture to have survived in Britain from the first half of the nineteenth century. It was a source of inspiration for the front of London's Royal Opera House'.

Manchester Free Trade Hall, Peter Street

'I don't believe you'. Dylan's response to the heckler's accusation that he was behaving like Judas.

This beautiful building boasts plenty of interesting Manchester history from corn laws to orchestras. But it might be most recognisable to music fans as the venue for "that Dylan concert" that helped change music history when he plugged in and attracted comparisons with Judas Iscariot for his troubles.

More significantly perhaps the Free Trade Hall stands witness to the atrocity that was the 1819 Peterloo Massacre being built on the site at St Peter's Field on land donated by Richard Cobden; its construction in 1850 remembers the passing of the Corn laws in 1846 while the liberal and radical tradition of Manchester is embodied in Richard Cobden and John Bright who promoted free trade there.

In 1905 suffragettes Christabel Pankhurst and Annie Kenney had their day here when they interrupted a meeting of the, ironically, Liberal Party by

Christabel at the Free Trade Hall in 1909

repeatedly demanding of then Liberal Winston Churchill an answer to the vexed question whether if elected, the Liberals would give the vote to women. Christabel showed her contempt for the inevitable lack of response by spitting at a policeman and was arrested.

The Free Trade Hall is now part-converted into a glassy hotel, but still worth checking out for its architectural beauty and history.

Lydia Becker, Cooper Street, Deansgate

As well as being a leader in the early British suffrage movement she was an ardent amateur scientist with interests in biology and astronomy and an acquaintance of Darwin

We know of the Pankhursts' work in fighting for women's suffrage in Manchester. But there is another woman who deserves much credit in championing that cause, and that woman is Lydia Ernestine Becker (1827 –1890) who as well as being a leader in the early British suffrage movement was an ardent amateur scientist with interests in biology and astronomy.

In 1867 she founded the Ladies' Literary Society in Manchester. She began a correspondence with Charles Darwin and soon afterwards convinced him to submit a paper to the society. Becker sent a number of plant samples to Darwin from the fields surrounding Manchester and gave Darwin a copy of her "little book", *Botany for Novices* (1864). Becker is one of a number of 19th-century women who contributed to Darwin's scientific work. She was also awarded a national prize in the 1860s for a collection of dried plants prepared using a method that she had devised so that they retained their original colours. She gave a botanical paper to the Biology Section (D) at the 1868 meeting of the British Association about the effect of fungal infection on sexual development in a plant species[1]. Botany remained important to her, but her work for women's suffrage took over: her involvement in promoting and encouraging scientific education for girls and women brought these two things together.

She it was who established Manchester as a centre for the suffrage movement when she convened the first meeting of women's suffrage in Manchester; and with Richard Pankhurst she arranged for the first woman to vote in a British election: a court case was unsuccessfully brought to exploit the precedent. The first public meeting of the National Society for Women's Suffrage was held on April 14, 1868, in the Free Trade Hall at which Becker moved the resolution that women should be granted voting rights on the same terms as men. Becker is also remembered for founding and publishing the *Women's Suffrage Journal* between 1870 and 1890 with Jessie Boucherett[2]. Lydia was opposed to the violent and media friendly means espoused by Emmeline Pankhurst which explains why she has been virtually forgotten in women's history.

What was the trigger? Diane Atkinson tells us that[3]
In autumn 1866 Becker attended the annual meeting of the National Association for the Advancement of Social Science, where she was excited by a paper from Barbara Bodichon entitled "Reasons for the Enfranchisement of Women". She dedicated herself to organising around the issue, and in January 1867 convened the first meeting of the Manchester Women's Suffrage Committee, one of the first organisations of its kind in England. She got to know there Dr. Richard Pankhurst, known as 'the red Doctor' whom Becker described as 'a very clever little man with some extraordinary sentiments about life in general and women in particular'. He married Emmeline in 1879.

Other pioneering firsts for women:

- Becker embarked on a lecture tour of northern towns and cities on behalf of the society[4].
- In June 1869, Becker and fellow campaigners were successful in securing the vote for women in municipal elections.
- Having campaigned for the inclusion of women on school boards, in 1870 she was one of four women elected to the Manchester School Board on which she served until her death.[5]
- In the same year Becker and her friend Jessie Boucherett founded the *Women's Suffrage Journal* and soon afterward began organising speaking tours of women – a rare thing in Britain at the time.[6]
- At an 1874 speaking event in Manchester organised by Becker, fifteen-year-old Emmeline Pankhurst experienced her first public gathering in the name of women's suffrage.[7]
- On 24 March 1877 Lydia appeared at a public meeting alongside J.W White, Henry Birchenough, Alice Cliff Scatcherd (subsequently one of the co-founders of the Women's Franchise League) and other early suffragists to discuss women's access to the vote in Macclesfield.[8]
- In 1880, Becker and colleagues campaigned in the Isle of Man for the right of women to vote in the House of Keys elections. Unexpectedly, they were successful and they secured for women voting rights in the Isle of Man for the first time in the elections of March 1881.[9]

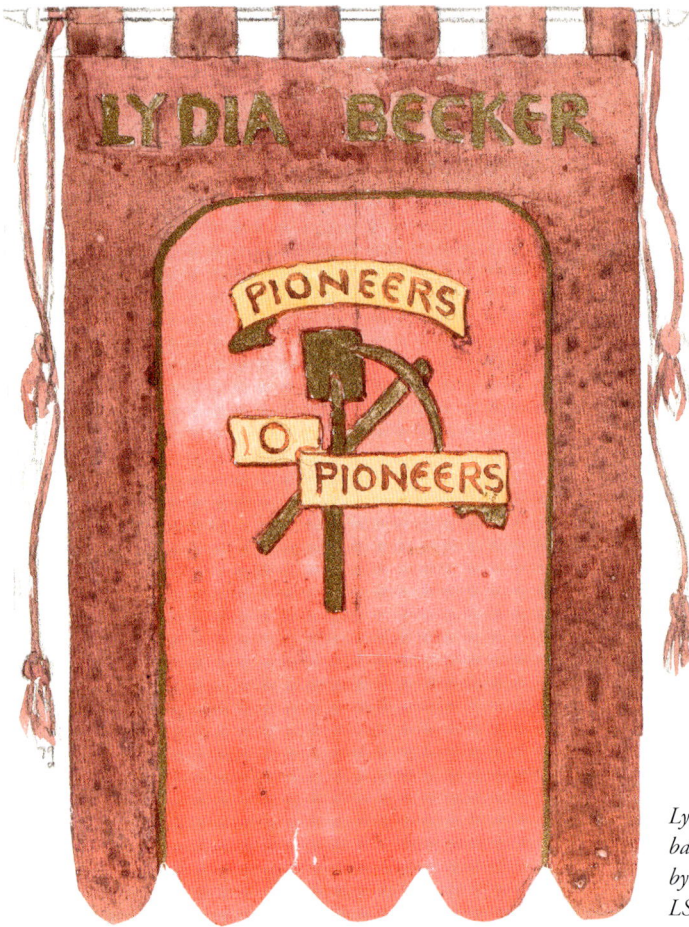

*Lydia Becker
banner designed
by Mary Lowndes.
LSE Library*

- Becker was voted chair of the Central Committee of the National Society for Women's Suffrage. This organisation had been formed in 1871 to lobby parliament.

According to the Chadderton Historical Society Becker differed from many early feminists in her disputation of essentialised femininity[10]. Arguing there was no natural difference between the intellect of men and women, Becker was a vocal advocate of a non-gendered education system in Britain. She also differed with many suffrage activists in arguing more strenuously for the voting rights of *unmarried* women. Women with husbands and regular sources of income, Becker believed, were less desperately in need of the vote than widows and single women. This stance made her the target of frequent ridicule in newspapers in both commentary and cartoons[11].

Lilly Maxwell

> *Lily is more than a mistake on the electoral roll. This Scottish former servant is part of the fabric of the long, hard fight for women to get the vote.*
>
> *- Sophy Ridge*

There was a near miss for the movement a few months after meeting Pankhurst when a widowed shop owner, Lilly Maxwell (c.1800 – 1876), appeared in error on the register of voters in Manchester. She was originally in domestic service before saving up enough money and setting up a shop selling a wide range of goods from crockery and candles to red herring at 25 Ludlow Street, Chorlton-upon-Medlock. On 4 April 1866 she made the newspapers when she was fined £1 in the Police Court for defrauding her customers with falsified weights and light measures.

The properties in Ludlow Street were of sufficient value to qualify their occupiers under the pre-1867 £10 household borough franchise. Consequently, her name appeared on the list of voters for Manchester because her name, Lilly, was mistaken for that of a man[12]. Her accidental inclusion on the list was discovered by one of the candidates for election, Jacob Bright, an ardent supporter of women's suffrage. Alongside his wife, Ursula Mellor Bright, he was a founder of the Manchester branch of the National Society for Women's Suffrage, in January 1867. Bright's election committee alerted Lydia Becker, the society's secretary, to Maxwell's appearance on the list, and she informed Maxwell of the situation. The outcome was a pivotal test case at the Court of Common Pleas.

Becker visited Maxwell and went with her to the polling station in Chorlton Town Hall. The returning officer found Maxwell's name on the list and allowed her to vote; reputedly the room erupted with cheers for Britain's first ever female voter. Becker immediately began encouraging other women heads of households in the region to petition for their names to appear on the rolls resulting in more than 5,000 more female heads of households applying for their names to appear on the electoral rolls; these claims were presented at the Court of Common Pleas (L.R. 4 C.P. 374) on 2 November 1868 by Sir John Coleridge QC and, as junior counsel, Richard Pankhurst (later the husband of prominent suffragette Emmeline Pankhurst)[13].

This was the first of the appeals brought in the Court of Common Pleas by women who had been struck off the voters register simply for being women. In this case, the court decided that women legally had no right to franchise. Byles J said in his judgment: 'I think it clear from the words of the Act 30 & 31 Vict. c. 102, that the word "man" in s. 3 does not include a woman but is confined to a man in the ordinary and popular signification of that word.' And so the loophole was closed and women's suffrage declared illegal.

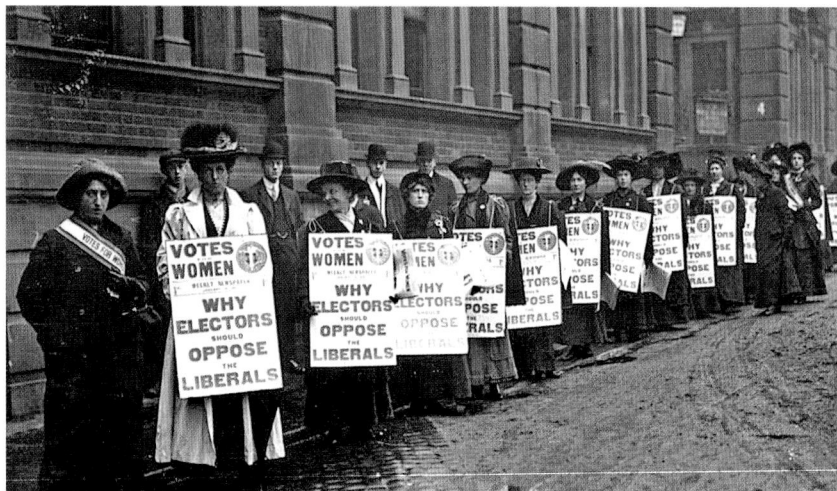

In January 1868 the *Englishwoman's Review* wrote of Lilly:
'It is sometimes said that women, especially those of the working class, have no political opinion at all. Yet this woman, who by chance was furnished with a vote, professed strong opinions and was delighted to have a chance of expressing them.'

Lilly was largely forgotten. She died in 1876 in the Withington Workhouse.

Becker's name and image, alongside those of 58 other women's suffrage supporters, are etched on the plinth of the statue of Millicent Fawcett in Parliament Square, London.

In Paris, a street is named after her, the 'Allée Lydia-Becker' near Montmartre, close to the rue Eva-Kotchever. In Chadderton, Oldham, a street is named for her, Lydia Becker Way. Becker's name is listed on the south face of the Reformers Memorial in Kensal Green Cemetery in London.

A collection of books by women, including some from Helen Blackburn's collection, her friends and from second hand sources, was placed in two bookcases decorated with paintings of Becker and Caroline Ashurst Biggs, who had been chairs of the Central Committee of the National Society for Women's Suffrage before Blackburn. These bookcases were given to Girton College, Cambridge[14].

'The Lydia Becker Institute of Immunology and Inflammation' was opened at The University of Manchester in 2018 - home to internationally renowned immunology and inflammation expertise in a vast array of basic and applied disciplines.

The institute is named after Lydia Becker because she was a celebrated natural scientist who interacted with Charles Darwin and because she firmly believed that women were intellectually equal to men and deserved the same opportunities.

Works:

- Botany for Novices (1864)
- "Female Suffrage" in *The Contemporary Review* (1867)
- "Is there any Specific Distinction between Male and Female Intellect?" in *Englishwoman's Review of Social and Industrial Questions* (1868)
- "On the Study of Science by Women" in *The Contemporary Review* (1869)
- "The Political Disabilities of Women" in *The Westminster Review* (1872)

1. *See Abir-Am, Pnina G.; Outram, Dorinda, eds. (1989). Uneasy careers and intimate lives: women in science, 1789–1979 (2nd, paperback ed.). New Brunswick; Ayres, Peter (2020). Women and the Natural Sciences in Edwardian Britain. Palgrave Macmilllan. p. 27*

2. *The Journal was the most popular publication relating to women's suffrage in 19th-century Britain. Roger Fulford, in his Votes for Women: The Story of a Struggle, writes: "The history of the decades from 1860 to 1890 – so far as women's suffrage is concerned – is the history of Miss Becker." The Journal published speeches from around the country, both within and outside of Parliament. Becker published her correspondence with her supporters and her opponents.*

3. *Atkinson, Diane (2018). Rise up, women!: the remarkable lives of the suffragettes. London. pp. 6, 14.*

4. *Herbet, Michael. Up Then Brave Women: Manchester's Radical Women 1819–1918. North West Labour History Society, 2012*

5. *Walker, Linda. "Becker, Lydia Ernestine (1827–1890), suffragist leader". Oxford Dictionary of National Biography (online ed.). Oxford University Press.*

6. *Phillips, Melanie. The Ascent of Woman: A History of the Suffragette Movement and the Ideas Behind It. London, 2004.p. 132.*

7. *Bartley, Paula. Emmeline Pankhurst. London, p. 22.*

8. *No. 868 Women's Suffrage Journal 1877". Women's Suffrage Journal. 8: 49. 1877*

9. *Herbet, p. 39*

10. *"Lydia Becker – The Life and Times". Famous Chaddertonians. Chadderton Historical Society. 25 May 2008.*

11. *Liddington, Jill and Norris, Jill. One Hand Tied Behind Us: The Rise of the Women's Suffrage Movement. Virago, 1978*

12. *Rix, Kathryn (26 November 2017). "'A woman actually voted!': Lily Maxwell and the Manchester by-election of November 1867". The Victorian Commons. Pugh, Martin (2000). The March of the Women: A Revisionist Analysis of the Campaign for Women's Suffrage, 1866–1914. Oxford. p. 21.*

13. *Some women voted 75 years before they were legally allowed to in 1918, Sarah Richardson, 18 March 2013, The Telegraph. In Praise of … Lily Maxwell, 19 March 2011, The Guardian; "The History Press Lily Maxwell: The first woman to vote".*

14. *Crawford, Elizabeth (2003). The Women's Suffrage Movement: A Reference Guide 1866–1928. Routledge. pp. 194*

Salford canal looking north to the Irwell. Author: Parrot of Doom

Manchester Salford Junction Canal Tunnel

Something of a 19th century tax avoidance scheme. Pennine Waterways tells us

The Manchester and Salford Junction Canal was built in 1839 to link the River Irwell and the Manchester, Bolton and Bury Canal to the Rochdale Canal. The canal was less than a mile long, with 4 locks and a tunnel below the Deansgate area. It was built to let boats get between the Irwell and the Rochdale Canal without having to pass through the Bridgewater Canal's Hulme link, the tolls for which were high.

In World War 2 it was drained and converted into a deep tunnel air-raid shelter running underground between Atherton Street and Watson Street. Capacity was a claustrophobic 5,000 people, working on the Home Office rule of 6 sq. feet per person and accessible to anyone within a 10 minute walk from the tunnel. Reassuringly, a bomb-proof dam was built across the entrance and 16 blast walls were built every 100 feet.

John Rylands Research Institute and Library, 150 Deansgate

A masterpiece of Victorian Gothic architecture

The John Rylands Research Institute and Library is one of, if not the, most beautiful buildings in Manchester: this masterpiece of Victorian Gothic architecture is more like a castle or cathedral. Architecture apart, highlights include the oldest known piece of the New Testament, the St John Fragment, magnificent illuminated medieval manuscripts and a 1476 William Caxton edition of Chaucer's *Canterbury Tales*.

We owe it all to the devoted, prescient and perceptive wife of John Rylands, Enriqueta. She was determined to give permanence to her husband's huge contribution to Manchester and Manchester's cultural life and so she bought some land on what is now Deansgate and built this monumental depositary for the some of the most important literary works in the land. Enriqueta based her collection on the Althorpe library which she purchased from the 2nd Earl Spencer and built it up magnificently as a start to the wonderful library we see today. Beautifully furnished and appointed with shades of an Oxbridge college the John Rylands Library is surely one of the jewels in the crown, not just of Manchester libraries but those of Britain and the world.

The 250,000 (and growing) volumes and one million plus archival items include rare manuscripts by Caxton and the personal archives of Elizabeth Gaskell and John Dalton.

courtesy of "Marketing Manchester/Rich J Jones"

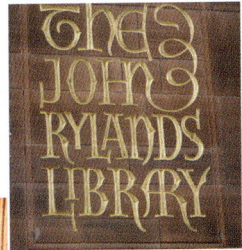

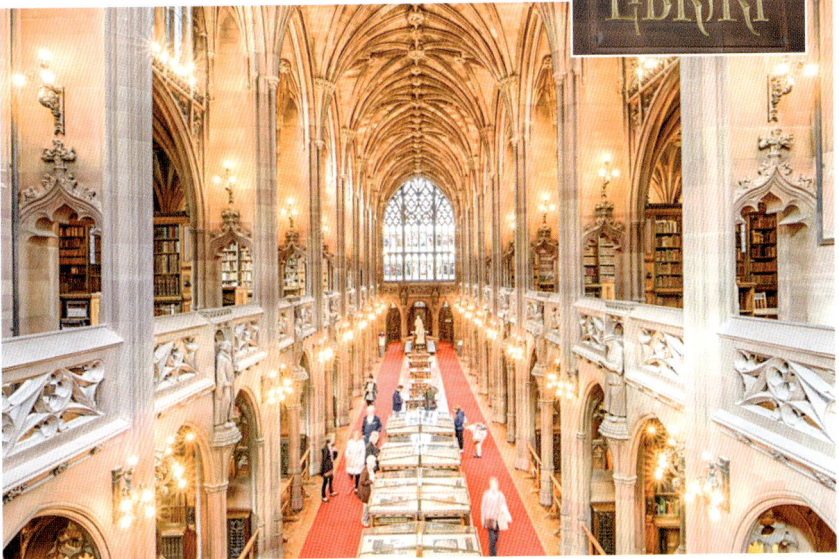

The Working Men's Church, Wood Street

there were also day trips to Southport leading to a seaside camp for 120 children

The church was commissioned by a charitable organization that sought to help those people who were ineligible for Poor Law relief. It is next to the Wood Street Mission and near to the Rylands Library. The plaque on the building indicates that it was rebuilt in 1905.

Today known variously as the Wood Street Mission, the Manchester and Salford Street Children's Mission and Working Mens Church was founded in 1869 by Alfred Alsop. Alsop's aim was to preach the Gospel in the slum areas of Deansgate, Salford and Hulme, once described as "the worst haunts of vice". As a social worker, Alsop realized that his zeal could not wholly eradicate hunger, poverty and destitution. Hence, he initiated a charitable movement that resolved to provide the basic necessities of life: food, shelter and clothing to the less fortunate.

Clothes and shoes were distributed and gifts were given at Christmas; there were also day trips to Southport leading to the building of a seaside camp for 120 children.

Seaside and queuing up outside the mission

Central Manchester

This relocated to Blackpool then, in1963, to an outdoor pursuits centre in the Derbyshire Dales. The Wood Street Mission continues to provide services to the community to this day, with particular emphasis on mitigating the effects of poverty and deprivation on children, young people, and their families in the Manchester and Salford areas.

The Frederyck Chopin statue, Deansgate

"My playing will be lost in such a large room, my compositions ineffective."

On 25 August 1848, Chopin travelled the eight hours to Manchester for a concert. When he arrived, he was horrified to find an audience of 1,200 at the Gentlemen's Concert Hall waiting to hear him play. He felt too weak to perform, saying to a friend, "My playing will be lost in such a large room, my compositions ineffective." He was pleased with his £60 fee, though - and the critics were not unkind to him.

(www.manchestersfinest.com tells us that the sculpture is about Poland, and about our own relationship with Poland and its people here in Manchester. Included in the statue is an eagle in flight- the symbol of Poland and behind Chopin is a battle scene which represents the Polish fight for freedom. Who's the woman then? One of his many muses (mistresses) - Baroness Aurore Lucile Dupon.

The British Pop Culture Archive, John Rylands Library

The British Pop Archive (BPA), is a unique collection of national significance dedicated to the preservation and research of popular music, popular culture, counter-culture, and youth culture. This ground breaking and innovative archive 'not only preserves the past but also serves as a dynamic resource for future generations to explore and understand the pivotal role of British popular culture on the global stage'. It is located in the John Rylands Library; launched in April 2021 it was a collaboration between the John Rylands Library and the John Ryland Research Institute.

The website https://ilovemanchester.com/did-you-know-manchester-holds-the-british-pop-culture-archive gives us an idea of what is included in the archive:

When we first opened the exhibition, we did an exhibit called Collection. It was a Manchester-focused archive...

- We had several of Ian Curtis's handwritten lyrics from Joy Division, including a notebook, some lyrics, and correspondence.

One of Johnny Marr's guitars

- We showcased one of Johnny Marr's guitars and materials from the archives of Tony Wilson. We've also got some stuff from Rob Gretton – manager of Joy Division and New Order.

- We included items from the Hacienda, City Life magazine founder Andy Spinoza, and photographer Kevin Cummins.

- Additionally, we incorporated materials from Granada Television's corporate archive and the personal archives of former Granada employees.

People's History Museum, Left Bank, Spinningfields

The Jo Cox Memorial Wall was on public display for the first time since Jo's murder in June 2016, alongside a specially commissioned virtual Wall of Hope to add your personal tribute message.

The national museum of working people, replete with items depicting the history of workers' rights, unions, women's suffrage, Peterloo, the dockers, democracy – the right to vote - and protest. The museum tells the history of workers' rights and democracy in Great Britain and people's lives at home, work and leisure over the last 200 years. The collection includes 2,000 posters focused on elections and political campaigns, 300 political cartoons, 7,000 trade union badges and tokens, as well as 95,000 photographs. With over 400 trade union and political banners, the PHM holds the largest banner collection in the world and visitors can see banners being conserved in Main Gallery Two in the Textile Conservation studio. This glorious museum is in fact the United Kingdom's national centre for the collection, conservation, interpretation and study of material relating to the history of working people in the UK.

The PHM also houses the Labour History Archive and Study Centre; collections include the archives of the Labour Party, the former Communist Party of Great Britain, the co-operative movement and the Department for Work and Pensions. It also contains documents relating to Chartism, general elections, the First World War, women's suffrage and the 1984–1985 miners' strike.

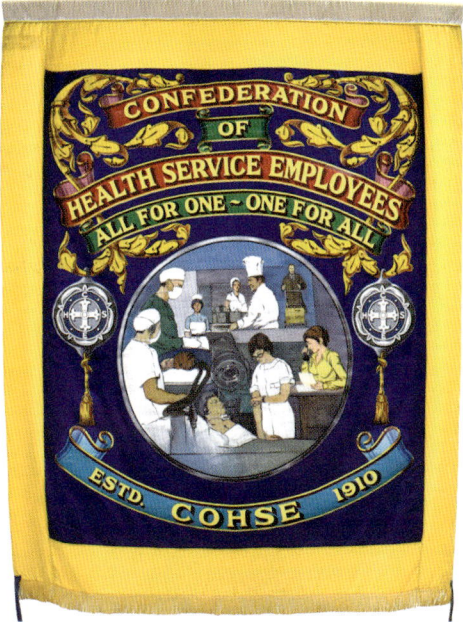
Image courtesy of People's History

Highlights have included More in Common: in memory of murdered MP Jo Cox. A recent special exhibition explored Jo Cox's life and legacy; the Jo Cox Memorial Wall was on public display for the first time since Jo's murder in June 2016, alongside a specially commissioned virtual Wall of Hope to add your personal tribute message.

Manchester Art Gallery, Mosley Street

'This is an art school for everybody, and for life – a free and accessible institution for the city and its people'.

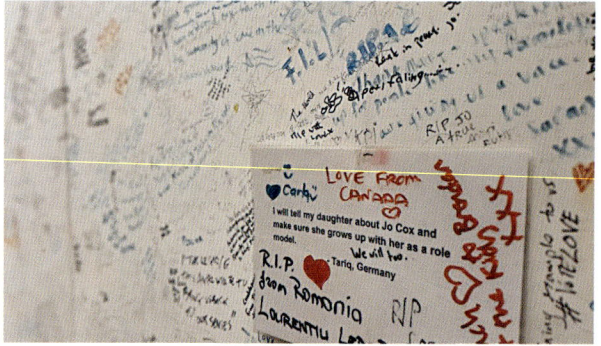

Manchester Art Gallery has been at the very heart of city life for 200 years, from its origins in the Royal Manchester Institution for the Promotion of Literature, Science and the Arts, founded in 1823, it's been proudly part of Manchester City Council since 1882. The gallery actively promotes art as a means to achieve positive social change.

It can boast a stunning collection of more than 25,000 objects; the first object acquired for its collection, James Northcote's A Moor - a portrait of the celebrated black actor Ira Aldridge - was bought in 1827.

'The Scapegoat' (1854) by William Holman Hunt depicts the "scapegoat" described in the 'Book of Leviticus'. On the Day of Atonement, a goat would have its horns wrapped with a red cloth – representing the sins of the community – and be driven off. Like Maddox Brown's 'Work' the Scapegoat is exhibited in two versions: one in the Lever Art Gallery, Port Sunlight; the other here, a smaller version in more vivid colours with a dark-haired goat and a rainbow. Hunt wrote that "the scene was painted at Sodom, on the margin of the salt-encrusted shallows of the Dead Sea. The mountains beyond are those of Edom." He painted most of the work on location in 1854, but completed the work in London in the following year[1].

Ford Madox Brown's Pre-Raphaelite masterpiece 'Work' is here for all to see. 'Work' (1852–1865) is generally considered to be his most important achievement. It exists in two versions: a smaller version is in Birmingham Museum and Art Gallery. The painting ambitiously and successfully attempts to portray, both literally and analytically, the totality of the Victorian social system and the transition from a rural to an urban economy.

The picture depicts a group of "navvies" digging up the road to build a tunnel. It is typically assumed that this was part of the extensions of London's sewerage system, which were being undertaken to deal with the threat of typhus and cholera. The workers form the centre of the painting; on either side of them are individuals who are either unemployed or represent the leisured classes. Behind the workers are two wealthy figures on horseback, whose progress along the road has inconveniently been halted by the excavations[2].

The painting also portrays an election campaign, evidenced by posters and people carrying sandwich boards with the name of the candidate "Bobus". A poster also draws attention to the potential presence of a burglar.

The setting is an accurate depiction of The Mount on Heath Street in Hampstead, where a side road rises up above the main road and runs alongside it. Brown made a detailed study of the location in 1852[3].

The Gallery of Costume, formerly at Platt Hall, has its own gallery here. See https://manchesterartgallery.org/costume/ for details, is coming to the Gallery, and will be the world's first dedicated museum of fashion and dress is coming in the guise of the Fashion Gallery.

Vibrant and vivid South Asian design

1. Bronkhurst, Judith, *Wiliam Holman Hunt, A Catalogue Raisonné*, vol. 1, p.180.

2. Biome, Albert, "Ford Madox Brown, Carlyle, and Karl Marx: Meaning and Mystification of Work in the Nineteenth Century", *Arts Magazine*, September 1981

3. Curtis, Gerald, *Ford Madox Brown's Work: An Iconographic Analysis*, "The Art Bulletin", Vol. 74, No. 4 (Dec. 1992), pp. 623–636

The Britannia Hotel, Portland Street

The six-storey building was originally Watt's warehouse, big players in the Lancashire cotton industry. It opened in 1856 as a textile warehouse for the wholesale drapery business of S & J Watts, and was the largest single-occupancy textile warehouse in Manchester. The building was designed to showcase Manchester's position at the centre of global trade, specifically a global centre for the cotton trade.

In 1979 Britannia Hotels bought the building: the famous entrance stairway, already a prominent feature of the building, was kept intact, giving a feel of elegance to the hotel's main lobby. The staircase and chandeliers remain one of the most impressive features of the Britannia Hotel.

Mr Thomas's Chop House, aka Sarah's Chop House, Cross Street (St Ann's Alley)

Women were forbidden – apart from the waitresses

Mr Thomas's Chop House was established in 1867 by Thomas & Sarah Studd, brother to Samuel Studd of Sam's Chop House. The interior is breathtaking, largely original, with its arches and Victorian floor tiling.

Back in the 1860s Manchester was a dynamic hub for industry, social revolution, enlightened thinkers and a frantic race for upwards social mobility. It became a magnet for people from all over the world searching for new opportunity and wealth.

A young chef from London, Thomas Studd, was one of those migrants starting his life in Manchester working in the kitchens of the ubiquitous Chop Houses doing good trade in Victorian England as meeting places for the leaders of industry and society to meet and do deals over flagons of beer, brandy, steaks, chops and sandwiches.

Women were forbidden – apart from the waitresses. While working in Brown's Chop House on Market Street, Tom met Sarah, one of the waitresses there. They shared the same ambitions, and soon they married and opened their own Chop House on Cross Street, opposite the original Town Hall and the Cross Street Chapel, it soon became one of the most popular establishments in town.

When, seven years later, Tom fell ill Sarah took over, running the Chop House and bringing up their eight children. Sarah was determined and introduced women to her clientele and even established a ladies room at the Chop House, in 1871 – a development way ahead of the time and certain to have caused outrage amongst some of her regulars.

In 1880 Thomas died, but not in vain as the output grew under Sarah to 400 covers per day.

To honour Sarah and her daughter, another Sarah, the current owners renamed Mr Thomas's Chop House to Sarah's Chop House on International Women's Day 2019. Almost 160 years later, Tom's, now Sarah's, remains a proud family-owned business.

St Mary's Church altar, by Anthony O'Neil Geograph

The Hidden Gem, St Mary's Catholic Church, Mulberry Street

"No matter on what side of the church you look, you behold a hidden gem"

'The Hidden Gem' is Manchester's oldest Catholic church, built in 1794. Its exterior is misleadingly unassuming and the only indication of the majestic interior is the doorway which features intricate carved designs. Inside, the church has a number of beautiful marble sculptures as well as wonderful architecture. Especially astounding is the Norman Adams 'Stations of the Cross', a number of paintings completed by commission in 1995 to celebrate Catholicism. There is also an impressive version of da Vinci's 'Last Supper'.

The Richard Cobden Statue, St Ann's Square

One of 11 children, son of a farmer, Cobden started out as a traveling salesman in the textile industry. He became one of the first elected aldermen on Manchester council and was voted MP for Stockport; he was a leading figure in the movement to repeal the Corn Laws and it was Cobden who recruited John Bright to speak at the rallies that were held nationwide. Along with Bright Cobden also went on to campaign against the Crimean War, for which they were derided; both lost their seats in Parliament in 1857.

But by 1859 though he was MP for Rochdale and went on to represent the British government in trade negotiations with France. He died of bronchitis in 1865.

By the way…

As well as the statue, a blue plaque is located on his former home on the corner of Byrom Street and Quay Street.

Science and Industry Museum, Liverpool Road

> *'take the best that exists and make it better. When it does not exist, design it'*
> *- Fredrick Henry Royce*

A goldmine of social and science history with a unique and extensive display of Manchester's textile heritage. It houses the world's oldest surviving passenger railway station and the world's first railway warehouse from 1830. You can see astonishing objects and learn about the men and women whose ideas changed the world. Daily demonstrations bring the museum's world class collection of textile and industrial machinery to life while there are interactive exhibits to explore and a regular programme of changing exhibitions to enjoy.

In 1978, Greater Manchester Council purchased the earliest part of the former Liverpool Road station from British Rail, which had been closed in 1975. The museum opened at this site in 1983 and later expanded to include the whole of the old station.

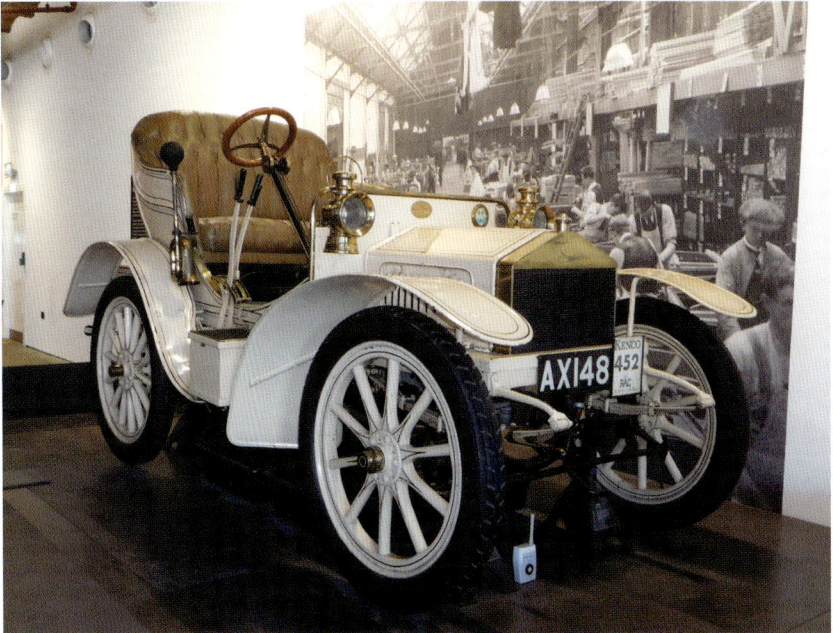

This beautiful machine epitomises Manchester's proud reputation for manufacturing excellence and finesse in design. As we have seen, Messrs Rolls and Royce met in the Midland Hotel to iron out the details of a company which was to lead the world in motor car manufacture and design. Built in 1905 in Hulme this was Henry Royce's own Roller.

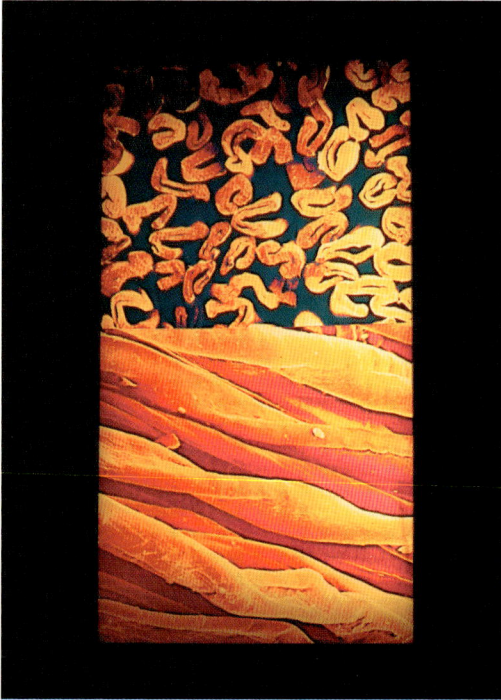

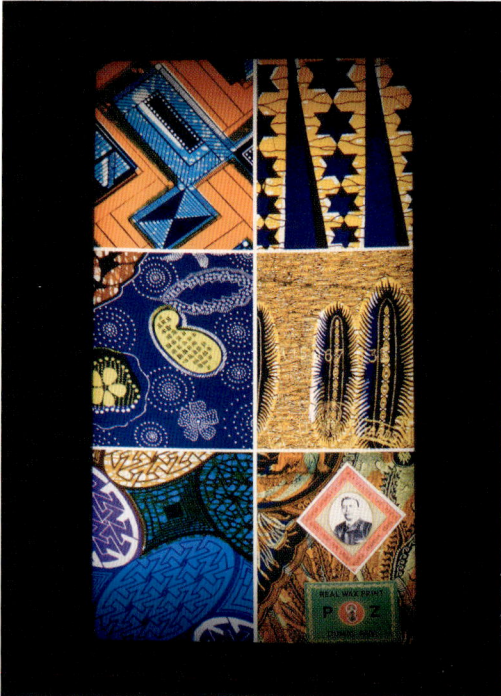

*SOME STUNNING
21ST CENTURY FABRIC
PHOTOGRAPHY IN THE
MUSEUM*

*High magnification photographs
of cotton fibres taken through a
microscope. Courtesy of Shirley
Technologies*

*ABC Brunnschweiler and
Paterson Zochonis fabric
patterns designed for the West
African market.*

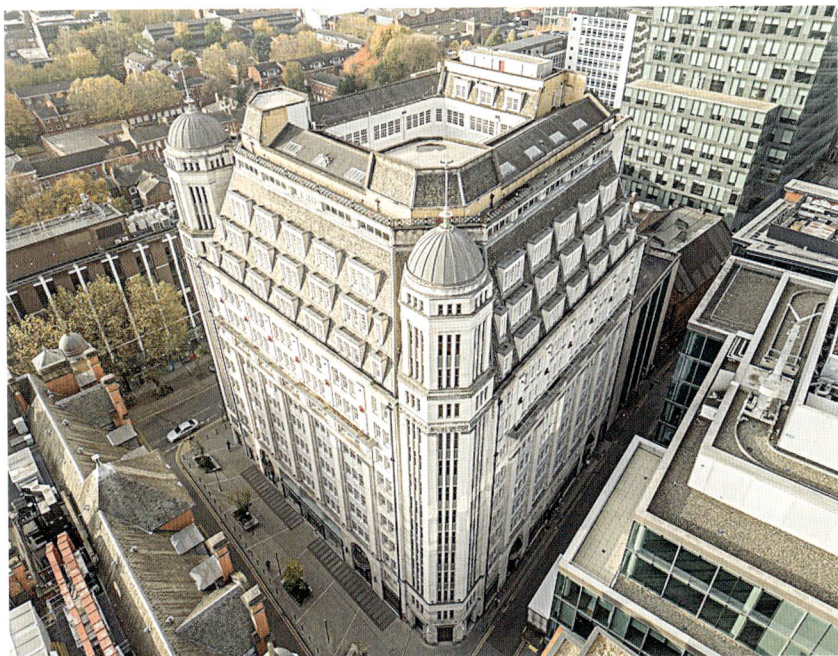

Sunlight House, Quay Street

'a soaring architectural statement'

Sunlight House is a stunning Grade II listed building in the art deco style completed in 1932 for developer, architect and entrepreneur Joseph Sunlight (1889–1978). At 14 storeys it was the first skyscraper to be built in the north of England and the tallest building in Manchester (reaching 200 feet from foundation to roof ridge) for a number of years until 1962 when the CIS Tower went up. Sunlight's turrets and multiple dormer windows and mansard roofs would enhance any skyline and make it a significant landmark in the city.

Sunlight was born in Russia as Josif Schimschlavitch. His new name was inspired by Lord Lever's pleasing model village at Port Sunlight.

Old Granada Studios, Quay Street

> *"Your starter for ten, no conferring", "fingers on buzzers",*
> *"I'll have to hurry you."*

The studios were the headquarters of Granada Television from 1956 to 2013; they are the oldest operating purpose-built television studios in the United Kingdom pre-dating BBC Television Centre by five years. As well as being the original home to Coronation Street, University Challenge and World in Action, the studios also held the Beatles' first television performance in 1962 and the first general election debate in 2010.

The studios closed in 2013, and ITV Granada and ITV Studios moved to Dock10's studios at MediaCityUK in Salford Quays. Later that same year, the Granada Studios was sold for £26 million to Allied London and Manchester City Council whose initial plans involved transforming the studios into residential space. However, plans were changed in 2017 to maintain the studio complex due to demand, and most studio spaces were reopened in 2018.

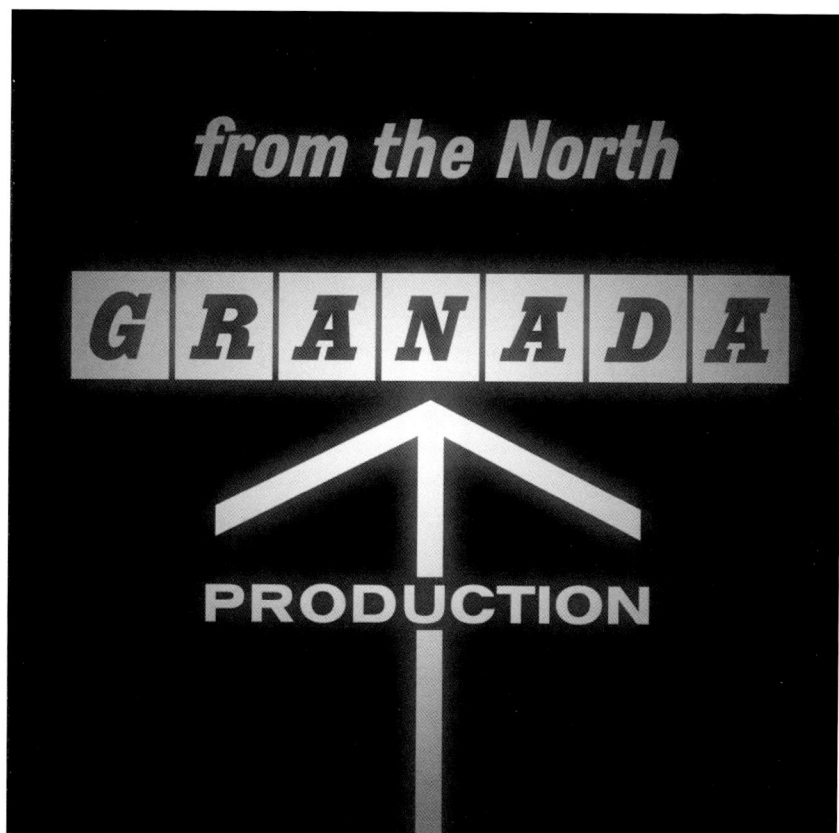

National Football Museum

Whether you like football or not, this really is social and cultural history at its best. Exhibits include Geoff Hurst's red England shirt and his hat-trick ball from the 1966 World Cup Final, view the infamous 'Diego Maradona Hand of God shirt'. The museum also has a statue of Lily Parr – a pioneer of women's football.

By the way…
see also the Football League Plaque on the site of the Royal Hotel.

The shirt worn by Diego Maradona when he scored two goals to knock England out of the 1986 World Cup, including the so-called "Hand of God" goal, sold for a record-breaking £7,142,500 at auction. Where was VAR when you needed it?

Lily Parr Statue, National Football Museum

We have come a long way since Lily Parr's days and she deserves recognition as a true pioneer of the sport.

- Marzena Bogdanowicz, head of marketing for women's football at the FA

Bogdanowicz continues 'Lily Parr was the first woman to enter the Football Hall of Fame, an iconic achievement in itself, so it's only fitting that she takes her place alongside other football legends and becomes the first woman [footballer] to be celebrated with a statue in her honour.'

The sculptor is Hannah Stewart, https://www. hannahstewartsculpture.co.uk/ figures-and-portraits/lily-parr

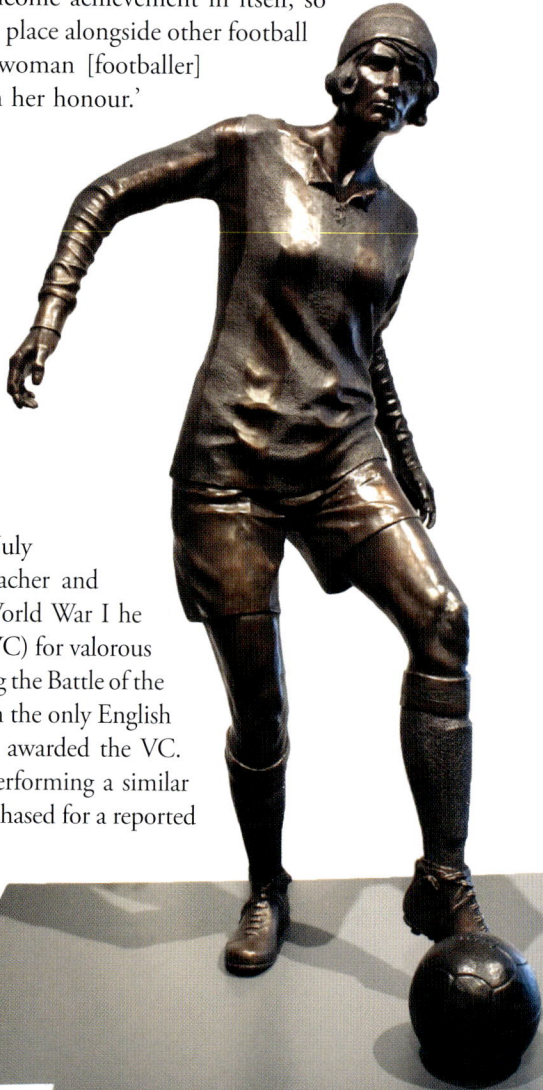

Donald Simpson Bell VC, National Football Museum

The Oxford Dictionary of National Biography tells us that Second Lieutenant Donald Simpson Bell, VC (1890 – 10 July 1916) was an English school teacher and professional footballer. During World War I he was awarded the Victoria Cross (VC) for valorous actions at Horseshoe Trench during the Battle of the Somme in mid-1916, making him the only English professional football player to be awarded the VC. Five days later Bell lost his life performing a similar act of bravery. His medal was purchased for a reported £210,000 by the Professional Footballers' Association and is on display at the National Football Museum.

Corporation Street and the IRA bomb

> *'A significant number of casualties (36, 18%) presented with emotional distress…'*

This is the street where the red and white Ford cargo van that contained the IRA bomb was, hazards flashing, illegally parked on double yellows outside Marks & Spencer and where, despite the best efforts of the British Army, it exploded at precisely 11.15 am on June 15, 1996[1]. The 1,500-kilogram (3,300 lb) bomb was the biggest bomb detonated in Great Britain since World War II[2].

The shockwaves travelled at 2,000 yards per second, apparently hurling people a quarter a mile away off their feet and showering the city with shards of glass. No one died, miraculously, but 212 people were injured and who knows how many would have suffered and still are suffering from PTSD[3]; the casualty profile report published in the *Journal of Accident & Emergency Medicine* reads as follows:

The Washington Post – democracy dies in darkness

OBJECTIVE: To produce a casualty profile for the Manchester bombing and to illustrate the potential uses of such templates in major incident planning. METHODS: A retrospective review of casualty notes from the Manchester bombing. RESULTS: A complete anonymous casualty profile for the Manchester bombing is given with AIS90 coded injuries. The majority (129, 62%) of casualties sustained minor injuries from flying glass. A significant number of casualties (36, 18%) presented with emotional distress or medical problems. A wide age range of casualties was involved. Few patients (19, 9%) required admission to hospital. There were no deaths and no casualties sustained major trauma. CONCLUSIONS: Casualty profiles may be useful in the planning and testing of health service major incident plans. Such information should be easily accessible to all emergency planners.

There was enormous damage to nearby buildings; a GPO post box at the scene survived more or less intact. The van ended up on the roof garden two stories up of a nearby Co-op building.

The Manchester Bomb. 15th June 1996.

Several buildings were irreparably damaged and were demolished, while many more were closed for months for structural repairs. Most of the rebuilding work was completed by the end of 1999, at a cost of £1.2 billion, although redevelopment continued until 2005. The silver lining, if we need one, is that the bombing has, however, been viewed by some as a "catalyst" for Manchester's mass regeneration, turning it into a modern "powerhouse" city with above-national average economic growth in the 20 years following the bombing[4]. Others say that's not true and the city was already engaged on a rigorous generation scheme. Moreover, the evacuation procedure carried out by the police and other emergency services when 75,000 people were evacuated was successful and a credit to their planning and organisation.

Ray King tells us how a search of the area for casualties involved a brief confusion when mannequins blasted out of shop windows were mistaken for bodies. Hospitals across Greater Manchester were made ready to receive those injured in the blast. The police commandeered a Metrolink tram to take 50 of the casualties to North Manchester General Hospital, which treated 79 in total; a further 80 were cared for at the Manchester Royal Infirmary, and many others were treated in the streets by ambulance crews assisted by doctors and nurses who happened to be in the city centre that morning[5].

Insurers paid out £411 million (£1 billion in 2023) in damages for what was at the time one of the most expensive man-made disasters ever, and there was considerable under-insurance[6].

According to Home Office statistics, about 400 businesses within half a mile of the blast were affected, 40% of which never recovered. The heaviest damage was sustained by the three buildings nearest the bomb:

- Michael House, comprising Marks & Spencer and a six-storey office block. Michael House was deemed beyond economic repair and demolished. Marks & Spencer took the opportunity to acquire and demolish the adjacent Longridge House, using the enlarged site to build the world's biggest branch of the brand. Things changed, however, during construction, and Selfridges subsequently co-occupied the building; Marks & Spencer leased part of the Lewis's store in the interim.[7]

- Longridge House, offices for Royal and Sun Alliance

- The Arndale Centre. The frontage of the Arndale was badly damaged and was remodelled when this area of the city centre was redeveloped.

Furthermore, the glass domes of the Corn Exchange and the Royal Exchange were blown to smithereens. The landlord of the Corn Exchange invoked a force majeure condition in the lease to evict all tenants, ultimately enabling him to convert the building into a shopping and restaurant emporium centre. The dome of the Royal Exchange shifted in the blast; its reconstruction took two and a half years and cost £32 million, paid for by the National Lottery.

"One Man's Fool", the closing track on Genesis' 1997 album Calling All Stations, was inspired by the bombing. Tony Banks stated in a SongFacts interview:

I remember I wrote the song "One Man's Fool", which was on the Calling All Stations album [1997]. If anybody hears it now, they would assume that lyric was referring to the bombing of the Twin Towers, but it wasn't. It was written four years before, and yet it sounds like we were recalling that. I was actually writing about a bomb attack in Manchester, in England, which was done by the IRA at the time, and the idea that people carry out these attacks and did they really believe that, all the destruction, that it really is worth it? But it still works, unfortunately, because we have this kind of terrorism still out there[8].

1. *Within three minutes a traffic warden had issued the vehicle with a parking ticket and called for its removal.*

2. *The device was a mixture of semtex, a military-grade plastic explosive, and ammonium nitrate fertiliser, a cheap and easily obtainable explosive used extensively by the IRA. Bits from what may have been a tremble trigger were also found later, designed to detonate the bomb if it was tampered with. See Oppenheimer, A. R. IRA: The Bombs and The Bullets. A History of Deadly Ingenuity. Irish Academic Press, 2009. p.131; Fleming, Nic (31 March 2004), "The Cheap and Easy Recipe for Bombs", Telegraph Media Group; King (2006), p. 6*

3. *Carley SD, Mackway-Jones K. The casualty profile from the Manchester bombing 1996: a proposal for the construction and dissemination of casualty profiles from major incidents. J Accid Emerg Med. 1997 Mar;14(2):76–80. doi: 10.1136/emj.14.2.76. PMID: 9132196; PMCID: PMC1342872.*

4. *Smithers, Dominic (15 June 2016), "Twenty years since the bomb and Manchester's property market", Manchester Evening News; Bounds, Andrew (14 June 2016), "Manchester's remarkable rise from the IRA rubble", Financial Times*

5. *King, pp. 21–22*

6. *Sengupata, Kim (28 March 1997), "£411m cost after Manchester bomb sets record", The Independent*

7. *Williams, pp. 86–87, 183–7, 218*

8. *Songfacts. "Tony Banks : Songwriter Interviews". www.songfacts.com.*

Further reading

King, Ray (2006), Detonation: Rebirth of a City, Clear Publications

Lesley-Dixon, Kenneth (2018), Northern Ireland: The Troubles from the Provos to the Det 1968–1998, Barnsley

Williams, Gwyndaf (2003), The enterprising city centre: Manchester's development challenge, Spon

By the way

Sadly, Manchester is no stranger to terrorist bombs; here are others which have afflicted the city:

- Manchester was hit by two nights of air raids on 22/23 and 23/24 December 1940. An estimated 684 people died and more than 2,000 were injured. On the first night of raids, 272 tons of high explosive bombs were dropped. The following night another 195 tons of high explosives devastated parts of the city. Almost 2,000 incendiaries were also dropped on the city across the two nights.

- In 1973 and 1974, firebombs damaged city centre businesses for which one man was later imprisoned.

- In April 1974, a bomb exploded at Manchester Magistrates' Court, injuring twelve.

- 1975, 27 January: An IRA bomb exploded at Lewis's department store in

Manchester. Following a warning telephoned to the Press Association at 16:07 pm, the bomb exploded 17 minutes later injuring 19 people, one of them seriously.

- In 1975, IRA bomb factories were found in Greater Manchester and five men were imprisoned for planning attacks in North West England

- On 3 December 1992, the IRA detonated two small bombs in Manchester city centre, forcing police to evacuate thousands of shoppers. More than 60 were hurt by shattered glass and the blasts cost an estimated £10 million in damage and business losses.

- 2009, 3 September: Manchester Piccadilly multiple suicide bomber plot. In 2009, Pakistani national Abid Naseer, was one of 12 suspects arrested on suspicion of being part of a Manchester Terror cell, after arriving in the UK a year before. All were released on insufficient evidence, but ordered to be deported from the UK. Naseer's deportation to Pakistan was prevented on human rights grounds, as he was ruled 'likely to be mistreated'. In 2013, on further evidence from Al-Qaeda sources, including documents from the bin Laden Raid, he was extradited to the US, and on 4 March 2015 was found guilty of masterminding an Al-Qaeda directed plot to synchronize multiple suicide bombings around Manchester's Arndale Centre and Piccadilly shopping centre in a coordinated attack involving other locations, including the New York Subway, with other cells.

- The Manchester Arena bombing occurred at 10:31 p.m. on 22 May 2017; it was an Islamic terrorist suicide bombing of the Manchester Arena following a concert by Ariana Grande. Perpetrated by Islamic extremist Salman Abedi and aided by his brother, Hashem Abedi, the bombing killed 22 people and

Muslim men pray for victims of the attack at Manchester Arena at a mosque in Manchester, May 23, 2017. Hindustan Times

injured 1,017, with the addition of severe psychological trauma and minor injuries. Of those hospitalised, 12 were children under the age of 16. In total, 112 people were hospitalised for their injuries, and 27 were treated for injuries that did not require hospitalisation. Out of this total of 139, 79 were children[1]. MI5 were 'profoundly sorry' that they missed an opportunity to stop the atrocity: the public inquiry released in 2021 found that "more should have been done" by British police to stop the attack, while MI5 admitted it acted "too slowly" in dealing with Abedi. Lessons learnt then? Hope so.[2]

- Grande hosted a benefit concert on 4 June entitled One Love Manchester, raising a total of £17 million towards victims of the bombing.

- 2018, 31 December: Mahdi Mohamud, a Dutch national from a Somali family, stabbed three in a knife attack at Manchester Victoria station. Mohamud shouted "Allahu Akbar!" and "Long live the Caliphate!" during the attack. Despite suffering from paranoid schizophrenia, Mahomud was convicted of a terror offence and attempted murder of three people due to his possession of significant amounts of extremist material and the attack's extensive planning.

1. Craigie RJ, Farrelly PJ, Santos R, et al Manchester Arena bombing: lessons learnt from a mass casualty incident BMJ Mil Health 2020;166:72–75.
2. Dark P, Smith M, Ziman H Manchester Academic Health Science Centre (MAHSC) Collaborators, et al Healthcare system impacts of the 2017 Manchester Arena bombing: evidence from a national trauma registry patient case series and hospital performance data Emergency Medicine Journal 2021;38:746–755.

Museum of Illusions Manchester, 58–66 Market Street

The Manchester museum is the first of this new and popular brand to open in the UK and joins a n established global chain with over 50 locations in 25 countries and more than 15 million visitors worldwide.

The website tells us that 'In addition to the museum's signature, most popular and photo-worthy exhibits, such as the Walk-in Kaleidoscope, Vortex Tunnel, and Infinity Room, visitors will be treated to custom-made installations that celebrate Manchester's unique culture and heritage. Examples include The Reversed Room—an interactive, tram-inspired illusion; The Following Eyes Illusion—where a famous

Lancashire Telegraph   October 1 2024

Manchester persona can't get their eyes off of guests; and The Building Illusion—where visitors can appear to hang from an iconic Manchester building. The Museum will also include some never-before-seen installations that will make their world debut in Manchester'.

Tabitha Wilson of the Lancashire Telegraph adds 'It promises a 'captivating' experience for all ages, featuring a range of exhibits from holograms and optical tricks to full-scale illusion rooms and mirror displays…Visitors are greeted with a sign reading 'Enter the Illusion' and can explore more than 65 exhibits. The museum is fully accessible, ensuring everyone can enjoy the experience'.

---

1. *Kennedy, Beccy (2015). "Outside Chinatown: the Evolution of Manchester's Chinese Arts Centre as a Cultural Translator for Contemporary Chinese art". Modern China Studies. 2016 (1). Center for Modern China: 58.*

St. Michael's Flags and Angel Meadow Park, Old Mount Street

"water oozed out of the swampy ground, pregnant with putrefying matter, and filled the neighbourhood with the most revolting and injurious gases."
- Friedrich Engels

This public park was, through the 18th century, a prosperous neighbourhood with Georgian houses overlooking the surrounding countryside. Towards the end of the century, in 1788, St Michael and All Angels' church was built. Within 20 years however, the industrial revolution had entirely altered the area's demographic and appearance. In only a few decades, the church came to be described in a local newspaper as "one of the ugliest churches in Manchester situated in one of the most crowded and notorious parts of the City…"

With over 30,000 people, many destitute and living in overcrowded houses and cellars, the area became rife with disease and squalor. It is said that cockroaches were welcomed as they would eat the rampant bed bugs. Unsurprisingly, the death rate rose significantly, at times reaching 175 per cent of the national average. What was once a small parish churchyard became the largest cemetery in Manchester. Outcast and unable to afford a proper burial, around 40,000 individuals were buried in mass graves and burial pits on the land.

Friedrich Engels described witnessing how "water oozed out of the swampy ground, pregnant with putrefying matter, and filled the neighbourhood with the most revolting and injurious gases."

Even after being closed to burials and covered over by flagstones for 30 years, during periods of heavy rain, bodies continued to be washed downhill. To combat this, in 1888 the entire space was enclosed by a wall and since this time St Michael's Flags became a popular park and football ground for local children, including 1966 World Cup winner Nobby Stiles.

See 'Angel Meadow: Victorian Britain's Most Savage Slum' by Dean Kirby.

Engels described Angel Meadow as 'hell on earth' in his 'The Condition of the Working Class in England'.

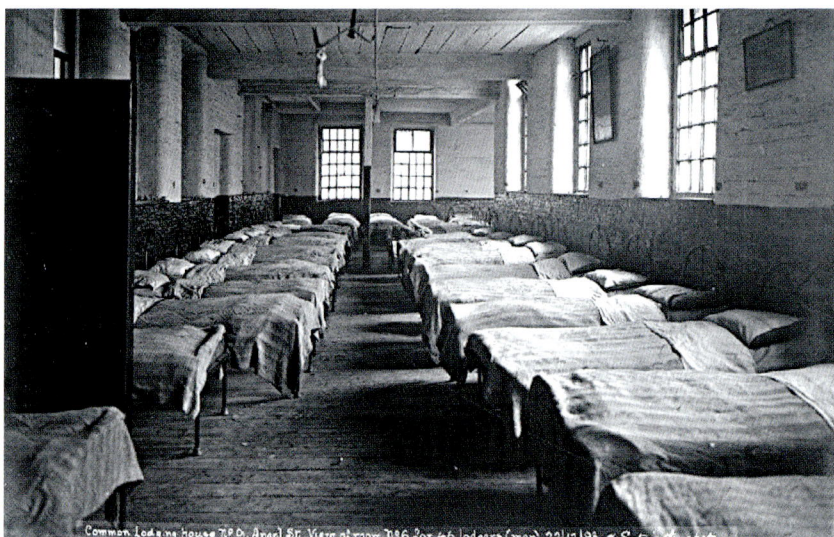

A typical lodging house in Angel Meadow where according to the 1881 census, there were just over 1000 inhabited dwellings in the region, the death rate was between 32 to 50 per 1000 per year. The average for the whole of England was less than 19.

Central Manchester

By the way…

Engels' House, Great Ducie Street

> *Plagued by spies in the German secret service everywhere he went while he was in Manchester and Salford*

Engels resorted to official addresses and unofficial secret addresses. No-one had a clue where all these were until Roy Whitfield uncovered a web of pseudonyms and covert lodging rooms… Engels arrived in Manchester in 1842 and stayed until 1844, before returning to Germany for 19 years in 1850 when it is assumed he took lodgings in Great Ducie Street, in front of the old Strangeways brewery, where he also definitely stayed at the start of his second stay in the city.

He returned to Manchester in November 1850. His address, according to the Census of 1851 and from letters sent to Jenny Marx, was 70 Great Ducie Street, where he lodged with Isabella Tatham, who he called "the old witch of a landlady". In 1852 the house was renumbered as 44, although Engels moved to number 48 with his landlady in October that year.

Further reading

Whitfield, Roy (1988) Frederick Engels in Manchester: The Search For A Shadow, Manchester,
Working Class Movement Library

See www.burynewroad.org/salford/the-secret-homes-of-friedrich-engels-revealed/

Castlefield Railway Viaduct

1830 saw Castlefield become the site of world's first inter-city passenger railway station: Manchester Liverpool Road - and during the following decades the area became the heart of Manchester's goods transportation network. Quite a position to be in, given that the Industrial Revolution (1760–1840) was still in full swing.

What is it? Castlefield Viaduct is a 330m redundant railway viaduct opened in 1892 to carry heavy rail traffic to and from the Great Northern Warehouse; it was built by Heenan and Froude, the engineers who built the Blackpool Tower. For the next 77 years the viaduct was used to carry heavy goods, until it finally closed in 1969; it has stood unused and increasingly dilapidated for more than 60 years.

June 2021 was a huge day for it was then that plans by the National Trust to turn it into a 'sky park' were unveiled, with work starting in March 2022. The first phase of the project began in July 2022 with the launch of a temporary urban park on the viaduct, to test ideas and invite visitors to share their ideas for the Viaduct's future. The longer-term aim is to "transform Castlefield Viaduct

David Dixon / National Trust 'Sky Park', Castlefield Viaduct, Manchester / CC BY-SA 2.0

into a free-to-access park and meeting place for people and nature. It will be a space that respects the listed structure, celebrates the nature, beauty and history of the viaduct, and complements existing plans for the city".

Despite the commercial wealth the viaduct obviously brought to the city, the construction came at a huge human cost, not least the forced displacement and relocation of more than 1,200 people (as usual the most vulnerable and the poorest) by the Cheshire Lines Committee. Moreover, the Roman fort (at Mamucium) and other priceless remains were ruthlessly destroyed in an act of culture vandalism that takes the breath away and ranks with the sack of Rome by the Gauls in 390 CE.

Mamucium and Castlefield Urban Heritage Park

Castlefield was the world's first urban heritage park

The canal sides have a series of towpaths that lead visitors by bridges, small pubs and picturesque canal boats.

The area has a reconstructed gateway and ruins of a Roman fort they called Mamucium. The area was an industrial hub from the 1700s and there are a number of restored Victorian warehouses as well as the Science and Industry Museum.

Overlooking the confluence of the Medlock and Irwell, the fort at Manchester (Mamucium or Mancunium) in today's Castlefield area was founded c.78 CE and became a hub of the regional transport network. One road ran east to west between Chester and York, the other ran north to Bremetennacum (Ribchester). It was garrisoned by a cohort of auxiliaries; a number of large civilian settlements grew up outside the fort.

Sadly, much of the fort was destroyed to make way for such developments as the Rochdale Canal and the Great Northern Railway. Part of the fort's wall along with its gatehouse, granaries, and other buildings from the vicus have been reconstructed (poorly) and are open to the public.

The Royal Exchange, St Ann's Square

'who seek to find eternal treasure must use no guile in weight or measure'

The Grade II listed building has had some bad luck over the last few years – it was damaged during the blitz and then again in the 1996 IRA bombing. It houses the Royal Exchange Theatre and the shopping centre.

The building we see today is the last of a number on the site which was used for commodities exchange, mainly, but not exclusively, of cotton and textiles. As such it embodies the concept of Manchester as Cottonopolis and its ramifications with slavery and colonialism, as well as with appalling workers' conditions of employment: the cotton industry was fed by cotton from the Caribbean which was landed at Liverpool and thence transported to Manchester and surrounding towns as the raw material needed to spin yarns and produce finished textiles. The raw cotton was processed in Manchester and thereabouts while Manchester Royal Exchange traded in spun yarn and finished goods on a truly global basis, including, ironically, Africa. Manchester's first exchange opened in 1729 but closed by the end of the century. As the cotton industry exploded, the need for a new exchange was clear.

In the new exchange of 1809 the exchange room where business was conducted also contained the members' library with more than 15,000 books.

The exterior of the circular theatre pod in the Great Central Hall.
David Dixon / Royal Exchange

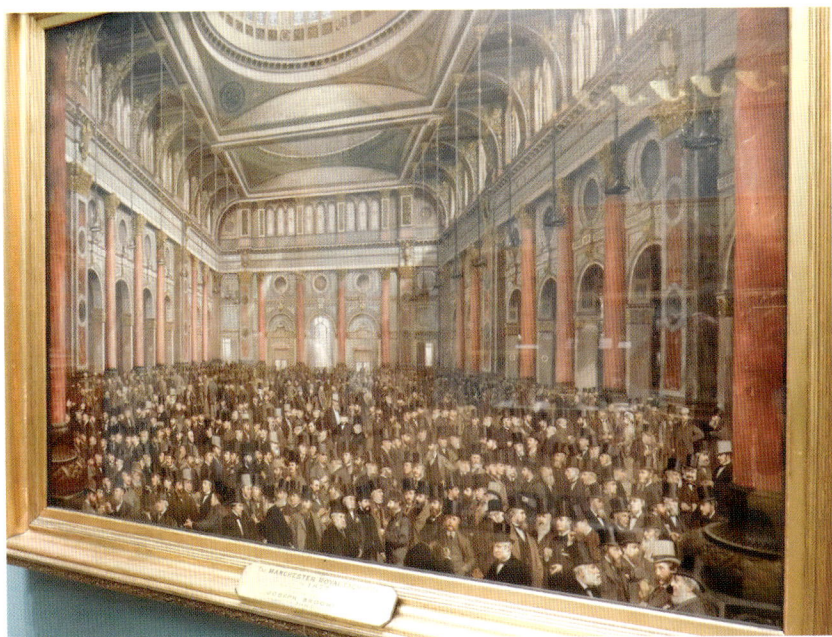

'Manchester Royal Exchange in 1887' as painted by
Joseph Broome; in Manchester Art Gallery

The basement housed a newsroom lit by a dome and plate-glass windows, its ceiling was supported by a circle of Ionic pillars spaced 15 feet from the walls. This second exchange was replaced by a third constructed between 1867 and 1874 and formed the largest trading hall in England. Trading came to an end in 1968, and the usual unenlightened threats of demolition ensued.

The metal and glass structure that is the theatre is in the form of a circular Elizabethan playhouse which is too heavy for the floor so it is suspended on four columns supporting the central dome.

You can still see some of the original trading boards showing the prices of different types of cotton – frozen in time from when trading ceased in December 1968.

The theatre was opened by Laurence Olivier on 15 September 1976.

St Ann's Church

Lady Ann Bland, daughter of Sir Edward Mosely, was the driving force behind this early 18th century church which she intended as a low church Whig alternative to the high church sermons being preached in the Collegiate Church - what is now Manchester Cathedral and, at the time, Manchester's only church. St Ann's was originally simple and plain, as befits the small rural place

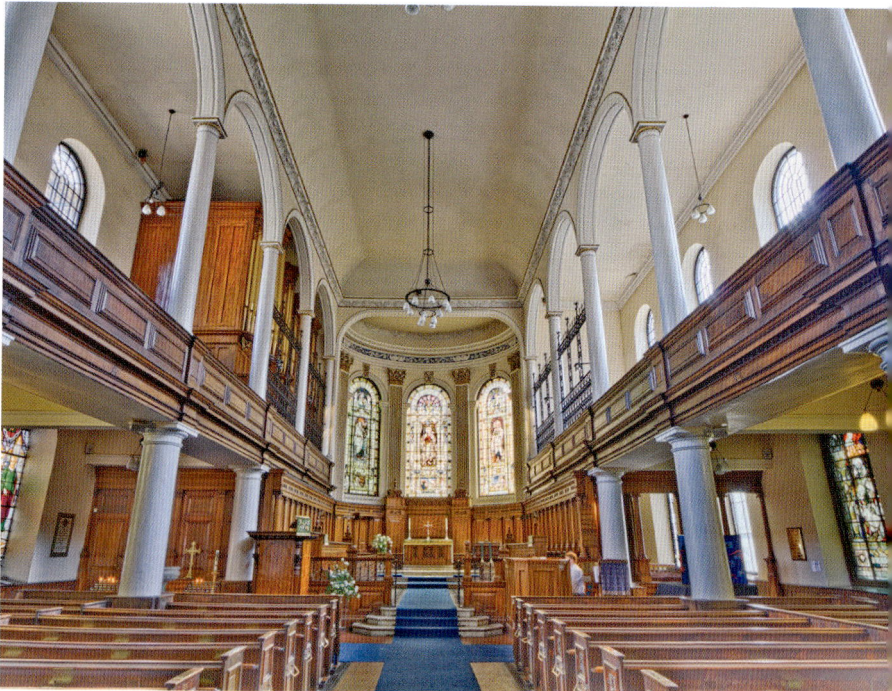

Photographer Mdbeckwith

Manchester was at the time but in the next century stained glass windows were installed – now the Church's jewels in its crown. Some of these were bespoke, and others were adapted from other churches. One such window, on the north side of the church, was designed and made by William Peckitt of York, the country's foremost glazier at the time. It was originally made for St John's, Deansgate and later moved to St Mary's, Hulme.

By the way…
The Homeless Jesus Statue

> *Nothing much has changed in the world since 30 CE when it comes to the destitute and margianlised*

A symbolic and evocative sculpture of Jesus Christ depicted as a homeless man on a park bench. Designed by Canadian artist Timothy Schmalz, the sculptures have been installed in cities around the world, with Manchester's the first in England.

Church of England leaders hope the poignant symbol will challenge the public to reflect and provoke them into action on the city's growing homelessness crisis.

'Jesus the Homeless' depicts a figure wrapped in a blanket lying on a bench, with its pierced feet indicating it is Jesus.

Planning permission was granted by Manchester council after an insensitive and socially ignorant Westminster City Council rejected an application for the sculpture near the Houses of Parliament. Should we be surprised?

The "Homeless Jesus" sculpture [of which there are a number around] the world is a visual representation of 'Matthew 25'. The sculpture suggests that Christ is with the most marginalized in our society. The Christ figure is shrouded in a blanket with His face covered with the only indication that the figure is Jesus being the visible wounds on the feet. The life-size version of the work provides enough room for someone to sit on the bench with Jesus, as it were, and is cast in bronze metal measuring 36"H x 84"L x 24"D.

Manchester Cathedral

Commonly, the groom and friends would decamp to a nearby alehouse while the bride kept place in the queue

On the banks of the River Irwell, Manchester Cathedral - officially the Cathedral and Collegiate Church of St. Mary, St. Denys, and St. George - dates mostly from 1422 to 1506. The octagonal chapterhouse, built in 1465, has murals that include a figure of Christ in modern dress.

As we know from churches all around Britain during the various blitzes, bombs and glass windows do not mix. Manchester Cathedral has been particularly unlucky. All the original Victorian stained glass was destroyed during the Manchester Blitz in 1940 and until the late 1960s, only two windows had been replaced, notably the Fire Window by Margaret Traherne (1966). To commemorate the restoration of the cathedral following an IRA bomb in 1996, the Healing Window by Linda Walton was installed in 2004.

In the 19th century the cathedral held a monopoly on the legal contracting of marriages in the parish officiated by the pastoral chaplain employed by the Warden and fellows; who from 1790 to 1821 was the eccentric Revd. Joshua 'Jotty' Brookes. Jotty in 1821 alone, solemnized some 1,924 marriages usually in batches of 20 or more at a time. In fact, he baptised, married, and buried

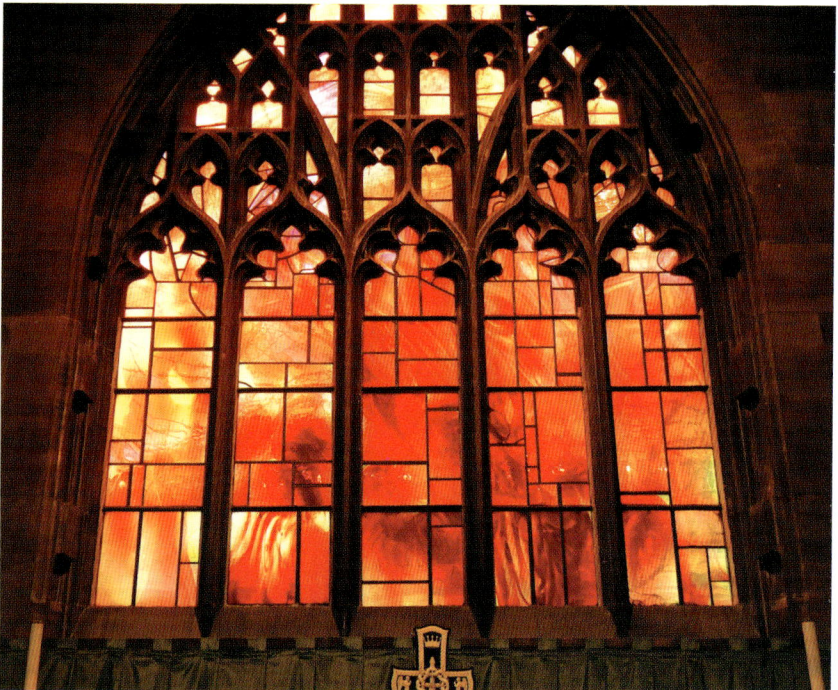

The glorious and vivid Fire Window

To commemorate the restoration of the cathedral following an IRA bomb in 1996, the Healing Window by Linda Walton was installed in 2004. Photo by Andy Read.

more persons than any clergyman, before and since. The Annals of Manchester tells us that

> 'the couples to be married were most often desperately poor but Brookes was no respecter of status, so all were subjected to his industrial 'production line' methods. Commonly, the groom and friends would decamp to a nearby ale-house while the bride kept place in the queue; but if there was one groom too few when a group of couples were lined up in front of the altar, Brookes would countenance no delay, but would continue the marriage with any passer-by (or even one of the other grooms) as a proxy stand-in'[1].

---

1. *Timperley, C.H. (1839), Annals of Manchester, Bancks & Co., p. 78. Joshua Brookes features in Mrs Linnaeus Banks' novel The Manchester Man. He is commemorated in the name of the Joshua Brooks pub in Princess Street, Manchester.*

The Glade of Light: *remembering the Arena bombing*

May 22, 2017 was a terrible day for Manchester; indeed, it was a terrible day for humanity. The 22 people who were killed and the 1,000 or so who were injured that night after an Ariana Grande concert are remembered here. The following evening saw a vigil in Albert Square while floral tributes remained in St Ann's Square for many months. Ariana Grande returned to Manchester two weeks later to host 'One Love Manchester' at Old Trafford Cricket Ground – an event which touched the hearts of the nation and indeed the world. This, along with a Red Cross Appeal raised at least £17 million for victims of the outrage and for their families.

The fifth anniversary, May 10 2022, was marked by the opening of a living memorial called the Glade of Light:

A white marble 'halo' ring forms the heart of the memorial and the names of those who lost their lives are engraved in bronze on it. Personalised memory capsules, filled with memories and mementoes of them provided by loved ones, are embedded within the stone.

This picture was taken from the east (main) side of the memorial towards the river Irwell and the city of Salford. The glass building in the background is 100 Embankment, on the Salford side of the Irwell. Photographer Tomasz "odder" Kozlowski.

The planting scheme is designed to reflect the changing seasons while providing colour and maximising light all year round. It uses only plants native to the UK countryside.

In all a fitting tribute to the many who suffered and are suffering still, offering "a tranquil garden space for remembrance and reflection".

The memorial can be found between Chetham's School of Music and Manchester Cathedral.

Barton Arcade

"a gorgeous glass and iron shopping arcade with glass domes..., the best example of this type of cast-iron and glass arcade anywhere in the country."

A Victorian shopping arcade built in 1871 located between Deansgate and St Ann's Square. The sympathetically restored Victorian arcade is "a gorgeous glass and iron shopping arcade with glass domes..., the best example of this type of cast-iron and glass arcade anywhere in the country."

Victoria Station

What a wonderful place Victoria station must have been in the mid-19th century…

…whether you were arriving or departing. It still retains a number of its original treasures, despite its somewhat strained annexation to Manchester Arena.

- The beautiful tiling still takes the breath away on the restaurant and bookshop, now the information office
- The wooden ticket office and booths
- The destinations on the exterior proclaiming journeys to the four corners of the nation, from York to… Blackpool, from Goole to… Fleetwood…
- The stunning interior and ceiling of the café
- The impressive tiled map showing the extent of the Lancashire and Yorkshire Railway. Beware though: this map does not show lines run by rival train companies so it gives a false impression of the best routes to take, resulting in unnecessarily long and circuitous journeys.

These maps were each made by Craven Dunill & Co of Jackfield in Shropshire. More can be seen, for example, at Saltburn, Hartlepool, Beverley, York, Whitby and Middlesbrough.

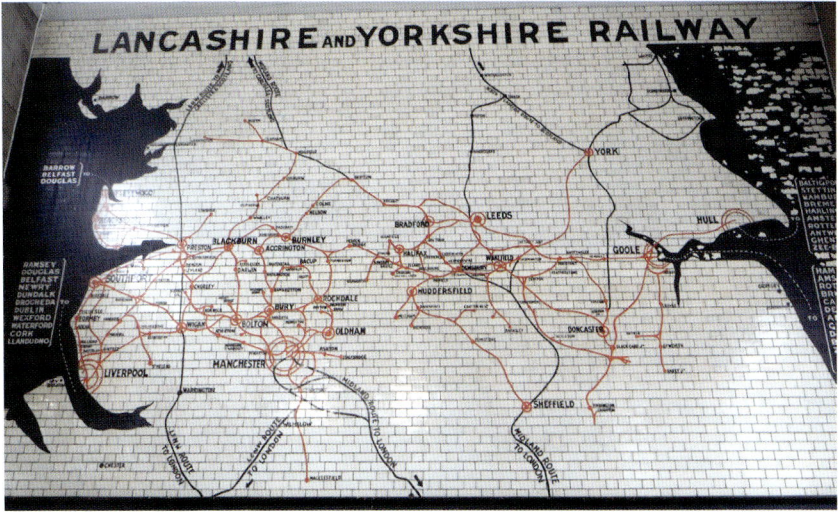

The Corn Exchange and The Corn Exchange Book Swap

Home to a rare book-vending machine

The Corn Exchange is now a food court with hotel but was originally a corn exchange previously called the Corn & Produce Exchange, and then The Triangle shopping centre.

In March 1996, to mark the anniversary of John Dee's death in 1609, a local paranormal group attempted to levitate the Corn Exchange. Why? Because the group were convinced that alchemist, mathematician, spy, magician and advisor to Elizabeth I ('Royal Advisor in mystic secrets'), John Dee (1527–1608), had lived for several years on the site of the Corn Exchange. He allegedly resided here while discharging his duty as the Warden of the town at nearby Chetham's Library.

Think of vending machines and we think of sweets, crisps, drinks and other snack options but over the years alternative options have been introduced like DVD's, socks and even false eyelashes. Elsewhere in the world you can vend bizarre items like live crabs (China), caviar (USA), cheese (Switzerland) and even more excitingly lettuce (Japan).

'The book vending machine is at the Fennel Street exit; simply bring in a book to one of our hosts on duty and they will swap it for a token that can be used in the machine. Visit for more information': https://cornexchangemanchester.co.uk/cornexreads/

The book vending machine at the Corn Exchange

Bombproof Corporation Street Postbox

The mail may often be late but this postbox is indestructible

We have said a lot about the destructive IRA bomb which exploded in Manchester on 15th June 1996. This quite normal red post box was one of the few things in the surrounding area left virtually unscathed.

The 1500kg bomb injured 200 people, tore through and destroyed a shopping centre and laid waste a large section of central Manchester. Although the IRA had sent warnings around an hour and half before the bomb exploded and more than 75,000 people were evacuated from the area, the bomb squad were unable to defuse it in time. It was the biggest bomb detonated in the UK since the Second World War.

Stephen Armstrong / Victorian Pillar Box, Corporation Street, Manchester / CC BY-SA 2.0

Chetham's Library

Part of Chetham's Hospital dates to 1422. Originally a residence for priests, it is now home to a music school and Chetham Library, the oldest public library

Chained books

in England. In continuous use since 1653, the library has in excess of 100,000 books, more than half of them printed before 1850. Chetham's is also famous as the meeting place of those two giants of political philosophy Karl Marx and Friedrich Engels during Marx's visit to Manchester in the 1840s. Engels had been sent to Manchester by his father to research the industrialisation in the city and its social impact. The result was the groundbreaking *Condition of the Working Class in England* in 1845. His family had established a factory in nearby Weaste, Erman & Engles.

John Dee was appointed warden of the library in 1595 at the age of 68. His time there was 'beset with money problems and his relations with the fellows of the Collegiate Church [Manchester Cathedral] were marked by antagonism that bordered on hatred. In 1605 he left Manchester weary of the struggle and returned home to Mortlake where he spent the remaining years of his life'[1].

As an antiquarian, Dee had one of the largest libraries in England at the time. As a political advisor, he advocated the foundation of English colonies in the New World to create a "British Empire", a term he is credited with coining[2]. According to Charlotte Fell Smith[3], in 1556 'Dee presented Queen Mary with a visionary plan for preserving old books, manuscripts and records and founding a national library, but it was not taken up. Instead, he expanded his personal library in Mortlake, acquiring books and manuscripts in England and on the Continent. Dee's library, a prodigious centre of learning outside the universities, became the greatest in England and attracted many scholars. His Mortlake library was the largest in the country before it was vandalised, and created at enormous, sometimes ruinous personal expense; it was seen as one of the finest in Europe, perhaps second only to that of De Thou[4].

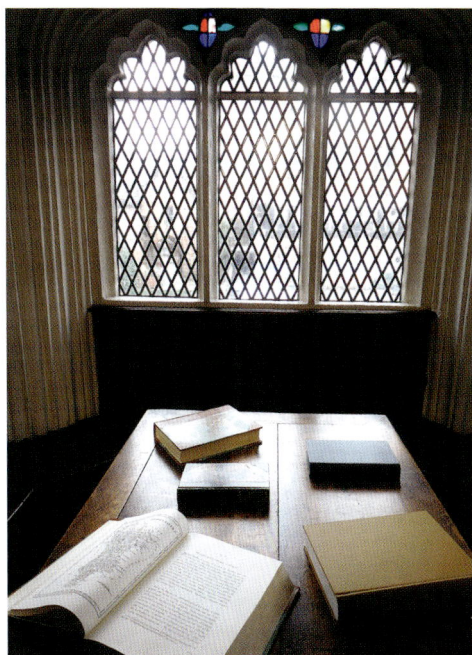

The desk where Marx and Engels worked

Chetham's has five books which once belonged to Dee including a work by the sixteenth-century Swiss physician and naturalist Conrad Gesner (*De remediis secretis* - a book of little-known remedies); it is signed 'Joannes Dee 1556' on the title page and is annotated throughout, including some marginalia of figures and apparatus.

Apparently, Dee actually took to signing his letters '007'

– a code to highlight that the letter was for the queen's eyes only – later adopted, of course, by Ian Fleming for Bond, James Bond.

One of the (thankless) tasks Dee took on was to sort out the boundaries of the parish and manor of Manchester. In 1596 Christopher Saxton, who had produced the first national atlas of England and Wales, was hired to carry out a survey of Manchester. All things related to the parish boundary were highly sensitive and attracted much opposition from local landowners and clergy.

John Dee "Sigillum Dei Aemeth". Dee was seeking practical knowledge of the profound laws governing the universe. He eventually found a collaborator in the mysterious Edward Kelley who was able to communicate with the spirit world, a gift that Dee himself never possessed. The Sigillum dei Aemeth 5 is the design incorporated on the wax discs that Dee and Kelley used with the "table of practice" during their Angelic Conversations. The complex design of the Sigillum was but derived from the Seal of the Truth of God which had first emerged in a 14th century grimoire. One disc was placed under each table leg, an a final one on the tabletop on which was placed the crystal ball.

In 1841 novelist Harrison Ainsworth published *Guy Fawkes, or The Gunpowder Treason: An Historical Romance*, in which Dee, Fawkes and Humphrey Chetham are described meeting in the warden's room, now the Library Reading Room. It is possible that Humphrey Chetham knew John Dee. Dee borrowed money from Humphrey's older brother Edmund who was master of the Grammar School from 1597 to 1602.

1. *https://library.chethams.com/collections/101-treasures-of-chethams/john-dee/*

2. *MacMillan, Ken (2001). "Discourse on History, Geography, and Law: John Dee and the Limits of the British Empire, 1576–80". Canadian Journal of History. 36 (1): 1–26.*

3. *Fell Smith, Charlotte (1909). The Life of Dr. John Dee (1527–1608). London: Constable & Co*

4. *Jacques Auguste de Thou (Thuanus) (1553–1617) was a French historian, book collector and president of the Parlement of Paris.*

5. *The Sigillum Dei Aemeth (seal of God, "Seal of Truth" or signum dei vivi, symbol of the Living God, called by John Dee the Sigillum Dei Aemeth) is a magical diagram, composed of two circles, a pentagram, two heptagons, and one heptagram, and is labeled with the names of God and its angels. It is an angelic magic seal with the magical function that, according to one of the oldest sources (Liber Juratus), allowed a magician to have the power to possess the Spirit of God and when activated can become the 'Living' God; or The Lord God itself; amongst humanity and all creation itself, communicate with spirits as well as angels and archangels, control all elements, control every creature's holy spirit on the planet including the Spirit of God itself; all except for the Archangels, and to control light itself. The intended user also possesses the true vision of God.*

Further reading

Roberts, Richard Julian (1990). "Preface". John Dee's Library Catalogue. London: The Bibliographical Society.

Roberts, Richard Julian ed. (2005). "A John Dee Chronology, 1509–1609". Renaissance Man: The Reconstructed Libraries of European Scholars: 1450–1700 Series One: The Books and Manuscripts of John Dee, 1527–1608. Adam Matthew Publications.

The Guardian Telephone Exchange, George Street

An iceberg of a building with much more below the surface than that which can be seen at street level.

The exchange was a covert underground telephone exchange built largely by Polish immigrants from 1954 to 1957 at the same time as the Anchor exchange in Birmingham and London's Kingsway Exchange – all apparently to provide communications in the event of nuclear war, as well as linking the UK government in London to the US Government in Washington, D.C. by means of a secure and hardened transatlantic telephone cable - making landfall near Oban and running through Glasgow, Manchester and Birmingham[1].

1. *Warrender, Keith (2007). Underground Manchester. Timperley: Willow Publishing. p. 49*

Entrance to the Guardian Exchange, Manchester. The entrance is on George Street, between Princess Street and Dickinson Street

Polish immigrants were used because they apparently had no English and were thus unable to divulge any secrets about the place. Surely not. Whatever, the place was covered by D Notice restrictions which prevented it being mentioned in publications until 1967.

Today, the underground site is used for telephone cabling. Built at a depth of 115 ft, the tunnels are about 80" in diameter and cost around £4million (approximately £130 million in today's prices), part of which was funded by the United Kingdom's NATO partners.

A large diameter, vertical shaft descends from an anonymous-looking yard on George Street. This contains a large goods lift and crane, by which all the equipment was installed and, subsequently, removed. In the event of hostilities, the shaft could be sealed by a huge 35 ton swinging concrete blast cover which could only be opened by hydraulic jacks from within. As well as the Trunk Telephone Exchange, the main complex also housed large diesel power generators, air scrubbers, sleeping quarters, kitchen, food storage and dining area and even a well furnished bar with Formica tables, banquette and stool seating, piano and pool table. Just as at the GPO Club, under the old Central Post Office in Spring Gardens, there were fake windows, with murals of outdoor scenes, to make it less claustrophobic.

Trouble was that nuclear technology swiftly moved on after 1954 and that if a thermonuclear device was exploded above the city in or after 1960 it would wipe out everything, including the bunker.

The Guardian Bunker has been called the "Best kept secret in Manchester" and its existence was only publicly acknowledged in 1968 14 years after it was first built. I would argue that the real 'best kept secret' was that the bunker was practically useless after 1960, some 31 years before the end of the Cold War (1947–1991).

Chinatown

Manchester's Chinatown is one of the largest not just in Britain and in Europe, but it is one of the biggest outside China. Obviously it's the centre of the city's Chinese community. The impressive Chinese Arch (paifang) in Faulkner Street went up in 1987; it was specially built in China and shipped over in three containers a year after the city of Manchester was twinned with Wuhan. The structure was a gift from Manchester City Council to the Chinese community.

The annual Chinese New Year festival in February is a highlight in the Manchester events calendar and it includes numerous stalls and dancing dragons in the famous parade.

Where did it all begin? The first Chinese settlers arrived in the city in the early 20th century; many set up in the laundry trade. Manchester's first Chinese restaurant, 'Ping Hong', opened on Oxford Street in 1948.

Sandy Tsin[1] tells how a surge of Chinese immigration wave began in the 1950s in a time of severe labour shortages, and in response to the British Nationality Act 1948 which allowed easier access into the country. The swift urbanisation back in Hong Kong led to local farmers' traditional homes being destroyed by rampant urban development causing many inhabitants deciding to migrate.

Chinese restaurants proliferated after the immigration boom and by the 1970s other Chinese businesses had opened, such as Chinese medicine shops, supermarkets and financial and legal services serving the area, including a Hong Kong government office and branch of The Hongkong and Shanghai Banking Corporation (later HSBC). In 1989, the Chinese Arts Centre opened in Chinatown (see above, esea). In 2013, the Bank of East Asia opened their first Manchester branch on Charlotte Street in Chinatown.

---

1. Tsin, Sandy. "History of Manchester Chinatown". Manchester China Archive.

Manchester Town Hall Murals

The neo-Gothic Town Hall (1877) offers excellent panoramic views of the city. Inside, the Council Chamber merits special attention, along with the cycle of Ford Madox Brown murals in the Great Hall that depict the history of the city (1879–1893). For this he moved from London with his family, living first at Crumpsall, then at Victoria Park. The Town Hall website tells us.[1]

---

1. https://www.manchester.gov.uk/info/500354/our_town_hall/7676/heritage_and_art/5

The choice of subjects stresses the importance of Christianity, commerce and the textile industry in our city's history. The murals are a monument to the ideals of the leaders of Victorian Manchester. Madox Brown did a great deal of research to check the details for accuracy, and he wrote the descriptions himself.

The murals, except for the last five, were painted directly on to the wall, not in true fresco as the pale colours would soon have become grimy, but using a Victorian technique, the Gambier Parry process of spirit fresco. The last five murals were painted on canvas after Brown's return to London.

By the way…

The world's first space oddity took place in Manchester: on July 12, 1961 the first human to walk in space, Soviet cosmonaut Yuri Alekseyevich Gagarin, came in out of the cold and appeared on the Town Hall balcony to a warm and rapturous reception and an unusual duet of the Red Fag fluttering in the Manchester wind alongside the Union Flag. A rare and brief thaw in the Cold War underlined by the crowd singing 'For He's A Jolly Good Fellow' for Yuri.

Gagarin's space suit

Manchester: Secret & Strange Places to Visit

121

Gagarin's visit to the UK, three months after his historic flight, was obviously a tentative and diplomatically cautious affair especially as Gagarin was accompanied by an official Soviet delegation. A foundry workers' union – in honour of Gagarin's former occupation – had invited the cosmonaut to Manchester which Gagarin accepted, extending his stay. "There's quite a famous moment when he's appearing in Manchester, and he stays in an open-top car even though it's raining, because, he says, 'The people have come to see me.'" Schoolboys dressed up in home-made space suits.

Gagarin's world tour took place a few months before the building of the Berlin Wall; a year later the Cuba Missile Crisis would bring the world closer to a nuclear confrontation than ever before and since (we think). Amid such tension, Gagarin's visit is a rare moment of celebration, and possibly a way of building detente.

Manchester Town Hall Restoration

£325m restoration of Manchester Town Hall is well underway, if a little late due to COVID.

Library Walk Link, Albert Square

The Link provides a marvellous connection between the two Grade II*
listed buildings, Manchester Central Library and Town Hall Extension. Akt-uk
describes the controversial passageway – a building in its own right - as follows:
'The centrepiece is the 'cloud', a 30-tonne polished stainless steel monocoque
roof composed of prefabricated panels welded together to form a seamless object.'
Interestingly, the floor of the Library Walk Link comprises a natural stone mosaic
with a Lancashire Rose motif. This incorporates 18 red, cast glass lenses within
the flowers, each inscribed with the name of a victim of the Peterloo Massacre.

At best the mosaic brings hope – that, in the words of Sarah Sayeed, 'one
thing remains with each flower. And that is a hope for humanity, for the future
lives of us all. May we never again have to experience such cruel death in the
face of air and truthful protest'[1].

1. *Paul Dobraszczyk and Sarah Butler, Manchester: Something Rich and Strange*

Greater Manchester Police Museum & Archives, Newton Street

The 1879 Police Station, complete with original cells and charge office also has a 1895 Magistrates Court as well as displays of equipment, murder weapons, machetes, vehicles, fingerprinting and incriminating evidence. A must for anyone who hasn't spent the night in a cell (yet).

Wooden pillows give an idea of the level of comfort, as does the fact that two-man cells were often crammed with up to 16 felons. Toilets were not provided, just the usual bucket.

By the way...
Women's Auxiliary Police Corps (WAPC)[1]

In early 1939 the Government published its National Service Handbook; conspicuous by their absence were women with no plans for enrolling women as Special Constables. However, the Women's Auxiliary Police Corps (WAPC) – known bitchily as 'waspies' by their male colleagues - was set up that August, for women between the ages of 18–55 for the duration of the war. Duties were wide-ranging and included clerical work at the police station, operating

the police control room, vehicle repairs, and driving duties. One of the most important tasks was documenting bomb sites and casualty numbers in the police station 'war room'. In October the Home Office notified forces that up to 10% of the local police forces could be made up of women.

In Manchester, Chief Constable John Maxwell reported to the City Council Watch Committee in late 1939 that six women were carrying out plain clothes police duties in the force – mainly taking statements from women and children, escorting female prisoners to court and dealing with "special enquiries of a delicate nature". Maxwell was living proof that vision and diversity were, albeit rarely, alive and well amongst some men in the higher echelons of public service.

He also referred to the Home Office report about the WAPC when he informed the Watch Committee that he had already had a number of applications from women to join the WAPC, and it was now time to reorganize women in the Manchester Police. He recommended that the existing six policewomen be given full police powers, granted the status of Constable and issued with a uniform. He also believed that the newly formed military camps in the area were attracting undesirables and causing problems with prostitution, which could best be dealt with by women police. He therefore recommended that twenty women be enrolled in the WAPC for the city. The report was acted upon in early 1940.

---

1. *Chrystal, Paul, Women at Work in World Wars 1 and 2 (2024), p. 185*

Anita Street, Ancoats

An insanitary cradle of the Industrial Revolution

Before it was Anita Street, Anita Street was known as Sanitary Street, a name that with some irony said it all; but, more positively, it reflected its original role as a site for much-needed public health initiatives in the 19th century.

Nowadays it is one of the most picturesque hidden gems in Manchester, a rare example of pristine terraced housing in a city centre these days better known for its posh apartments. But it wasn't always like this. In the 1790s, as plans for the Rochdale canal were drawn up, industrialists decided Ancoats would be the ideal place to locate their mills. As they did so, a new dystopian neighbourhood surreptitiously grew around them – a dark, tight network of shabbily constructed back-to-back terraces, in which droves of weavers and mill-workers crammed in to filthy rooms and cellars with their families, all there to provide workforces for the mills all around. By 1815 Ancoats was the most populous district in Manchester. Streets of back-to-back houses and court dwellings were rapidly built. For the poorest members of the community, houses were split and cellars let separately.

And so Ancoats became the world's first industrial suburb, or, as Friedrich Engels said of the neighbourhood in 1845:

Anita Street today

"It must be admitted that no more injurious or demoralising method of housing the workers has yet been discovered than precisely this. The working man is constrained to occupy such ruinous dwellings because he cannot pay for others, and because there are no others within the vicinity of his mill."

So bad was it that public health actually became a concern; a survey motivated by the fear of a cholera outbreak showed that over half of homes in Ancoats had no private plumbing, and over half of streets were not cleaned. In response, a series of public health campaigns aimed at improving living conditions and reducing the spread of disease were initiated, one of which was the creation of a network of streets designed specifically for the purpose of improving public health.

Sanitary Street was one of the streets created and designed with wider footpaths, better drainage, and other features that were intended to reduce the spread of disease. The name "Sanitary Street" remained in use until the early 20th century.

Manchester Central Library, St Peter's Square

Sex and the index system

A truly beautiful building comprising a columned portico attached to a rotunda domed structure, loosely based on the Pantheon in Rome. The library collections include over 30 incunabula (books published before 1500) and

The stunning ceiling decorations include the arms and crests of the Duchy of Lancaster, the See of York, the See of Manchester, the City of Manchester, and Lancashire County Council.

many first and early editions of major works. Anthony Burgess, the author of A Clockwork Orange, was a regular visitor to the library during his school days. In a volume of his autobiography, Little Wilson and Big God (1987) he recounted his visit to the index system, then in temporary accommodation in Piccadilly, Manchester, where he met an older woman who took him to her flat in Ardwick where she seduced him.

By the way…
Ahmed Iqbal Ullah RACE Centre and Education Trust

This important collection and research centre can be found in Manchester Central Library

The website tells its laudable aims and scope best:

The Ahmed Iqbal Ullah RACE Centre and Education Trust is a specialist open-access library and archive, focusing on the study of race, migration and thinking about race, anti-racist activism and the fight for social justice.

Reading Race, Collecting Cultures: Collections at the Ahmed Iqbal Ullah Race Relations Resource Centre

We are recognised as a centre of excellence in oral history work, Global Majority community-led collecting and ethical community engagement. We work ethically and sensitively with Global Majority communities to explore, document and share their histories, cultures and experiences.

We work with the heritage sector to deliver ethical and anti-racist collections-based practice, and to build anti-racist organisations.

Rise up, women: the Emmeline Pankhurst Statue, St Peter's Square

The statue is Rise Up, Women by Hazel Reeves. We all know that Paul Rotha's classic 1947 documentary, A City Speaks, celebrates the great and good responsible in no small part for the post-war resurrection of Manchester in science, industry, culture and politics. Only problem was that they were all men and it took 70 years before their monopoly on the city's statuary was broken by a woman. A sign of the times? Not really: what a number of Manchester women had achieved (and were busy achieving making them worthy of a statue in line with their male counterparts) had been going on for at least a century. How did it finally happen? Usual thing: man (Manchester City councillor Andrew Simcock) and woman (Anne-Marie Glennon) meet in the Town Hall Sculpture gallery; over coffee she had remarked "these (busts) are all men. Where are the women!"

Emmeline owes her exalted position to a 2015 vote which saw her win over fellow eminences such as Labour MP Ellen Wilkinson and Elizabeth Gaskell[1].

The full list of runners-up:
- **Lydia Becker** (1827–1890): suffragist, botanist and astronomer
- **Louise Da-Cocodia** (1934–2008): nurse and social campaigner
- **Margaret Downes** (d.1819) killed at the Peterloo Massacre
- **Elizabeth Gaskell** (1810–1865): novelist and social reformer
- **Annie Horniman** (1860–1937): theatre patron
- **Sunny Lowry** (1911–2008): English Channel swimmer
- **Kathleen Ollerenshaw** (1912–2014): mathematician, educationalist and Lord Mayor of Manchester
- **Christabel Pankhurst** (1880–1958): leading suffragist
- **Sylvia Pankhurst** (1882–1960): leading suffragist
- **Mary Quaile**: Trade Unionist
- **Elizabeth Raffald** (1733–1781): businesswoman and author
- **Esther Roper** (1868–1938): suffragist and trade unionist
- **Enriqueta Rylands** (1843–1908): founder of the John Rylands Library
- **Olive Shapley** (1910–1999): radio broadcaster
- **Shena Simon** (1883–1972): educationalist and political reformer
- **Marie Stopes** (1880–1958): birth control pioneer
- **Ellen Wilkinson** (1891–1947): MP and mental health campaigner
- **Emily Williamson** (1855–1936): co-founder of the RSPB

In 2014 International Women's Day and LGBT Month saw the worthy busts in the Town Hall temporarily transitioned into women by the appliance of crochet masks when Warp & Weft (artist Helen Davies and heritage researcher Jenny White) devised the Stature project, 'yarnbombing eight male portrait busts with crochet masks depicting local historical women of achievement…'

The unveiling which was attended by those 6,000 people including many who had marched from the Pankhurst Centre. The event marked exactly 100 years since the first women voted and stood as candidates in a general election. Two marches set off from two symbolic locations – the People's History Museum and the Pankhurst Centre – converging at St Peter's Square, which was attended by 6,000 people including 1,000 local schoolchildren. In July 2018, the Portland stone Pankhurst Meeting Circle was unveiled, designed to encircle the bronze statue.

The Cenotaph and other war memorials

Manchester was late in commissioning a First World War memorial compared with most British towns and cities; the city council did not convene a war memorial committee until 1922. Here are two less prominent memorials to the often forgotten, lest we forget. We can add Korea to these.

Memorials to the nuclear testing guinea pigs, and to the Russians who helped us win the war

The Adrift Statue (1907) – St Peter's Square

Yes, it surely could be a vivid description of a small boat fighting to reach a land of opportunity in the Mediterranean or the English Channel.

This is how the Public Monument and Sculpture Association National Recording Project, describes 'Manchester's first modern figurative outdoor sculpture', by John Cassidy who had a studio on Plymouth Grove in Manchester:

Bronze sculpture of a family clinging to a raft in a stormy sea. The central figure is a half-naked man, holding a sheet aloft in his raised right hand, calling for help. Arranged around him are the figures of his wife and three children. His wife is shown leaning over and kissing their infant son. To the left, is the daughter, her raised arm held in her father's left hand. At the rear is the prone figure of a youth, the elder son, holding his breast. Parts of the raft are visible in the waves which make up the base.

John Cassidy himself described the work as follows:

Humanity adrift on the sea of life, depicting life's sorrows and dangers, hopes and fears, embodying the dependence of human beings upon one another, the response of human sympathy to human needs and the inevitable dependence upon divine aid.

Sound familiar? Yes, it surely could be a vivid description of a small boat fighting to reach a land of opportunity in the Mediterranean or the English Channel.

Courtesy of Aidan O' Rourke

Erinma Bell with her statue at Manchester Town Hall. Credit: X, Erinma Bell

The Erinma Bell MBE Statue, Town Hall Gallery

The one and a half life-sized bust is, and this is what takes your breath away, made out of 50 lethal firearms seized by police or surrendered during gun amnesties.

The year 2017 saw the first woman intrude into the male dominated gallery: Erinma Bell MBE got in thanks to her unstinting work to give young people positive alternatives to street and gun crime. Erinma, who grew up in Moss Side, was honoured in 2017 with a sculpture designed by Manchester-based artist Karen Lyons. The one and a half life-sized bust – is, and this is what takes your breath away, made out of 50 lethal firearms seized by police or surrendered during gun amnesties. The weapons, after being made safe, were melted down and fashioned into the sculpture – astonishingly the first-ever sculpture of a woman in the building.

Detail from 'The Massacre of Peterloo', or 'Britons Strike Home' by George Cruikshank
Speech balloon top left: Down with 'em! Chop em down my brave boys: give them no
quarter they want to take our Beef & Pudding from us! — & remember the more you kill
the less poor rates you'll have to pay so go at it Lads show your courage & your Loyalty

The Peterloo Massacre Memorial, Windmill Street

This commemorates those who were slaughtered or injured on August 16, 1819. It was unveiled just before the 200th anniversary of the atrocity.

Jeremy Deller is the designer and he has achieved what the proud Peterloo Memorial Campaign has described as 'a respectful, informative and permanent Peterloo Memorial at the heart of Manchester'.

What caused the massacre?

At the time, the ending of the Napoleonic War four years earlier had led to a period of economic depression in which unemployment was rife, with wages of textile workers slashed by half. In addition, the passing of the Corn Laws imposed tariffs on imported grain. This, in turn, caused rising food costs and famine.

On Monday August 16, 1819, more than 60,000 people gathered at St Peter's Field to listen to a speech by Henry Hunt, a charismatic pioneer of working-class radicalism and an advocate of universal suffrage. They had walked for hours from the towns and villages surrounding Manchester, bearing banners with slogans such as "Universal Suffrage" and "Liberty and Fraternity." Wanting to make it abundantly clear that they were respectable, law-abiding citizens protesting in peace, the attendees came in their Sunday best. Local magistrates had declared the gathering illegal, not surprising since they supported Lord Liverpool's government – a government fervently opposed (in true-self-serving style) to any extension of the franchise.

The Peterloo Memorial

ST. PETER'S FIELDS
THE PETERLOO MASSACRE
On 16th August 1819 a peaceful rally of 60,000 pro-democracy reformers, men, women and children, was attacked by armed cavalry resulting in 15 deaths and over 600 injuries.

118

The Manchester and Salford Yeomanry along with the 15th Regiment of Light Dragoons were deployed at the edge of the field. Hunt had barely started to address the crowd from the hustings when they moved to arrest him. Events quickly spiralled out of control, with the Yeomanry drawing their sabres and slashing wildly at the unarmed attendees. The sheer numbers of people made it impossible for the protesters to escape. Hundreds were injured, with estimates as high as 600. It is believed that 18 people died, either on the field or later of their injuries. A high price to pay for the right to vote. An attempted cover-up failed.

By the way…

The massacre is also celebrated in the mosaic floor between the Central Library and the Town Hall where five-petalled red and orange flowers remember the dead with 18 of the flowers adorned with names of the casualties. Easily missed, the tiles could do with better signage.

'Four days before the Peterloo Massacre, a cartoon entitled The Belle-alliance, or the female reformers of Blackburn!! was published, depicting the Blackburn Female Reform Society speaking at an open air meeting. Despite the women being well organised and sober, the cartoon depicts them as bawdy, licentious, and ugly women; their children lay abandoned, their clothes are dishevelled, and the drawing is peppered with sexual innuendo, implying that women who got involved with politics were merely looking for sexual favours.

The argument of the Female Reform Societies, however, was sound. Though they did not demand the vote for themselves, they recognised the impact of having a household member – their husbands and fathers – being able to vote would make a massive difference on matters such as income, wages, and working conditions'.

- People's History Museum https://phm.org.uk/blogposts/the-women-of-peterloo/

By the way….

Margaret Downes

Margaret was one of the many women dressed up in their bonnets and long dresses, expecting a good day out for a good cause. They could have had no idea of the carnage which awaited them; certainly Margaret Downes would have had no reason to believe that she would later that day be 'dreadfully cut in the breast [with a yeomanry sabre]… secreted clandestinely away, and cannot be heard of, supposed to be dead'.

Hundreds of people were injured as the yeomanry charged the crowds, who fled the field, crushing each other to escape the sabres of the volunteer militia. Included in the list of dead were, apart from Margaret Downes, Mary Heyes, and Martha Partington.

The Portico Library, Mosley Strvet

Another marvellous Manchester library: a veritable hidden treasure in the Greek revival style in 1806 which takes its name (originally the Portico Library & Newsroom) from the splendid portico which fronts the building and is based on the north elevation of the Temple of Athena Pallas at Priene.

The Portico Library occupies the upper floor; its collection of over 25,000 mostly 19th-century books includes many first editions and represents the interests and wisdom of Manchester's most influential Georgian and Victorian people. Built at the height of British colonialism, the books and archives offer 'a collection that reflects the innovations, but also the exclusions and inequities of its time.' In addition to the books, it held over 100 newspapers, journals and

The reading room; photographer Michael D. Beckwith. This file is made available under the Creative Commons CC0 1.0 Universal Public Domain Dedication.

magazines including the London papers. The ground floor is a pub, The Bank, which takes its name from the Bank of Athens that leased the property in 1921.

The gold lettered signage is fascinating with one showing 'Polite literature', that is novels, poetry and drama suitable for 'polite society', or 'educated people'.

The Portico is an independent subscription library. The first secretary was Mark Roget, he of the Thesaurus of English Words and Phrases, who was obviously blessed with a plethora of primary sources for his research. Famous members included Robert Peel snr, de Quincey, Richard Cobden, John Dalton and the Rev. William Gaskell - Mrs Gaskell was not a member as women were not allowed to join - until the Married Women's Property Act of 1870 – and Eric Cantona.

By the way…

In 1913 the Gallery was subject to attack by militant suffragettes, resulting in the imprisonment of Lillian Forester (1879–1973) née Williamson, (a student at Owens College) for three months for malicious damage and Evelyn Manesta for one month. They (with Annie Briggs) attacked the glass of thirteen paintings including two by John Everett Millais and 'The Last Watch of Hero and Captive Andromache' by Lord Frederic Leighton.

FAC 251, Charles Street, Oxford Road and Tony Wilson's headstone

"I felt an enormous responsibility, because it [the headstone] would be there for eternity. There is a permanence to it and that was a little intimidating"
- Peter Saville

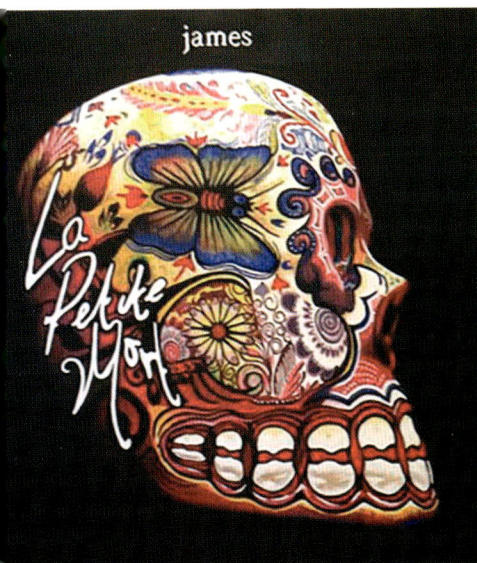

Factory Records was a Manchester based independent record label, established in 1978 by Tony Wilson and Alan Erasmus, which had on its books several significant acts such as Joy Division, New Order, Happy Mondays and (for a short while) Orchestral Manoeuvres in the Dark and James.

Fac 251 is the latest reincarnation of the building formerly known as Paradise Factory, Industry and as the home of Factory Records.

A quotation from the famous Isabella Banks novel, Manchester Man:

James' album cover La Petite Mort comes courtesy of Simon James Crossley; www.simonjamescrossley.com.

'Mutability is the epitaph of worlds / Change alone is changeless / People drop out of the history of a life as of a land though their work or their influence remains'

forms the epitaph on the Southern Cemetery tombstone of Tony Wilson (grave number 118 in Plot B).

Regarding the headstone Peter Saville, the designer, says

"It was the first time that I had ever been to a burial. I realised during Tony's memorial service, which was held in a remarkable little church in the centre of Manchester called The Hidden Gem, that there was a coffin there. There was a coffin there – with Tony in it. That was quite odd and quite upsetting. I had known him for such a long time and he had played such a pivotal role in my life, so that was strange. Then we went to Southern Cemetery in Manchester where his coffin was lowered into the ground and I had quite a profound feeling about it.

Isabella Burley adds:

Tony Wilson's death in 2007 marked a sombre moment for independent pop culture. Saville was asked by Wilson's family to design a headstone for his burial plot in Manchester's Southern cemetery. The process took three years and resulted in a beautiful design that captured the spirit of Factory Records and of course, Tony Wilson. It was numbered FAC-501, marking the last ever Factory art work.

https://www.anothermag.com/art-photography/2651/peter-saville-on-tony-wilsons-headstone
see also https://www.mdmarchive.co.uk/artefact/16769/Tony-Wilson-Photograph-2007B

By the way…
New Order's "Blue Monday" (FAC 73) was, as we know, an international chart hit in 1983. However, the label did not make any money from it since the original sleeve, die-cut and designed to look like a floppy disk, was so expensive to make that the label lost 5 pence on every copy they sold.

The Northern Quarter
& North Manchester

Northern Quarter street art:
1   The "Make Do Mend" mural by Nomad Clan on Port Street reflects the area's rag trade.
2   Next to Sweet Mandarin Chinese restaurant is a mural by Akse P19. The mural is of Debra Williams, an Operating Department Practitioner. It's a homage to the hard work of all the medical staff during the coronavirus pandemic.
3   A unique giclee art print of the 'Tyger Tyger Mural' painted by Jim Vision in 2019. This painting is a visual representation of William Blake's poem of the same name.

22 Bees

Twenty-two bees buzz busily over Manchester's Northern Quarter; this is the highly symbolic and moving bee mural by Qubek in Stevenson Square. They're part of a two-storey mural painted to commemorate the victims of the Manchester Arena bombing. On May 22, 2017, a suicide bombing at an Ariana Grande concert caused the deaths of 22 visitors and the injury of 139 others, more than half of them children. In the immediate aftermath, the Manchester Bee was quickly adopted as a symbol of public unity, which spread quickly via social media after illustrator Dick Vincent posted a bee on Instagram captioned with the life affirming caption 'stay strong our kid'. The Manchester bee went viral, enforcing its status as a symbol of Manchester resilience to partner with the existing symbol of Manchester industriousness. A Manchester Tattoo Parlours Qubek (AKA Russ Meehan) was launched almost immediately by Stalybridge tattoo artist Sam Barber, in which tattoos parlours offered tattoos of the bee for a £50 donation to victim-supporting charities.

Manchester first joined forces with the world of bees to symbolise the pivotal part Manchester played in the industrial revolution. The bees speak of the industriousness of the city's "worker bees" in the cotton mills, themselves dubbed "beehives". The greatest honour came in 1842 when the city officially adopted the bee and bees swarming across a globe were added to its coat of arms.

Around 100 years of bees quietly getting on with their endless work saw some discreet appearances: on bollards and bins in the city, on the Victorian Palace hotel's clock face (now the Kimpton Clocktower Hotel), the Boddingtons Brewery logo, and in the black and gold on one of Manchester City's recent away kits.

The bees on the coat of arms showing, among other things, global influence. The motto translates as 'good planning and hard work'.

By the way…The Bee Mural

Commissioned by the *Manchester Evening News*, the mural was painted just days after the bombing by artist Russ Meehan. Meehan had been painting bees on walls across Manchester for a number of years, but his artwork took on new significance in the wake of the attack.

The mural on the side of The Koffee Pot on Oldham St took only 2 days to complete. It features 22 Manchester worker bees swarming around a honey heart, a remarkable tribute to the 22 victims of the terror attack.

Isabella Banks

she gave birth to the Manchester Man

Isabella Banks (*née* Varley; 1821–1897) is also known as Mrs G. Linnaeus Banks. She was a novelist and poet. Born at 10 Oldham Street she is mainly remembered today for her classic book *The Manchester Man*, published in 1876.

Things started to take off when *The Manchester Guardian* published her poem *"A Dying Girl to her Mother"* in 1837. Around the same time she began to frequent the Sun Inn on Long Millgate in Manchester, a pub popular with poets, writers, and other working class intellectuals, and became part of a poetry collective known as *the Sun Inn Group* alongside figures such as *Samuel Bamford, John Critchley Prince, John Bolton Rogerson, Robert Rose, Elijah Ridings*, and *Robert Story*. However, shyness prevented her from taking an active part in the Group's meetings, preferring instead to hide behind a velvet curtain at the back of the room during readings, and asking others to read her own works aloud on her behalf. She contributed to the Sun Inn Group's only published anthology, *The Festive Wreath*, in 1842.

The Sun Inn (also known as Poet's Corner), located on Long Millgate in central Manchester, England. Taken in 1866. View is from outside Chetham's Library, looking east towards the junction with Todd Street. Two figures are partially visible standing in the doorway. Source: Chetham's Library.

Varley was paid for her writing for the first time through the Sun Inn Group, when she was commissioned by Rogerson, editor of *Oddfellows' Magazine* from 1841 to 1848. She also met her husband, *George Banks* - a journalist and editor who reported from across the UK — when both worked for the magazine. They married in 1846, after which she usually published under the name of "Mrs G. Linnaeus Banks," although she sometimes still wrote under her maiden name. Her first collection of poetry, *Ivy Leaves*, was published in 1844.[1]

Her output includes *Bond Slaves – the story of struggle* (1893), a *social novel* about Luddites in the north of England.

But it is *The Manchester Man* for which Isabella Banks is best remembered which was first serialised in *Cassell's Magazine* between January and November 1874, before being published in three volumes in 1876. It remains an important social and historical novel, charting the rise of Jabez Clegg, the eponymous "Manchester Man", from the time of the *Napoleonic Wars* to the first *Reform Act*. His personal fortunes, from the near tragic snatch of his crib from the River Irk, create a tale of romance and melodrama, his life from apprentice to master and from poverty to wealth, mirroring the growth and prosperity of the city. This is achieved in a politico-historical setting, with vivid accounts of the *Peterloo Massacre* of 1819 and the Corn-Law riots (the *Anti-Corn Law League* was formed in Manchester in 1838). In 1896, the year before she died, an illustrated edition of *The Manchester Man* was published with forty-six plates and three maps.

What's it all about?

An orphaned child is rescued by a tanner and his daughter from the *River Irk* during a storm. Simon, the tanner learns that the child's family did not survive the flood and Bess, his daughter, decides to foster the child herself. They christen him Jabez Clegg and he is educated as a Blue Coat Boy at *Chetham's Hospital School* under the supervision of clergyman *Joshua Brookes*. Jabez meets his antagonist, the wealthy Laurence

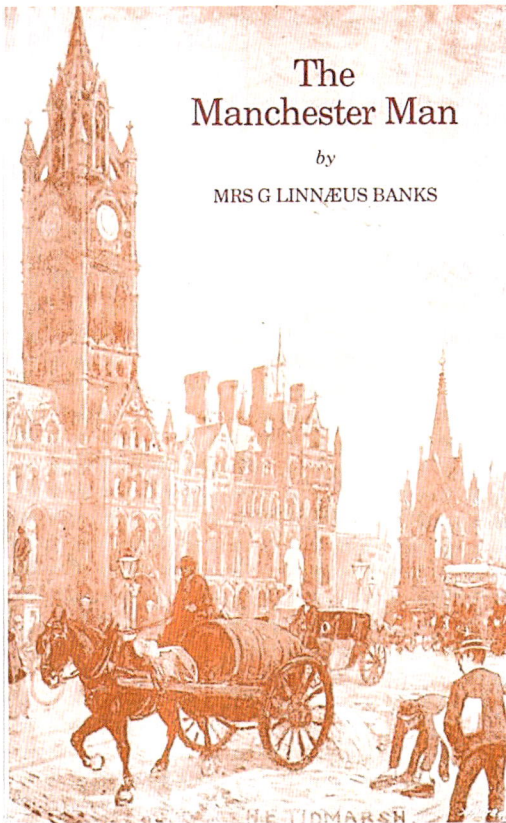

Aspinall, who is to be a rival for the rest of his life. Meanwhile, Bess is longing for the return of her lover, Tom Hulme, who is fighting in the Napoleonic wars. On his return, he sees Bess with the child and assumes that she has forgotten about him and remarried. Later, Jabez rises up the social ladder to become apprentice under Mr Ashton, whose daughter Augusta catches the eye of Jabez. A love diamond is created by Jabez, Augusta, Aspinall and Augusta's cousin, Eleanor.

The Manchester Man is remarkable for its historical detail.[2] It contains vivid accounts of early 19th century textiles and fashions, historical characters, and historical events including *Peterloo* and the sinking of the *Emma* [3], based on unpublished eye-witness accounts. The novel includes appendices in which the author delineates the historical versus fictional content.

The book is still read throughout the world and remains in print while its heroes, Jabez Clegg and Joshua Brooks, are commemorated locally in the names of Manchester *public houses*.[4] A quotation from the novel ('Mutability is the epitaph of worlds / Change alone is changeless / People drop out of the history of a life as of a land though their work or their influence remains') forms the epitaph on the Southern Cemetery tombstone of *Tony Wilson*, one of the founders of *Factory Records* in Manchester [5].

The Modernist, 58 Port Street

A shop, a magazine, a society, an online bookshop (https://the-modernist. org/pages/online-books), a newsletter, the Modernist offers talks, tours, exhibitions and films.

The Modernist gives us its mission statement, aims and scope:
We organise city mooches, talks, film screenings and exhibitions; we publish pamphlets, zines, photo books and magazines; we are specifically focused on raising awareness of modernist architecture and design and support a network of city 'chapters' in Birmingham, Leeds, Liverpool, Huddersfield, Manchester, Sheffield & Swansea… oh and we also run a gallery-bookshop!

Our publishing arm '*The Modernist*' was established in 2011, initially publishing as a quarterly printed magazine. The Modernist has now developed into a small press, publishing limited editions about 20th century architecture and design as well as evolving into a gallery and a shop.

1. *Van Ardsel, Rosemary T. (2004), "Banks, Isabella Varley (1821–1897)", Dictionary of National Biography, Oxford University Press*

2 *Brill, Barbara. Some Manchester Chroniclers, Library Review, Vol. 24 No. 4, pp. 147-153 1973.*

3 *https://en.wikipedia.org/wiki/Emma_(1828_ship)*

4 *'Jabez Clegg', Dover Street, M13; 'Joshua Brooks', 106 Princess Street, M1*

5 *Burgoyne, Patrick (22 October 2010). "Saville and Kelly's memorial to Tony Wilson". https://www.anothermag.com/art-photography/2651/peter-saville-on-tony-wilsons-headstone*

Courtesy of Gemma Parker of the Modernist Society and Magazine

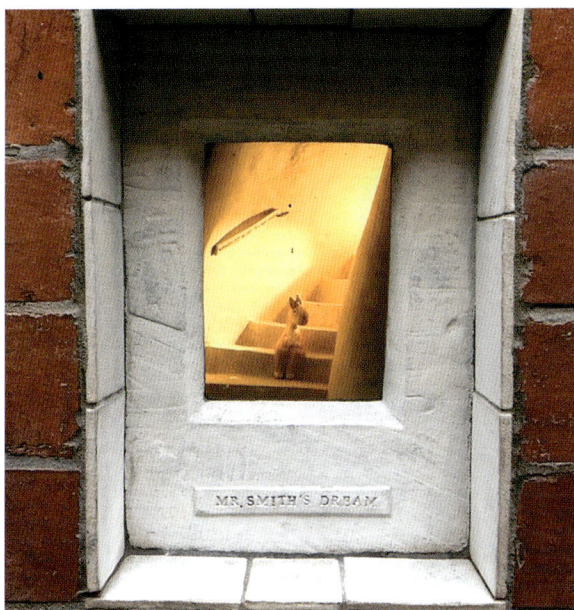

https://www.atlasobscura.com/places/mr-smiths-dream

Mr Smith's Dream and Manchester Craft & Design Centre

> *A tiny, heartwarming piece of art hiding in plain sight*
> *- Atlas Obscura*

Who better to tell us all about this than Atlas Obscura?

'Built into the brickwork of the Manchester Craft & Design Centre, this tiny piece of art is easily missed. Mr Smith's Dream is a true hidden gem and brings a smile to everyone who stumbles across it. Look at the piece, and you'll see a miniature staircase spiralling out of sight. The soft glow of the installation's backlight makes you wish you could shrink and enter the enticing secret world to which the stairs lead. The artwork was inspired by the many pet shops that once filled Manchester's Northern Quarter. It pays homage to a man named Mr. Smith, who once ran a pet shop in the area and often dreamt of his animals. It was designed by ceramicist Liz Scrine and commissioned by the Manchester City Council'.

The Centre was formerly a fish market, and the stunning glass roof allows the handicrafts and jewellery on display to be bathed in light.

Atlas Obscura advises: 'The artwork is on the Copperas Street side of the building and is visible at any time. If you're approaching from Oak Street, you'll see it beneath the fourth window you pass. It is opposite the tone MCR salon'.

Out House, Stevenson Square

What do you do with a depressingly ugly, dilapidated public toilet block if you don't demolish it? The former toilets in Manchester's Northern Quarter had been abandoned as repulsive concrete eyesores for decades before two artists turned the forgotten bathrooms into the vibrant, constantly evolving street art gallery known as Out House.

When Stevenson Square went into decline the brutalist restrooms were closed, leaving behind nothing but garish concrete. Enter two local artists, Tasha Whittle and Ben Harrison, to turn the decaying water closets into a vibrant art space. Thus, the blank urban canvases became the Out House project which allows local artists the chance to come and display their work. Every three months, a new group of artisans decorates the site with large-scale artworks.

Smithfield Market Hall, Swan Street

Smithfield Market Hall is a renovated *market hall* which houses a *food hall* known as Mackie Mayor. The hall reopened in 2017 after years of dereliction.

The area now known as part of the Northern Quarter in Manchester was named Smithfield Market in May 1822 because the potato market had moved to the area in 1820. Built between 1857 and 1858 and roofed over with iron trusses in 1865 the hall replaced an earlier butchers' shambles on the same site. As the area continued to expand a retail fish market was built the same year; the building has since been demolished however its extension built in two stages has survived. Smithfield Market was closed in 1972 and parts of the complex were demolished. Today it is a food lover's paradise with specialist independent kitchens serving up in the wonderful glass-roofed market hall.

Panoramic picture of the inside of Smithfield Market Hall, home to food hall Mackie Mayor; photographer Duncan Hull

Images courtesy John Mee for permission to use his stunning photos of Afflecks as at https://www.johnmeephotography.com/ return-to-afflecks-palace/

Afflecks

The Affleck & Brown Emporium opened in the 1860s as a drapery business in Oldham Street, closing in 1973 when the shopping landscape moved on and away to St Ann's Square and Deansgate. But you can't escape the past and Manchester's version of retro land came back in a blaze of glory with Affleck's Palace, later just Affleck's.

It was first opened in 1982 by James and Elaine Walsh offering those with enough get up and go affordable rent and no long-term contracts. A licence agreement allowed them to pay for space on a weekly basis. Affleck's chimed with the 1990s 'Madchester Summer of Love' period, when local bands reached dizzying heights.

By the way...

Mark Kennedy's totemic 'On the 6th day God created MANchester' mosaic on Affleck's wall in Short Street was restored in 2021.

The Tib Street Warp & Weft Mural

When public art tells a story - the history of the Northern Quarter in mural form
- Hayley Flynn

Hayley Flynn tells us how 'Installed in 1998 as part of the Tib Street Trail, a public arts trail dominated by ceramics, the mural is one of the most elaborate pieces of storytelling in the city'. *www.theskyliner.org/blog-1/the-warp-and-weft-mural* She continues 'the level of detail on the piece is fascinating.

Installed in 1998 as part of the Tib Street Trail, a public arts trail dominated by ceramic's...Liz Scrine's 'mural, found on Silver Jubilee Walk, is meant to be the peeled away, faded wallpaper of Ducks and Potts Mill which formerly occupied the site before it was replaced with the existing council houses... sometime around 1980. At this time the area was nameless and a sad sort of place, coined by Tony Wilson as 'our fucking Detroit".

Installed in 1998 as part of the Tib Street Trail, a public arts trail dominated by ceramics, the Liz Scrine's mural is one of the most elaborate pieces of storytelling in the city. Image by Arielle Vey, on Silver Jubilee Walk.

How the mural was composed is a fascinating story in itself; here's another extract from Hayley Flynn's piece:

Details within the mural reflect the history of the immediate area - the imprint of oak leaves for Oak Street, which would have once been a green space before the city expanded and it became dominated by the fish and poultry market (now Manchester Craft and Design Centre). The imprint of lace and jute for the weavers in the area, most of the original weavers' cottages can be found all over the Northern Quarter and many of these are listed giving the NQ the highest density of listed buildings within Manchester. There are buttons on the eyes of birds for button makers, and some tiles replicate business signs from the Victorian era. Just before the mural was created Steve Little, a researcher on the project, discovered some old pet shop adverts and letters under the floorboards of a former pet shop on Tib Street and a selection of these, from 1912 and earlier, have been transferred onto the pale tiles within the mural itself. You can see adverts for live tigers and read a letter of complaint about a mail order macaw who arrived with only one eye and a broken wing.

Manchester Craft & Design Centre, Oak Street

For more than 40 years, Manchester Craft & Design Centre has been home to 'some of the region's most talented independent designers and makers. Selling textiles, jewellery, accessories, ceramics, glass, prints and homeware, each of the 20 studios offers much more than just a shopping experience'.

The centre runs a free *exhibitions programme* that promotes and celebrates regional, national and international Craft talent. They also run a regular series of craft workshops

The superb building where all this happens is worth a trip alone. Housed in a former Victorian fish and poultry market, this light and airy space has retained some of its wonderful original features such as the fishmongers' booths on the ground floor.

A gem of an outlet here is **Valé et Oli** - a joint venture between Valery Touchet & Olive Youmbi. - Olive has kindly given permission to use two of her beautiful, colourful handmade fabrics, based on the cultural references of African wax print.

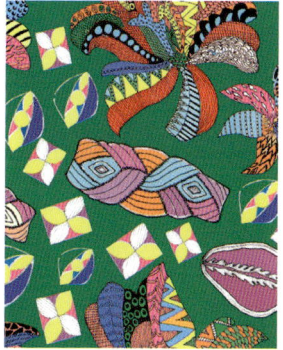

Olive surrounded by her vividly coloured African fabrics

Hallé St Peter's, Blossom Street

The Industrial Revolution transformed rural, villagey Ancoats into an area overwhelmed by cotton factories and warehouses; Ancoats was henceforth the beating heart of Cottonopolis.

Founded in 1858, the Hallé, Manchester's symphony orchestra, now ranks among the UK's top symphonic ensembles but when St. Peter's was built the following year, Ancoats had become an overcrowded and insanitary industrial slum endured by its poor population of more than 50,000. In the 1990s the church was closed and years of vandalism and decay ensued: in short, St Peter's was left to rot, a symbol of the wider neglect and dereliction of Ancoats. But restoration was at hand…

Since 2013 the deconsecrated Grade II listed Hallé St Peter's church has been the principal rehearsal and recording venue for the Hallé Orchestra, Choir and other Hallé ensembles. The striking 2019 three-storey Oglesby Centre hosts much of the orchestra's rehearsal activity with practice rooms and performance spaces, and incorporates the Victoria Wood Hall which became the new home for the Children's Choir of which she was patron.

The Hallé has been associated with Manchester since 1857 when German immigrant Charles Hallé formed a band in the city to perform at the Art Treasures Exhibition. The band became permanent and had as its home the Free Trade Hall until its move to the Bridgewater Hall in 1996.

One of the many stunning candle lit concerts held at St Peter's

The Printworks, Withy Grove

Sensitively restored after the 1996 IRA bomb with an eye on preserving its industrial history as far as possible. Built in the 1870s it was home to newspapers such as the *Manchester Evening Chronicle* and northern editions of Fleet Street nationals. By the 1920s it was Europe's biggest printing press.

In 2024 it relaunched with another European first: it is now home to the largest digital ceiling in Europe. The website *https://printworks-manchester.com/ printworks-refurb-2024/* tells us all about it:

Printworks has revealed a stunning 1000m² screen on its ceiling, the first of its kind in Europe. The centre has been transformed into an immersive, interactive digital family-friendly space with state-of-the-art digital screens flooding the central walkways with colour and sound. The experience is free of charge for our guests to enjoy and must be seen to be believed.

Nine actors, eight dancers, six dogs, four rabbits, three snakes, three swimmers, two tarantulas, one baby and one Coronation Street star were all filmed for over 250 hours to create the content over 12 months. In addition, stunning CGI content will run throughout the day and night at specially programmed times. We hope that every time you visit you'll see something new!

A digital gaming screen has also been added where passers-by can use their phones to play multi-player games against each other. Look out for the gaming screen on the hour for a new session, plus we'll be hosting some gaming events…

Another big surprise, however, is the roof garden. Featuring Happy Mondays' Bez's beehives, a chicken coop, wildflower meadow, orchard and herb garden, the award-winning urban retreat is something not to be missed. The garden's hives were first launched by Bez in August 2013 during his campaign to get bees back into the city centre. Altogether there are now four hives – housing around 240,000 bees. They are tended by The Printworks staff, who have become trained beekeepers.

Now there is a hotel providing shelter and habitat for around 100 common ground beetles.

The project has also raised hundreds of pounds for homeless charity The Booth Centre through the sale of its hen's eggs.

An allotment containing strawberries, rhubarb, cauliflower, potatoes and carrots is also used to make soup and other meals for the charity.

The Manchester Mural, Dantzik Street

A huge mural celebrating Manchester's best, its inspirational daughters and sons and its cultural landmarks is resplendent before our eyes.

The Printworks commissioned famous Manchester artist Justin Eagleton to create a lasting piece of nostalgic artwork, celebrating the city's rich and vibrant history. The result is a huge 4.8m wide by 2.4m high mural which is now on display on Dantzig Street.

The artwork includes famous landmarks including Belle Vue Circus, Beetham Tower, the Royal Exchange and the repurposed cotton mills that populate the city's landscape. Music heroes and legendary comedians such as The Stone Roses, Oasis, Victoria Wood, Peter Kay and Steve Coogan also make an appearance.

Charter Street Ragged School & Working Girls Home

The Ragged Schools offered Sunday school teaching, basic education, food and clothing to children who were too "ragged" to go to regular Sunday schools and church services.

Located on the corner of Dantzic Street and Little Nelson Street, Charter Street Ragged School which opened in 1861 was built on the site of the first industrial school in Manchester which had opened in 1847. The former Industrial School had become a dancing saloon "of the lowest class" and "a meeting house for thieves and prostitutes" with gaudy decorations. In 1862, the Charter Street School felt compelled to buy the building so as not to have to compete with the saloon. In the meantime, the school moved to Nelson Street and took with it the Band of Hope Friendly Society, soup kitchen and a savings bank.

Mervyn Busteed and Paul Hindle in their *"Angel Meadow: the Irish and Cholera in Manchester"* write that the school, "provided food, clogs and clothing

for children, and a Sunday breakfast for destitute men and women; medical services were also provided" all of which assisted around 3,000 people every year. The girls' home helped keep girls off the streets and for a small fee provided a bedroom and various facilities. They add that the school was, "intended to convey not only literacy but basic skills such as carpentry to the boys, and home making and cooking to the girls in order that they might become respectable, useful and productive citizens".

Volunteer workers were escorted to and from the school by the police, such was the social deprivation in the neighbourhood.

By the way…
Sharp Street Ragged School

> *"every boy in Manchester should be taught to darn his own socks and cook his own chops."*

This school was established in 1853 by evangelical Christians; the current building dates from 1869. The ground floor was for the reception class where "wild and subdued children" were segregated. The basic curriculum included the teaching of simple arithmetic, writing and reading, along with Bible-based religious and moral instruction. The school was eventually taken under School Board control in 1870. After World War II Sharp Street enjoyed strong connections with the cast of Coronation Street, particularly Violet Carson (Ena Sharples), who became President of the school - an example of life imitating art as her character was a caretaker in a mission hall similar to Sharp Street school. The building is now Grade II listed.

The charity Lifeshare tells us of the good and bad intentions surrounding the schools:

> Both schools met with resistance when they first started, from people with a vested interest in keeping the population of Angel Meadow ignorant and in want. The archives highlight that one group of people offered a higher rent for the original Sharp Street building to try to price out the school. It is pleasing to know that both schools are still standing and Charter Street is still providing free meals for the destitute via the charity Lifeshare.
> *www.lifeshare.org.uk*

Lydia Becker stood for the Manchester School Board as an independent member, receiving 15,000 votes and remaining a member until her death. As with her suffrage activities, her education work gave her a high public profile as she gave speeches and attended the opening of new Board Schools.

Laying the foundation stone of a new school in Burgess Street, Harpurhey she said

> "it was a great mistake to suppose that domestic duties were limited to girls and women, every boy in Manchester should be taught to darn his own socks and cook his own chops."

The school was eventually called Burgess Becker primary school, but the Becker part was dropped as parents would phone the school and call it Burgess Boris Becker School.

Some shocking facts:

1862 Annual Report: Soup kitchen opened with help from Cotton Famine Relief Committee (cotton famine caused by over production, and disruption of import of baled cotton by American Civil war). 20 beer houses closed in the area with help from the school. The Old Victory now a boys hostel/night refuge. Number of thieves diminished.

1865 Annual Report describes filthy narrow dangerous streets and overcrowded alleys and courts, damp cellars and rickety stairs leading to obscure garrets. Beds of orange boxes and straw with 3 families sleeping in 1 room.

1869 Annual Report – Surrounded by vice, crime and ignorance. 151 in infants class, sewing class introduced and a library with 350 books.

1900 300 children were given clogs, stockings and in certain circumstances entirely reclad. 300 were given toys & drums etc

Jewish Children for Redbank and Cheetham Hill received gifts at New Year to avoid religious sensitivies.

Local mortality rate was 50 per 1000 against a national average of 19.

Source:
https://raggeduniversity.co.uk/2014/09/26/ragged-schools-angel-meadows/

No 1 Angel Square – Co-operative Group Head Office

Every day something like 3,000 employees troop in an out of this stunning building. It is part of a marvellous regeneration of the once notorious Angel Meadow area - a 19th-century slum once described by Friedrich Engels as "hell on earth". No 1 Angel Square was finished off in 2013. The landmark building is 238 ft tall and forms the centrepiece of the £800 million NOMA development in the Angel Meadows area of Manchester city centre. The building cost at least £105 million to construct.

It remains is one of the most sustainable large buildings in Europe and is built to a BREEAM 'Outstanding' rating powered as it is by a biodiesel cogeneration plant using rapeseed oil to provide electricity and heat. No 1 'makes use of natural resources, maximising passive solar gain for heat and

One Angel Square as viewed from the CIS Tower nearing completion in October 2012. https://www.geograph.org.uk/photo/320617. David Dixon

using natural ventilation through its double-skin façade, adiabatic cooling, rainwater harvesting, greywater recycling and waste heat recycling'.[1]

In December 2012, the scheme surpassed its pan-European sustainability aims and achieved a world-record BREEAM (Building Research Establishment Environmental Assessment Method) score of 95.32%.[2] It is also an energy-plus building, producing surplus energy and zero carbon emissions. The building has received numerous awards for its striking aesthetic and sustainability aims.

HMP Strangeways, Cheetham Hill

One of the better known prisons in Britain, Strangeways is different from the other locations in this book in that access is strictly restricted and, in the short term, is usually one-way if indeed you do manage to get in. Nevertheless, the name resonates with natives and visitors alike and speaks Manchester, as one of its most infamous buildings with, of course, a fine main entrance and façade.

Notoriously, the prison boasted an execution chamber before the abolition of capital punishment in the United Kingdom in the 1960s. Originally, the prison contained an execution shed in B wing and after World War I a special execution room and cell for the condemned criminal was built. Strangeways was one of the few prisons to have permanent gallows. The first execution at Strangeways was that of 21 year old murderer Michael Johnson, who was hanged by William Calcraft on 29 March 1869. The last execution at the prison took place in 1964[1]. Gwynne Owen Evans was hanged by the executioner Harry Allen at 8:00 am on 13 August 1964, assisted by Royston Rickard. At the same time, Peter Allen was hanged at Liverpool's Walton Prison by Robert Leslie Stewart, assisted by Harry Robinson. Those were the last two judicial executions of death sentences in Britain.

Between 1 April and 25 April 1990, 147 staff and 47 prisoners were injured in a series of riots by prison inmates. There was one fatality among the prisoners, and one prison officer died. The riots resulted in the Woolf Inquiry, after which the prison was rebuilt and renamed Her Majesty's Prison, Manchester. Repair and modernisation cost more than £80 million after the riot, and rebuilding was completed in 1994.

The prison has a poor reputation for a high suicide rate following its reopening in 1994. From 1993 to 2003, Strangeways had the second highest number of suicides among inmates of any prison in the United Kingdom and, in 2004, Strangeways had the highest number of suicides in the country.

---

1 *"Low Carbon Office design". forty4consulting.*

2 *"The UK's Most 'Outstanding' Green Building", designbuildsource.com.au. 21 December 2012.*

Some notable inmates:

- *Joey Barton,* footballer jailed for assault.
- *Brendan Behan,* Irish republican, playwright and poet, imprisoned in Strangeways in 1947 for attempting to free an IRA prisoner.
- *Ian Brady,* held for theft prior to the Moors murders.
- *David Britton,* author of *Lord Horror,* the last publication to be banned under the Obscene Publications Act.[25]
- *Charles Bronson,* a criminal who has been referred to in the British press as the "most violent prisoner in Britain" and "Britain's most notorious prisoner".
- *Ian Brown,* musician and singer-songwriter jailed for "air rage". Wrote three songs inside: *"Free My Way"*, *"So Many Soldiers"*, and *"Set My Baby Free"*. Released in December 1999.
- *Valdo Calocane,* perpetrator of the 2023 Nottingham attacks in which three people were stabbed to death and three others were injured. Held at HMP Manchester briefly whilst awaiting trial before later being transferred to Ashworth Hospital.
- *Thomas Cashman,* convicted of shooting dead nine-year-old girl in Liverpool in August 2022.
- *Connor Chapman,* the gunman from the Christmas Eve 2022 Wallasey pub shooting.
- *Emily Davison,* suffragette, sentenced to a month's hard labour in 1909 after throwing rocks at the carriage of chancellor David Lloyd George. Hunger strike led to force feeding. Blockaded herself in her cell and sued Strangeways for using a water cannon.

- *David Dickinson,* TV presenter specialising in antiques, imprisoned for fraud in pre-celebrity days.
- *Benjamin Mendy,* French football player.
- *Christabel Pankhurst,* suffragette, was held for a week.
- Gordon Park, convicted in 2005 of murdering his first wife, Carol Park, in 1976.[35]
- *Harold Shipman,* serial killer, who was held there on remand whilst awaiting trial.
- *Reynhard Sinaga,* an Indonesian serial rapist found guilty of assaulting 48
- *Ray Teret* – former radio DJ and friend of *Jimmy Savile* convicted of a series of sexual offences, including seven rapes, for which he was sentenced to 25 years in prison. Died at HMP Manchester in 2021.
- *Catherine Tolson* and *Helen Tolson,* suffragette sisters imprisoned in 1909 for breaking glass at White City in Manchester.

The prison keeps cropping up in popular music, for example:

- *"Strangeways"*, a track on the 1987 rock album The House of Blue Light by Deep Purple.
- Strangeways, Here We Come, 1987 album by The Smiths.
- *Ian Brown*, see above.
- In the song *"There Goes a Tenner"* from the album The Dreaming, *Kate Bush* sings of being "a star in Strangeways". The song is about a botched bank robbery.

It features in an episode of Hancock's Half Hour when *Bill Kerr* defends Sid James's character with the words - "He's not a criminal - he's just got strange ways". And it's mentioned by *John Cooper Clarke* in his poem *"Are You the Business?"* when John Cooper Clarke asks "Is Strangeways full of prisoners?".

During the reign of Henry VIII (1509–1547), as many as 72,000 people are estimated to have been executed[2]. In Elizabethan England, the death penalty applied for treason, murder, manslaughter, infanticide, rape, arson, grand larceny (theft of goods worth more than a shilling), highway robbery, buggery, sodomy and heresy. Hanging was the method used for all but treason, which was punished by drawing, hanging and quartering for men, burning for women, and beheading for the nobility; and heresy, which was punished by burning. About 24% of those facing trial for such offences were actually executed. About 75% of hangings were for theft.

---

1 *In 1965, the death penalty for murder in Britain was suspended for five years and in 1969 this was made permanent. However, it was not until 1998 that the death penalty in Britain was finally abolished for all crimes. The last people executed in the UK were Peter Allen and Gwynne Evans on 13 August 1964.*

100. Manchester Jewish Museum, Cheetham Hill

Cheetham Hill has been a magnet for immigrants and refugees for centuries providing refuge and sanctuary for, for example, the Irish fleeing the 19th century potato famine and British oppression; and the Jews escaping Russian anti-Semitism and then the Nazis; and Afro-Caribbeans and south Asians doing us a colonial favour by lending us their help in rebuilding a country shattered by, again, the Nazis. Today, this is a place where more than 150 languages are spoken – and that speaks volumes about the multi-ethnicity and multiculturalism of the place. It is now home to the Irish World Heritage Centre.

The Manchester Jewish Museum is housed in a former synagogue: built in 1874 in unmistakeable Moorish-style architecture: the museum first opened in 1984, housed in a Grade II* listed 1874 (former) Spanish and Portuguese synagogue. This building is the oldest-surviving synagogue in Manchester

offering breathtaking original stained glass windows and ornate ironwork. Inside, the museum explores and celebrates the lives and importance of Jewish people in Manchester, through a number of permanent collections. You can learn about Jewish life in the city through items, documents, photographs and spoken stories, providing an immersive understanding of the role Manchester's Jewish community played in the city's growth: in short, a unique insight into Manchester's Sephardi Jewish history. The website tells us that the collection is considered to be of national and international significance.

The museum is home to over 31,000 items documenting the story of Jewish migration and settlement in Manchester. It includes over 530 oral history testimonies, over 20,000 photographs, 138 recorded interviews with Holocaust survivors and refugees and many other objects, documents and ephemera.

Gabby Jahanshahi-Edlin grew up in Hale, Trafford – her roots are in Eastern Europe. She started Bloody Good Period in 2016, when she found out that very few food banks and asylum seeker drop-in centres were providing period products— despite an obvious, desperate need. She successfully developed BGP from a Facebook whip-round for products to a growing, trailblazing charity. It is now linked to over 100 drop-in centres for asylum seekers and refugees around the country. See https://www.manchesterjewishmuseum.com/wp-content/uploads/2023/08/ ilovepdf_merged-8.pdf

The Museum of Transport, Cheetham

Greater Manchester has much to offer in transport terms; we had the first purpose-built canal in 1761, the first bus service in the UK in 1824, the world's first public passenger carrying railway in 1830 and one of the first extensive tramway networks in Britain. All of this is displayed and recorded here with historic buses, coaches, trams, objects and displays inside a 1930s bus garage.

An early project of the society was the restoration of Manchester Corporation Tramways 765, which had been found on a farm near Huddersfield.

By the way…

The Tramways Museum, Heaton Park

The Manchester Transport Museum Society (MTMS) was founded as a registered charity in the early 1960s, with the aim of the preservation of documents and artifacts relating to public transport in the Manchester region. An early project of the society was the restoration of Manchester Corporation Tramways 765, which had been found on a farm near Huddersfield.

The Ukrainian Cultural Centre, 31 Smedley Lane

Manchester Ukrainian Cultural Centre or 'Dnipro' has been at the heart of the Ukrainian Community in Manchester and the surrounding areas for over 60 years; it is a valuable asset in the development of Ukrainian culture, education and traditions for all communities across Manchester.

"20 Days in Mariupol," directed by Mstyslav Chernov, has won an Oscar Award as the 2024 Best Documentary Feature. This is the first Oscar in Ukrainian history.

Manchester Ukrainian Archives tells us

'The first record of Ukrainians in Manchester is an entry in the Aliens Register in Salford of J. Koyetsky from Brody, Ukraine in 1897. Some 100 families settled in Manchester before WWI after which a community centre was established. Towards the end of WWII and after a large number of Ukrainians (mainly displaced persons from camps in Germany) arrived in Manchester and the surrounding towns. Ukrainians were integrated into the UK as European Voluntary Workers, while Ukrainian POWs from the Polish and German armies were also demobilised and settled in the Manchester area as well as other parts of the UK'.

It goes on to say that 'The size of the Ukrainian community in the late 1940s was up to 10,000 persons in the Greater Manchester area, with 3,000 of them in Manchester alone. The community integrated with the early migrants (1890s) at the community centre in Cheetham Hill'.

The Manchester Branch of the Association of Ukrainians in GB (AUGB) was established during the late 1940s as well as a Ukrainian Women's' Organisation (OUZh), a Ukrainian Youth Organisation (CYM), Plast (Ukrainian Scouts) and a Ukrainian Former Combatants Organisation.

Nowadays the Manchester Cultural Centre provides facilities for the main community groups of AUGB.

It was on Smedley Lane that the orator and activist Henry Hunt stayed (in Smedley Cottage which was behind St Luke's Church) with Joseph Jackson, the organiser of the tragedy which we know as the Peterloo Massacre.

Hannah Beswick: the Manchester Mummy

Hannah died in 1758 and is buried in Manchester General Cemetery in Harpurhey; but it was a long and circuitous underworld journey which finally got her there in 1868 over a century after her demise. Hannah Beswick

'The Premature Burial' (1854) by Antoine Joseph Wiertz in the Museum of Antoine Wiertz in Ixelles, Belgium

The Northern Quarter

(1688 – 1758), of *Oldham*, was a woman of means whose life was spoiled, to say the least, by her pathological fear of *premature burial, or taphephobia*; in laymen's terms she was terrified of the prospect of being buried alive: she told her doctor this and set up what was the opposite of a DNR, 'do not resuscitate'. Following her death in 1758 her body was *embalmed* and kept above ground, to be periodically checked for signs of life. The embalming probably involved a blood transfusion using a mixture of *turpentine* and *vermilion*.[1]

The body was then stored, aptly, in an old grandfather clock case in the house of Beswick's doctor in Sale, *Dr Charles White*. Dead as she was she became a local celebrity, and visitors were allowed to view the corpse at Dr White's house who eventually out-died her at which time the mummified body was bequeathed to the *Museum of the Manchester Natural History Society*, where she enjoyed yet more celebrity on display in the entrance hall there next to a *Peruvian* and an Egyptian *mummy*.

The "cold dark shadow of her mummy hung over Manchester in the middle of the eighteenth century", according to *Edith Sitwell* [2]. Some time later the museum's collection was transferred to *Manchester University* (or Owen's College as it then was) when it was decided in 1867, with the permission of the *Bishop of Manchester*, that Beswick should finally be buried since she had displayed all the symptoms of being dead for over a century and none of the symptoms of being alive . The funeral took place on 22 July 1868, more than 110 years after her death in an unmarked the grave.

Further reading:

Bondeson, Jan (1997), A Cabinet of Medical Curiosities, I. B. Taurus

Bondeson, Jan (2001), Buried Alive: the Terrifying History of our Most Primal Fear, W. W. Norton & Company

Cooper, Glynis (2007), Manchester's Suburbs, Breedon Books

Dobson, Jessie (1953), "Some Eighteenth Century Experiments in Embalming", Journal of the History of Medicine and Allied Sciences 8 (4): 431–441

---

1 *The veins and arteries would have been injected with a mixture of turpentine and vermilion, after which the organs would have been removed from the chest and then the abdomen placed in water, to clean them and to reduce their bulk. As much blood as possible would then have been squeezed out of the corpse, and the whole body washed with alcohol. The next stage would have been to replace the organs and to repeat the injection of turpentine and vermilion. The body cavities would then have been filled with a mixture of camphor, nitre and resin, before the body was sewn up and all openings filled with camphor. After a final washing, the body would have been packed into a box containing plaster of Paris, to absorb any moisture, and then probably coated with tar, to preserve it.*
   See Zigarovich, Jolene (2009), "Preserved Remains: Embalming Practices in Eighteenth-Century England", Eighteenth-Century Life, 33 (3): 65–104

2 *Sitwell, Edith (1933), The English Eccentrics, London*

By the way…

Throughout January, 1880, the nation was both shocked and fascinated by the murder of a servant girl, which took place on Wednesday, 8th January, 1880, in Harpurhey. The victim was Sarah Jane Roberts, an eighteen-year-old girl from Pembroke in South Wales.

The sorry story reveals some interesting details about coroners and post-mortem examination and optography at the close of the 19th century.

The Manchester Courier, on Friday, 16th January, 1880, reported that the police were examining the victim's eyes in the hope that they might be imprinted with an image of the murderer… Mr. Superintendent Bent, we understand, proposes making a microscopic examination of the eyes of the murdered girl from the portrait which was photographed shortly before her interment.

The portrait, as stated in yesterday's Courier, has already been examined by the electric light, but although the eyes were each magnified to the size of half a sheet of ordinary notepaper, there was nothing visible which would furnish the slightest evidence as to the features of the murderer [1].

Optography is the process of viewing or retrieving an optogram, an image on the retina of the eye. A belief that the eye "recorded" the last image seen before death was all the rage in the late 19th and early 20th centuries, and was a frequent plot device in fiction of the time, to the extent that police photographed

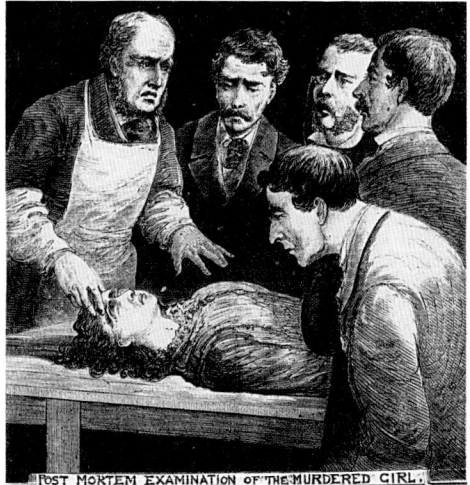

From The Illustrated Police News, Saturday, 31st January, 1880.

the victims' eyes in several real-life murder investigations, just in case the theory was true. The concept has been repeatedly debunked as a *forensic* method.

Further reading

Ang JL, Collis S, Dhillon B, Cackett P. The Eye in Forensic Medicine: A Narrative Review. *Asia Pac J Ophthalmol (Phila).* 2021 Sep 14;10(5):486-494

Atreya A, Ateriya N, Menezes RG. The eye in forensic practice: In the dead. *Med Leg J.* 2024 May 1:258172241230210.

Gerstmeyer, K. et al.: *The last image. On the history of optography*, European Society of Cataract and Refractive Surgeons.

Ogbourne, Derek: *Optography and optograms,* The College of Optometrists.

Ogbourne, Derek (2008). Encyclopedia of Optography. Muswell Press.

---

1 My debt here is to the https://www.jack-the-ripper-tour.com/generalnews/the-murder-of-sarah-jane-roberts/ posted by Robert Jones, January 8, 2020

From The Illustrated Police News, Saturday, 31st January, 1880.

The Manchester Martyrs Memorial, St Joseph's Cemetery, Moston

'I dare not, I must do my duty' attributed to Sgt Charles Brett

In 1858, a young man by the name of James Stephens founded a secret society which he called the Irish Republican Brotherhood (an early forerunner of the IRA). This soon became known as the Fenian Movement, derived from the Fianna Eirann, a legendary band of Irish warriors led by Fin MacCoul. The object of the Fenians was to overthrow British rule in Ireland and it was their basic belief that this would be impossible to do by political means alone: armed insurrection, they believed, was the only solution.

In December 1866 James Stephens' role was taken over by an Irish American, a veteran of the American Civil War, Colonel Thomas J. Kelly, originally from Galway. He had, as his second in command, Captain Timothy Deasy, also a war veteran. There were, by now, a number of Civil War veterans in Great Britain, including Captain Edward O'Meagher Condon, who came to Manchester in 1867 to rejuvenate the nine Circles there and who was soon *de facto* Head Circle for the north of England.

One evening in September Kelly and Deasy were ambushed by the police after a meeting in Manchester. Deasy drew a pistol, but this was wrestled from him before he had a chance to use it. Kelly, too, was overwhelmed before he could use his revolver and was taken, with his companion, to the nearest police station. Once at the station they did themselves no favours with odd, evasive answers as to how they had arrived in England and the magistrate had no compunction in remanding them in custody for a week.

The Manchester Martyrs were three *Irish nationalists* – William Philip Allen, Michael Larkin, and Michael O'Brien – who were *hanged* in 1867 following their murder conviction after an attack on a *police van* in *Manchester*, in which a *police officer*, Sergeant Charles Brett, was accidentally shot dead, an incident known at the time as the 'Manchester Outrages'.

The red plaque marking the location of the Fenian Ambush, on Hyde Road

This monument, raised by public subscription, was erected to the memory of the Manchester Martyrs and stands in the Roman Catholic Cemetery in Moston

The three men were members of the *Irish Republican Brotherhood*, the *Fenians*, an organisation devoted to ending *British rule in Ireland* and fomenting an uprising in Britain; they were among a group of 30 to 40 Fenians who attacked a horse-drawn police van transporting two arrested leaders of the Brotherhood, *Thomas J. Kelly* and *Timothy Deasy*, to *Belle Vue Gaol*. Police Sergeant *Charles Brett*, travelling inside with the keys, was shot and killed while looking through the keyhole of the van as the attackers attempted to force the door open by shooting the lock.

Kelly and Deasy were sprung after one of the women in the van took the keys from Brett's body and passed them to the group outside through a ventilation grill; the pair were never recaptured. According to Paul Rose (p. 42) such was the zeal of the police in the search that one man with a strong Irish accent surrendered himself to the magistrates "as the only means I have of saving myself from being arrested over and over again wherever I go, as a Fenian". Allen and Larkin admitted taking part in the attack, but none of the defendants was accused of firing the fatal shot; they were convicted on the basis of "joint enterprise" for taking part in a criminal enterprise that ended in the killing. At the time, the Irish community in Manchester accounted for more than 10 per cent of the population, and one contemporary estimate put the number of Fenians and Fenian sympathisers living within 50 miles of the city at 50,000[1].

It all started when in the early hours of September 11, 1867, police arrested two men found loitering in Oak Street, Shudehill, suspecting them of planning to rob a shop. Both were charged under the Vagrancy Act and held in custody. The Manchester police were initially unaware of their identities, until their colleagues in the Irish police identified them as Kelly and Deasy.[2]

According to the Sullivans, on 18 September 1867, Kelly and Deasy were being transferred from the courthouse to Belle Vue Gaol on Hyde Road, Gorton. They were handcuffed and locked in two separate compartments inside a police van escorted by a squad of 12 mounted policemen. The van contained six prisoners: a 12-year-old boy who was being taken to a reformatory, three women convicted of misdemeanours, and the two Fenians.[3] As it passed under a railway arch, a man darted into the middle of the road, pointed a pistol at the driver and told him to stop. Simultaneously, a party of about 30–40 men leaped over a wall at the side of the road, surrounded the van and seized the horses, one of which they shot.[4] The unarmed police were described by O'Meagher Condon, who organised the attack on the police van,[5] as "a miscellaneous lot, apparently embracing the long and short and the fat and lean of the Manchester force"; they offered little resistance and soon fled.

The trial took place in what was described as a "climate of anti-Irish hysteria" by the radical British weekly Reynold's Newspaper, which described it as a "deep and everlasting disgrace to the English government", the product of an ignoble panic which seized the governing classes. A yell of vengeance, it said, had issued from every aristocratic organ, and that before any evidence had been obtained the prisoners' guilt was assumed and their executions had been demanded. The Irish historian F. S. L. Lyons, writing in the 1970s, said that the men were convicted "after an unsatisfactory trial, and on evidence that, to say the least, was dubious"[6]. More recently, the events have been described as "accidental murder, public panic and rumour-mongering, elaborate trial... and lingering doubts about a miscarriage of justice[7]."

Allen, Larkin and O'Brien were publicly hanged on a temporary structure built on the wall of *Salford* Gaol, on 23 November 1867, in front of a crowd of 8,000–10,000. A platform had been built about 30 feet above ground, through the outside wall of the jail facing New Bailey Street, to support the *gallows*. The spectators were "well supplied by the gin palaces of Deansgate and the portable beer and coffee stalls".[8]

The authorities were at pains to discourage any rescue attempt. Over 2,500 regular and special police were deployed in and around the prison, reinforced by a military presence which included a detachment of the *72nd Highlanders* (later the 1st Battalion, Seaforth Highlanders) and a squadron of the Eighth Hussars. All traffic in and out of the city was stopped.[9]

Sadly, this was to be one of the first in a history of wrongful convictions of alleged Irish terrorists, culminating in the Birmingham Six (1974) and Guildford Four (1975) miscarriages of justice and cover-ups.

Police Sergeant Brett was buried in Harpurhey Cemetery; the words "I will do my duty" are engraved on his tombstone. There is also a memorial tablet to him in *St Ann's Church, Manchester*.

---

1 Rose, Paul (1970), *The Manchester Martyrs: The Story of a Fenian Tragedy*, Lawrence & Wishart. See also Glynn, Anthony (1967), *High Upon the Gallows Tree: The story of the Manchester Fenian Rescue of 1867 and of Allen, Larkin and O'Brien*, Anvil Books and Kee, Robert (1972), *The Green Flag Vol. II: The Bold FenianMen*, Penguin Books.

2 Rose p. 17

3 Sullivan, T. D.; Sullivan, A. M.; Sullivan, D. B. (1953) [1882], Ua Cellai, Seán Ua Cellaigh (ed.), *Speeches from the Dock*, Dublin: M. H. Gill & Son

4 Sullivans p. 337, 338

5 Rose, pp. 32- 36

6 Lyons, F. S. L. (1985). *Ireland since the Famine*. London

7 Busteed, Mervyn (November–December 2008). "The Manchester Martyrs: a Victorian melodrama". *History Ireland*.

8 Rose, p. 10

9 See Chrystal, Paul, *The Seaforth Highlanders* (2024)

Heaton Park

Covering some 600 acres, Heaton Park is the largest park in Manchester and the largest municipal park in Europe. Heaton Hall lies at the very heart of the park famous for its Orangery. It is Grade I listed, neo-classical and built in 1872.

Despite the great pleasure that can be had here with the animal farm, boating lake, golf course, bowling green, Transport Museum, zip wire, picnics and cafes Heaton Park is replete with historic buildings and has something of a recurring military history. In World War I the Pals Battalions of the Manchester Regiment trained here, not very representative of the sucking bogs of the trenches which awaited them; the Hall itself became a Military Hospital and in World War II the RAF came in their hundreds of thousands for combat training.

And then there was the Cold War and the Heaton Park Tower when the British government proposed a communications network that would (theoretically anyway) survive a nuclear attack. Radio stations (including the 72m high Heaton Park Tower) would maintain national and international communications before, during and after a nuclear emergency, transmitting microwave radio signals in a network known as Backbone. Whether or not the Backbone network plan was realized is classified, but HM Government denied in Parliament that the tower's function was secretive[1].

Beside the tower was a monitoring station (one of hundreds across the country) to record the blast and fallout in the event of a nuclear war. The station provided for three men from the *Royal Observer Corps* (ROC) to live underground whilst recording what was happening above ground during a nuclear strike[2].

Heaton Park Colonnade. The Colonnade dates back to 1822, when Francis Goodwin designed it as the façade of the Old Town Hall on King Street. Photo: Steven Haslington @ Geograph, Creative Commons.

1 *"CONCRETE RADIO TOWERS (Hansard, 18 December 1962)". Parliamentary Debates (Hansard). 18 December 1962.*

2 *"Heaton Park in World War Two and World War One" - www.lancashireatwar.co.uk.*

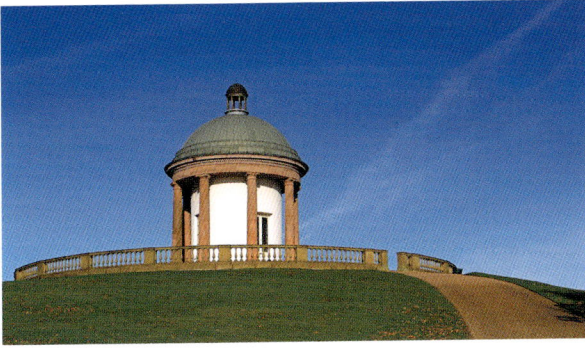

Heaton Park Temple. It was built in the 19th century and provides panoramic views of the city. A sign reads: "The Temple stands at the highest point in the City of Manchester." It doesn't.

https://www.silverkris. com/guide/uk/man/do-manchester/heaton-park/

The Colonnade was from originally from Manchester Town Hall.

The Temple Folly dates from around 1800.

Edgar Wood, Middleton

'The boldest building of the early 20th century in England is without doubt Wood's First Church of Christ Scientist (in Manchester's Victoria Park). It is a pioneer work, internationally speaking, of an Expressionism halfway between Gaudi and Germany about 1920. (It is) one of the most original buildings anywhere.' So wrote Nikolaus Pevsner, no less. The melding of Arts and Crafts (1860-1910) with Art Nouveau and 'marrying them to create something 'modern' and different, yet still beautiful, was one of Wood's hallmarks, and resulted in something unique in Europe'.

The Arts & Crafts Church, Middleton - Edgar Wood Society

Edgar Wood's First Church of Christ Scientist (in Manchester's Victoria Park).

Wood was born and brought up in Middleton, the son of a cotton manufacturer. The intention was that he join the family business but he wanted to be a fine artist. The trade-off with the family was that he apply himself to the art of architecture.

He was a founder of the Northern Art Workers' Guild in 1896, one of the major provincial societies within the Arts and Crafts Movement and was president of the Manchester Society of Architects from 1911 to 1912. Wood retired in 1921 with 21 of his architectural works listed.

By 1892, his practice was flourishing and he moved into new premises at 78 Cross Street in the centre of Manchester. He would arrive for work attired in a large black cloak, lined with red silk, a flat, broad-brimmed hat and brandishing a silver handled cane. He said, "If an architect is not allowed to advertise his name he must advertise his personality."

We have Wood to thank for salvaging the colonnade from Manchester's first town hall. The Colonnade formed the entrance facade of the Old Manchester Town Hall in King Street, built between 1822 and 1824. When the Old Town Hall was demolished in 1912 the Colonnade was moved to Heaton Park.

Wood raised a public appeal and prepared a scheme for the re-erection of the colonnade in *Platt Fields park*, and when this was rejected he drew up another for a site in *Heaton Park* where the colonnade now stands, "a magnificent Ionic wide screen and a fine parkland feature."

Salford & West Manchester

Gaythorn Street

The area known around Gaythorn Street near the Medlock has been defined by its huge, ugly, noisome gas cylinders which prevailed for a century or so and the 1832 cholera outbreak. The desperate community there were described as feral, existing as they did in damp and disease-ridden hovels ten feet by nine with ten souls crammed in, and toilets serving them and 250 neighbours. During the cholera epidemics in the 1840s the authorities bricked up the 'houses' and sealed the area up as a disease containment measure.

L.S. Lowry on Gaythorn Street with Oldfield Road Dwellings in the background

The only good to come out of this dire place was the good, philanthropic work it encouraged by people such as Dr James Philip Kay and Jacob Venedy as well as *The Origin and Progress of the Malignant Cholera in Manchester* by Henry Gaulter. Kay described the residents as 'the haunt of hordes of thieves and desperadoes who defy the law and is always inhabited by a class resembling savages in their appetites and habits'. Venedy, a German social historian, observed how

'hundreds were evicted from their cellars. Hundreds rotted alive next to the unburied dead. And the endless pestilence that was raging there had taken such a grip that all fumigation and cleaning were useless and the decision had to be taken to brick up many of these pits'.

Salford Museum and Art Gallery, Peel Park

Opened to the public in November 1850 as the Royal Museum and Public Library devoted to the history of Salford and *Victorian* art and *architecture.*

This superb museum gives a rare opportunity to walk down a Victorian Street, a street fixed for over 100 years in the past. Lark Hill Place is a mock-up Victorian street, complete with genuine street signs and fittings that allow museum visitors the chance to feel as though they've been transported back to 1897. A range of Victorian businesses line the street, including a chemist, blacksmith, toy shop, and printers, all fitted out with genuine Victorian artifacts salvaged from Salford and Manchester. And a pub, The Blue Lion Tavern.

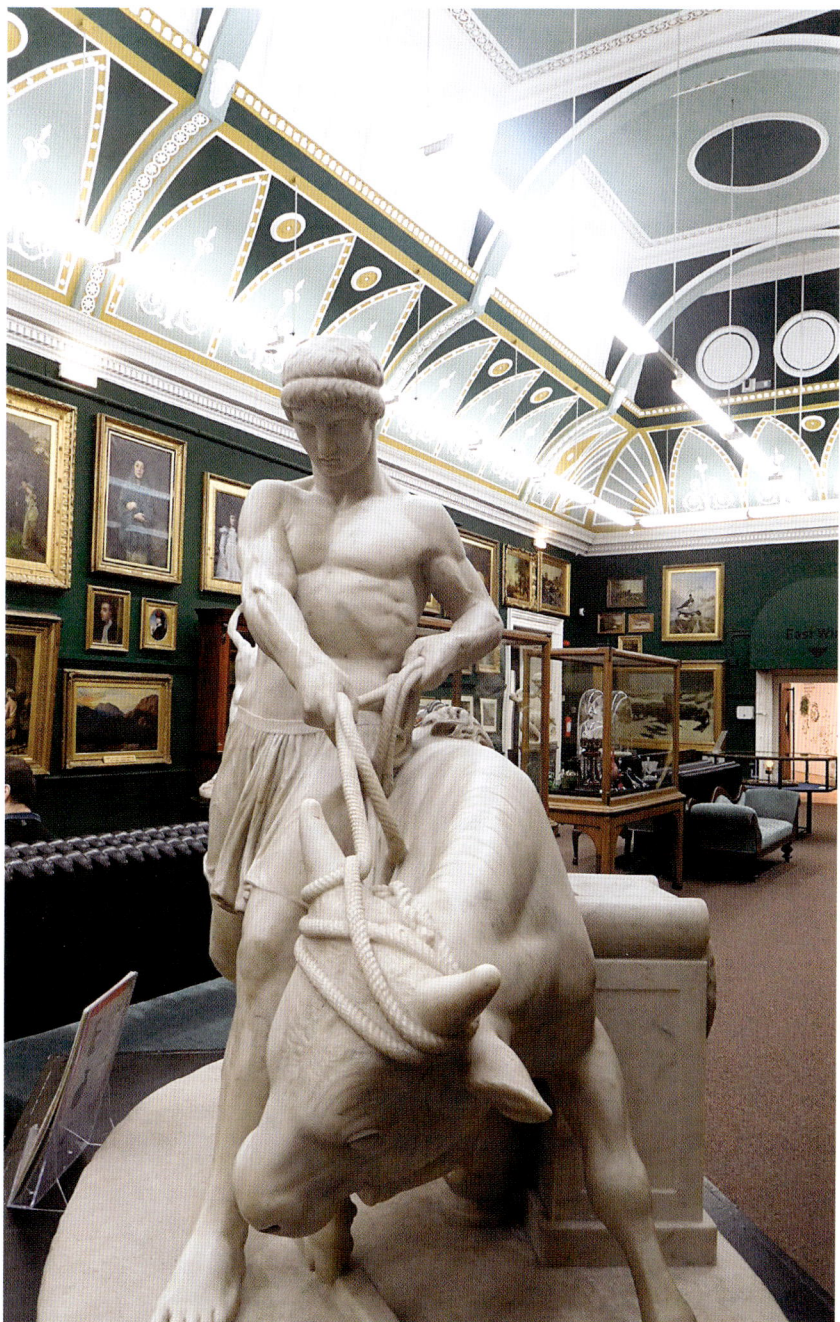

The beautiful ceiling and 'Greek hero leading a bull to be sacrificed'. Alfred Gatley (1816–1862).

'Salford Museum and Art Gallery holds a fantastic collection of **Pilkington's Lancastrian Pottery** which was made at the Clifton factory in Salford. The items span almost the entire history of the factory from 1889 to 2008 and is evidence of one of the most successful and longest surviving of the British art potteries founded in the late Victorian period'.

Corbett, A & B (2016). *Pilkington's Lancastrian and Royal Lancastrian Pottery. A guide for collectors.* Pilkington's Lancastrian Pottery Society

Flora's train tiles, designed by Walter Crane

See https://www.pilkingtons-lancastrian.co.uk/history.htm

The Females of the Factory: Women's contribution to Pilkington's Tiles and Pottery, Lancaster Arts'

By the way:

William Burton (1863–1941)

The company was established in 1892 at Clifton Junction, alongside Fletcher's Canal. William Burton was a chemist with the Wedgwood Company at the Etruria Works in Stoke-on-Trent, with an extensive knowledge of the ceramics industry. It was he who suggested that the red clay and marl found at Clifton was suitable for production of ceramic tiles.

> *'A distinctive type of ware produced in the last years were glazed with a formula including uranium compounds, which gave a bright orange colour, but have the disadvantage of being slightly radioactive; "it has been suggested by experts that one should not store a large number of such pieces in a closed cabinet. Opening the door after a prolonged period could be equivalent to receiving an X-ray"'.*
>
> Bergesen, Victoria (1992). *Bergesen's Price Guide: British Ceramics*. Barrie & Jenkins.

Burton was a boss who cared about the well-being of his workers, many of whom were factory girls and women labouring in toxic and life-shortening conditions. There were annual free day trips to the seaside and milk was dispensed in a bid to offset the debilitating impact of the chemicals and lead used. Pilkington's paid for young artists to go to art school.

Two highly contrasting but similar images of Salford life. The one on the left with the Salford woman in a rainy steet was shot by Nick Hedges; on the right is Michael Goodger's 'Woman in Pink Sweeping'… Michael recalls 'asking for (and obtaining) permission to take this photo but, remarkably it wasn't posed or 'done for the camera'. This young woman really was sweeping the street outside her house as part of what I presumed was a regular routine, even though she looks more dressed up for a day out'.

The Working Class Movement Library, 51 The Crescent

a charity with a social conscience and a fascinating history

A unique and unsurpassed collection of books, periodicals, pamphlets, archives and artefacts, relating to the development of the political and cultural institutions of the working class created by the Industrial Revolution, in Salford.

As the website (*https://www.wcml.org.uk/about-us/*) reminds us 'Working people have always struggled to get their voices heard. The Working Class Movement Library is a treasure trove with records of over 200 years of organising and campaigning by ordinary men and women'. Established in a former nurses' home, the Library began life in the 1950s as the personal collection of Edmund and Ruth Haines who were more than 'proud that their love of books created a unique and valuable resource for people wanting to know more about working people's lives and political beliefs'. In 1953 the two bibliophiles, Eddie (Edmund) Frow and Ruth Haines, had met at a Communist Party Summer School. In 1956 they set up home together and the merger of their book collections saw the beginning of the Working Class Movement Library. They spent their spare time and money travelling around Britain, squirrelling new items for the collection.

By the 1980s their house had reached 'bursting point and so Salford Council agreed to house the magnificent library in a Victorian building called Jubilee House on the Crescent in Salford. The collection has been here ever since'. The three main parts are the trade union movement, the co-operative movement and the political parties and campaigns of the left. The WCML houses 30,000 books as well as journals, newspapers, pamphlets, leaflets, banners, ceramics, photographs, personal papers, archives of organisations, trade union emblems, badges and other artefacts. The collection includes much related cultural material including poetry, novels, prints, playscripts, songbooks and audio-visual material.

The library encapsulates many points of view to tell the story of Britain's working classes from the beginning of industrialisation to the present day with the oldest items dating from the 1760s; the collection includes some of the earliest trade union documents to have survived, from the 1820s.

They have artefacts and historically significant records about
- Thomas Paine and the Radical Movement of the 1790s
- Chartism, ILP and Clarion Movement
- The Peterloo Massacre of 1819
- Fascinating Insights into the lives of the Suffragists and Suffragettes
- The General Strike, National Unemployed Workers' Movement
- International Brigades and moving accounts of life on the front line in the Spanish Civil War
- the Miners' Strike of 1984–85
- real life stories of tradesmen and women struggling to make ends meet
- while mainly concerned with Britain, the library also has a major collection on Irish history from the late 18th century onwards

A particularly invaluable item is the first edition of Samuel Bamford's autobiographical *Passages in the Life of a Radical*. Bamford (1788–1872) hailed from Middleton, just north of Manchester, campaigned for social justice and was present at the Peterloo Massacre. Like many others he, despite being opposed to activism that involved violence, was arrested on fabricated charges of treason and spent a year in Lincoln jail. Bamford, however, was not just a political writer but also a widely popular poet and was the author of poetry (mostly in standard English) but also in dialect, several showing sympathy with the conditions of the working class. Cunningly, the first issue of *Passages in the Life of a Radical* came to an abrupt end in the middle of a sentence so readers had to buy the next volume just to find out how the sentence, and the story ended.

Various campaign groups are represented, as well as collections of archive material from bodies as diverse as the *National League of the Blind and Disabled*, Manchester *CND*, Manchester Unity Theatre, Big Flame and the Jubilee Group.

Salford Lads' Club, Coronation Street

Provided an alternative lifestyle 'for the roving gangs of teenage thugs that had been plaguing English cities'.

Established in 1904 by Chief Scout Robert Baden-Powell, the iconic Salford Lads' Club initially worked to provide an alternative lifestyle for the roving gangs of teenage thugs that had been plaguing English cities. The club (the only one of many in Manchester and Salford to survive) offered activities such as boxing, billiards, bagatelle, a handful of outdoor sports, and even checkers, at the time a bar room game. Regular camping holidays to Wales were also on the agenda: Salford Lads' Club first camp was at Llanddulas in 1904, when 173 boys took part. The camps have been held during Whitsun since 1934. 'Wayward' youths were given a second chance on the straight and narrow. The club was financed by James and William Groves, founders of the local brewery.

The club continued to the later 20th century eventually serving as an early practice space for Graham Nash and the Hollies, and possibly most famously serving as the backdrop to the album art from The Smiths album, *The Queen Is Dead*. The club's history rubbed off on the young Smiths almost as much as their fame did on the club, helping to define the bands image as troubled youth. The club was also home to future Joy Division and New Order bassist Peter Hook. Apart from this roll call of popular music royalty, Albert Finney was also one of the 25,000 lads to have passed through its doors.

In the Smiths Room

In October 2024, the club announced that it needed £250,000 by the end of November to keep going. The resulting overwhelming response included contributions from global superstars, local businesses, and over 1,400 community members, highlighting the club's importance as both a cultural landmark and a lifeline for young people in one of the country's most deprived areas.

Salford Council pledged £100,000, while Graham Nash contributed £10,000, calling the club his "second home." Morrissey donated £50,000 while the auction of one of Noel Gallagher's guitars helped exceed the target on November 28, 2024. Phew!

Engels' Beard

it also doubles as a climbing boulder for students to clamber over

Engels' Beard is a 5m high fibreglass sculpture at the University of Salford's Peel Park campus outside what was the New Adelphi building, the new home for the School of Arts and Media. The artwork was unveiled on 22 September 2016; it also doubles as a climbing boulder for students to clamber over, 'standing on the shoulders of giants' (Isaac Newton) and making the whole thing more interactive. The signature luxuriant beard which is the focus of the sculpture (rather than Engels' face) is a symbol of wisdom and learning. Ask any ancient Greek poet or philosopher.

Walter Greenwood and the cast of Love on the Dole walking down Ellor Street. From Good Times in Old Salford by Tim Ashworth and Tony Frankland

Tom Greenwood in the doorway of his hairdressing shop

The University had commissioned Salford based Engine Arts Production Company led by Jai Redman and Ian Brownbill; the idea had existed for much longer – they had come up with the idea with their former business partner Simon Chislett, after reading *Manchester, England* by former Haçienda DJ, Dave Haslam. Haslam referred to a failed plan in the mid 1980's to relocate a statue of Friedrich Engels from an unspecified former Eastern bloc country to Manchester City Centre.

By the way...

Engels lived a sort of double-life. On the one hand we know him as an ardent and diligent researcher of the indescribable poverty in Manchester and the causes of that poverty; on the other hand, however, he moved with ease amongst the Manchester gentry. He was a fully paid up member of the Albert Club, as founded in 1874 as a club for gentlemen and now a vibrant social and tennis club, integral to the local West Didsbury society where today they admit women. Engels also rode with the Cheshire Hunt, rubbing shoulders with wealthy capitalist Manchester merchants who never tired of reminding our Marxist friend of the money to be made there despite, or rather because of, the poor and their poverty.

Ellor Street and *Love on the Dole*

Walter Greenwood's 1933 novel was written during the early 1930s as a response to the widespread unemployment, which was hurting great swathes of people locally, nationally, and internationally. It is set in Hanky Park, an industrial slum in *Salford*, where Greenwood was born and raised. The novel begins around the time of the *General Strike* of 1926, but its main action takes place in 1931. After the death of his hairdresser father when Greenwood was nine-years old things got progressively worse for the family. After leaving school aged 13, Walter worked in many low-paid jobs, including a pawnbrokers, a draper's shop, the Ford factory at Trafford Park, and dismantling wooden packing cases.

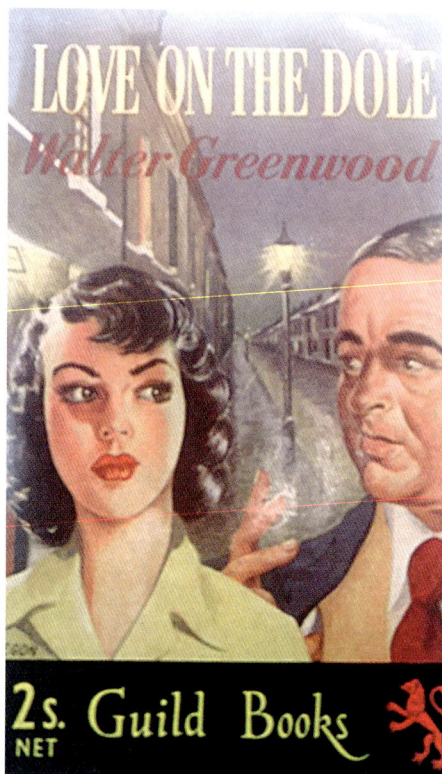

1952 edition

The novel follows the Hardcastle family as they are torn apart by mass unemployment. After 17-year-old Harry Hardcastle of Mansfield, a student in Lincoln, is attracted to the prospect of working in the engineering factory Marlows Ltd, he is, after seven years working there as an apprentice, laid off in the midst of the Great Depression, and is unable to find work. The novel's climax focuses on an actual march, in which the *NUWM* marched on Salford Town Hall in October 1931. As Chris Hopkins[1] writes

Even more successful [than the novel] was the play version, co-written with the Manchester writer *Ronald Gow* in 1935, and ever since then *Love on the Dole*, Walter Greenwood, and Salford have been remembered together... his first and last books were firmly set in Hanky Park, a place he could never completely leave behind... Ellor Street was replaced by Walter Greenwood Court (and two other skyscrapers)... Not that many writers have buildings named after them, let alone writers with working-class roots, and even fewer then suffer the indignity of the dedicated building being demolished within 35 years of its completion.

---

1 *Emeritus Professor of English from Sheffield Hallam University where he was Head of the Humanities Research Centre from 2003 until 2020. https://hub.salford.ac.uk/modern-salford/2022/08/26/from-love-on-the-dole-to-walter-greenwood-court/*

Ordsall Hall, Salford

Ordsall Hall is a once moated large Tudor mansion in Salford and is one of the most impressive half-timbered houses in the north west. It dates back more than 750 years, although the oldest surviving parts of the present hall were built in the 15th century. The most important period of Ordsall Hall's life was as the family seat of the Radclyffe family, who lived in the house for more than 300 years.

In 1380 the Hall was described as having a hall, five chambers, a kitchen and a chapel. It was associated with two stables, three granges, two shippons (cattle sheds), a garner (granary), a dovecote, an orchard and a windmill, together with 80 acres of arable land and six acres of meadow.

Michael D. Beckwith. This file is made available under the Creative Commons CC0 1.0 Universal Public Domain Dedication.

Since its sale by the Radclyffes in 1662 it has seen life as a working men's club: the area was by now subsumed by industrial housing and factories. Its future was uncertain until 1875 when it was let to Haworth's Mill (a cotton spinning factory on Ordsall Lane) for use as a Working Men's Club, a school for clergy, and a radio station during World War 2. The clergy school transferred to Egerton Hall in 1908 as Manchester Theological College, but an associated men's social club survived until 1940.

Over time Ordsall had is fair share of prestigious visitors, one of who was the Dutch humanist and theologian Erasmus in 1499, he described it as follows:

'...the floors are made of clay and are covered with layers of rushes, constantly replenished, so that the bottom layer remains for 20 years harbouring spittle, vomit, the urine of dogs and men, the dregs of beer, the remains of fish and other nameless filth...'

The house was bought by the old Salford Council in 1959 and opened to the public in 1972, as a sensitively restored period house with an innovative garden, and local history museum. Historic fruit varieties grow in the organic garden; there is a herb garden with medieval and Tudor herbs.

Archie Street, Ordsall and Coronation Street[1]

The street became well known for its association with the programme and was nicknamed "Coronarchie Street".

The story of Coronation Street and the minutiae relating to it would fill at least one voluminous book all of its own[2]. Archie Street was a terraced street in the Ordsall district of Salford which provided the design and inspiration for the look and feel of the fictional Coronation Street when the serial began in 1960. It all started when Archie Street was chosen by Tony Warren and designer Denis Parkin in the autumn of 1960 as they drove round Ordsall looking for a suitable location on which to base the programme's set designs. The street was used in the first title sequence for the programme and also in various end-caption photographs. A filmed shot used throughout most of the 1960s from a high vantage point on Manchester Ship Canal dock buildings on Ordsall Lane also showed St. Clement's Church in the distance.

It is interesting to know that Salford artist Harold Riley, a friend of Tony Warren, was present when these sequences were shot as attested by him on an etching that he and L. S. Lowry collaborated with on 5th December 1960, just five days before the programme began: here is an extract of his text:

I walked with Lowry on the 5th of December 1960 through the Ordsall area of Salford…After Gertrude St (tea-leaf alley) we stopped at Archie street where Eddie Colman (a Busby Babe killed at Munich) had lived. He was much taken with it, with the church at the end and the corner shop. We sketched briefly and then went to my studio and drew it again on a litho-stone… He added some figures to my drawing to see how they came out. He was delighted with the 5 pulls, taking one and leaving me with 4 others [3].

Archie Street in 1961

By the way:
There are 74 other Coronation Streets in the kingdom, including one in Openshaw.

The 'Coronation Street' set at the MediaCityUK set, with the Rovers Return pub in the foreground. Manchester: Coronation Street by Lewis Clarke

---

1   I am indebted to the https://coronationstreet.fandom.com/wiki/Archie_Street website for much of the granular detail and Byzantine complexity recounted here.

2   Eg: Kemp, Abigail (2020) 60 Years of Coronation Street

3   The street was also well known as being the birthplace, at No. 9, of Manchester United "Busby Babe" Eddie Colman on 1st November 1936. The street has been referred to as the "spiritual home" of the Busby Babes and fellow player Bobby Charlton has spoken eloquently of spending Christmas Day with the Colmans, their friends, neighbours and extended family who all congregated at 9 Archie Street with jugs of beer supplied from the off licence at the corner shop. Colman later died in the Munich air disaster on 6th February 1958.

The Mark Addy Memorial, Weaste Cemetery

a courageous Salford publican and oarsman who saved the lives of 50 or so unfortunates who found themselves floundering in the foul waters of the polluted River Irwell

If any one individual embodies the spirit, the bravery and the selfless desire to help we see embodied in the RNLI in their sterling work saving lives at sea, then it is Mark Addy (1840 – 1890) – a courageous Salford publican and oarsman who saved the lives of 50 or so unfortunates who found themselves floundering in the foul waters of the polluted River Irwell. He made his debut aged 13 when he rescued a friend, John Booth, who had fallen into the Irwell, which ran along the side of his house. Although Mark, astonishingly, was not himself a swimmer he waded out up to his chin and pulled Booth to the bank. Carelessly, the same boy had to call on his friend some time later, when he fell into a pool of deep water, and Addy floated out on a plank to rescue him.

Mark learnt to swim, took up rowing, married and became the landlord of the Old Boathouse Inn in Everard Street, because it was near to the river. When the Suez Canal was opened in 1869, the Irwell was wittily renamed the "Sewage Canal".

Rescue followed on rescue; perhaps the most dramatic was when a boatman alerted him that a woman was drowning in the river. Rushing out in his night-clothes, he rowed out to the woman but was unable to get her into the boat as she weighed over

17 stones so, holding her head out of the water with one hand, he rowed the boat to the bank with the other.

About 1,000 people attended the unveiling of the granite obelisk; on the front was inscribed:

'1890 in the 52nd year of his age. He saved more than 50 persons from drowning in the River Irwell, for which he received amongst other rewards, the Albert Medal (1st class) from H.M. the Queen. Life's work well done; life's races well won. He rests in peace. Erected by public subscription'. 'Sacred to the memory of Mark Addy, the Salford hero who died 9 June'.

Old Trafford

There were 44 people on board, 20 of whom died at the scene

You can sit in the manager's seat in the dugout, walk through the players' tunnel towards the pitch and find the peg of your favourite player in the dressing room.

But it is the poignant **Munich Clock** which gets the spine tingling. The clock remains permanently frozen at 3.04 p.m. on February 6, 1958, for that was the time and date when a plane carrying the Manchester United team crashed on take-off from Munich airport.

The Munich air disaster occurred on 6 February 1958 when British European Airways Flight 609 crashed on its third attempt to take off at Munich-Riem Airport in Munich. The aircraft was carrying the Manchester United football team, nicknamed the "*Busby Babes*", along with supporters and journalists. There were 44 people on board, 20 of whom died at the scene. The injured, some unconscious, were taken to Munich's Rechts der Isar Hospital, where three more died, making 23 fatalities with 21 survivors.

Stephen Morrin adds some detail [1]:
Thain (one of the two pilots) had flown the "Elizabethan"- class Airspeed Ambassador (registration G-ALZU) to Belgrade but handed the controls to Rayment for the return. At 14:19 GMT, the control tower at Munich was told the plane was ready to take off and gave clearance for take-off, expiring at 14:31. Rayment abandoned the take-off after Thain noticed the port boost pressure gauge fluctuating as the plane reached full power and the engine sounded odd while accelerating. A second attempt was made three minutes later, but called off 40 seconds into the attempt because the engines were running on an over-rich mixture, causing them to over-accelerate, a common problem for the "Elizabethan". After the second failure, passengers retreated to the airport lounge. By then, it had started to snow heavily, and it looked unlikely that the plane would be making the return journey that day. Half-back Duncan Edwards sent a telegram to his landlady in Manchester, reading: "All flights cancelled, flying tomorrow. Duncan."

Emirates Old Trafford Cricket Ground

One of England's great Test Match cricket grounds, home of Lancashire Cricket Club, exuding over 150 years of cricket history

The site first heard the unmistakeable sound of leather on willow in 1857, when the Manchester Cricket Club moved onto the meadows of the de Trafford estate. Despite the construction of a large pavilion (for the amateurs—the professionals used a shed at the opposite end of the ground - Old Trafford's first years were somewhat tenuous it being accessible only along a footpath from the railway station; the ground was effectively out in the country with small crowds. However, When W.G. Grace came with Gloucestershire in 1878, 28,000 showed up.

In 1884, Old Trafford became the second English ground, after The Oval, to stage Test cricket. The ground was purchased outright from the de Traffords in 1898, for £24,372, as crowds continued to increase, with over 50,000 spectators attending the 1899 Test match.

---

1 Morrin, Stephen R. (2007). The Munich Air Disaster. Dublin: Gill & Macmillan

During the Second World War, Old Trafford was requisitioned as a transit camp for troops returning from Dunkirk, and as a supply depot. Despite bomb damage, cricket resumed promptly after the war, with German PoWs being paid a small wage to prepare the ground.

Its capacity is 22,000 for Test matches, for which temporary stands are erected, and 15,000 for other matches. Since 1884, it has hosted 84 Tests, the third-highest number in England, behind Lord's and The Oval.

Media City – Footbridge and BBC Offices.

BBC News at One, June 2024

The Studios, Media City UK, Broadway, MediaCityUK, Salford

Since 2011 the BBC and ITV have radio and television studios here as part of the Media City development. It is also home to the set of the world's longest-running soap opera, ITV's *Coronation Street*.

At the BBC about 3,200 staff work in twenty-six departments, producing thousands of hours of content for television, radio and online.

BBC Manchester transferred its base to MediaCityUK in 2011, two miles west of New Broadcasting House, in Salford Quays.

Fascinating tours are available and you can join the set of 'Blue Peter' or read the weather.

In December 2010, Granada announced it would move to the Orange Building in Media CityUK next to the *University of Salford*. It planned to build a studio to produce *Coronation Street* on the opposite bank of the ship canal on Trafford Wharf. ITV Granada moved to Media CityUK in March 2013.

By the way…
Coronation Street

Coronation Street has been shown on *ITV* since 9 December 1960. The programme is all about the shenanigans which consume a cobbled, terraced street in the fictional *Weatherfield*, a town based on inner-city *Salford*. The show currently averages around five million viewers per episode. It had its 10,000th episode on 7 February 2020 and celebrated its 60th anniversary later that year.

Quote of the series, from the prescient Ken Barlow: in an episode from 1961, Barlow declares: "You can't go on just thinking about your own street these days. We're living with people on the other side of the world. There's more to worry about than *Elsie Tanner* (*Pat Phoenix*) and her boyfriends." William Roache who plays Ken is the only remaining member of the original cast.

60. The Lowry, Pier, 8 The Quays, Salford

'a cultural beacon situated on the vibrant Salford Quays waterfront renowned for its striking modern architecture and commitment to the arts'

What is it? Two theatres, including the Lyric (with the largest stage in England outside London) and one of the best galleries in England showcasing, among other artists, a stunning collection on permanent exhibition of Lowry's work; pieces such as 'The Cripples', 'The Fight' and 'The Fever Van' will make you look twice.

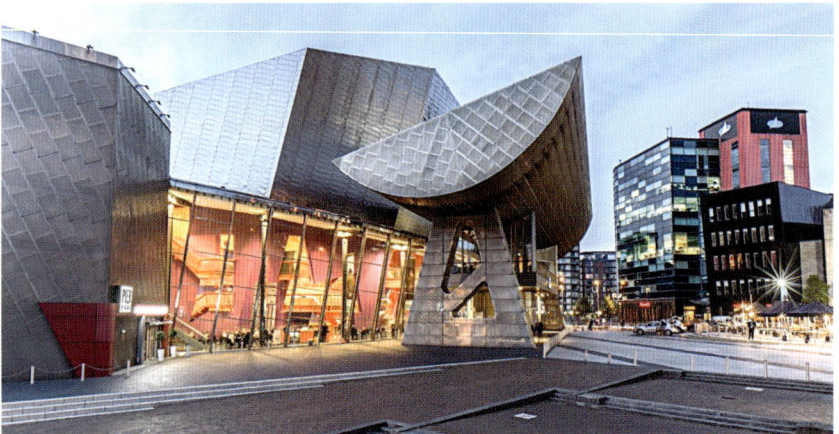

A mangled Twin Towers remnant

Imperial War Museum North, Trafford Wharf Rd, Trafford Park, Stretford

Among the 2,000 fascinating and unique exhibits here are the First World War 13-pounder field gun that fired the opening British round on the Western Front, a Russian T-34 tank, a United States Marine Corps AV-8B Harrier jet and a 23ft section of twisted rusty steelwork retrieved from the rubble of the World Trade Center in New York.

You can lose yourself in the 'award-winning 360-degree cinematic Big Picture Shows that bring a broad range of perspectives into poignant focus, reflecting not only on the immediate effects of war, but also on what happens when the guns stop firing'.

Lancashire Mining Museum,

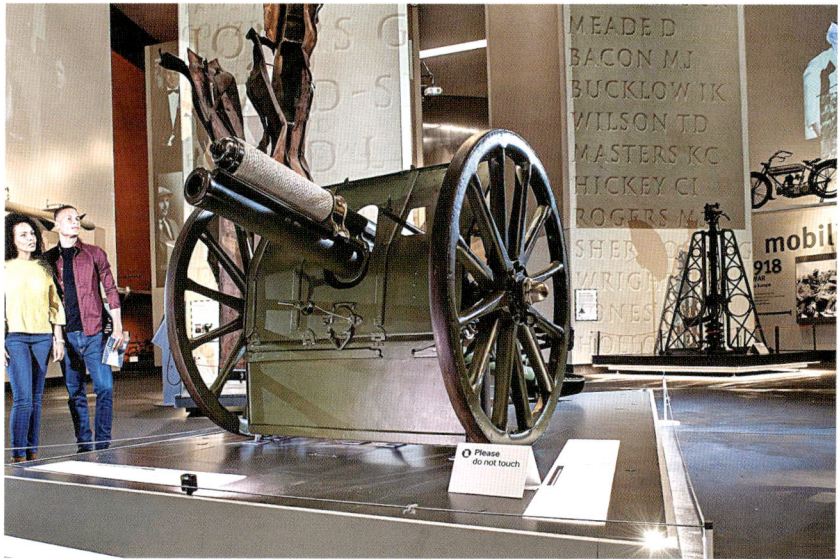

13 pounder gun that fired the first Allied shot of WWI, Imperial War Museum North, File: QF 13 pounder IWM North.jpg

Astley Green near Tyldesley

Before it was an exciting and interesting museum of vanishing industrial and social history, the site was a working colliery that turned out coal from 1912 to 1970. Here you can see the last surviving headgear and winding house in the entire Lancashire coalfield. Apart from this the museum houses many exhibits, not least of which is the collection of 28 colliery locomotives, the largest collection of its type in the United Kingdom.

RHS Garden Bridgewater, Worsley, Salford

New in 2022 the breathtaking 154-acre estate and gardens is centred on Worsley New Hall. It is one of Europe's largest gardening projects. As well as the restoration of the walled kitchen garden, other highlights include the recreation and development of historic features such as the tree-lined Garden Approach, and a reworking of the Lost Terraces.

The RHS have also built a new Learning Centre here for schools to enhance

their horticultural knowledge; a space for communities to come together with plant experts, a Plant Centre and space for a personal RHS Gardening Advice Service giving people scientific-based expert knowledge to help them garden at home.

St Mark's Church, Worsley

> *at 1 o'clock the church clock strikes thirteen... to prevent his workforce returning late from their lunch hour*

By any measure this is a truly outstanding church, as the photograph of the awe-inspiring chancel shows so well.

Completed and consecrated in 1846 the architect was Sir George Gilbert Scott (1811–1878). The windows are a marvel: 12 were acquired by Scott from France, Belgium or Italy depicting saints, two others were made by the studios of Edward Burne-Jones and the aisle windows are Powell's cast glass.

The church clock is a wonder in itself: it strikes thirteen at 1 o'clock by means of a device invented by the Duke of Bridgewater to signal to his workers that it was time to return to work. He had noticed that the workforce started their lunchbreak on the stroke of midday, but were less fastidious in returning at 1.00 pm. The somewhat lame excuse was they did not hear the single 1pm chime due to noise in the yard. So, to prevent his workforce returning late from their lunch hour he alerted them with an unmissable 13 chimes. The mechanism was transferred from the Bridgewater estate yard at Worsley Green to the church tower in 1946.

Worsley Village and the Bridgewater Canal

The canal linked the Duke of Bridgewater's mines in Worsley to Manchester, providing the coal needed to fuel the Industrial Revolution. Beautiful black and white buildings abound, and there is one of the oldest dry-docks in the country.

The main buildings of interest are the Bridgewater Estate Offices, the

Worsley Packet House, overlooking the
Bridgewater Canal in Worsley

Alphabet bridge, the humpback bridge, the Nailmaker's House, Rock House, Packet House, Court House and former Police Station (The Old Nick). If you stroll through Worsley woods you can see The Aviary, a splendid mock Tudor house.

By the way…
Worsley Delph, a former quarry, now a scheduled monument, was the entrance to the Duke's underground mines. Two entrances, built years apart, allowed access to the Starvationer boats, the largest of which could carry 12 tons of coal. *See https://lancashirepast.com/2021/07/17/worsley-delph-salford/*

Barton-Upon-Irwell RC Church

It's not the church but the associated overgrown burial ground which is of interest here because the gravestones reveal a lot about medical science as practiced in the late 19th century. Cause of death was sometimes etched on the gravestones and a selection here of the 270 interments reveals some fascinating diseases and medical conditions, as well as euphemisms for death:

- A condition related to pregnancy described as **'frog on the stomach'**: the frog test is a pregnancy testing method relying on frogs to show the pregnancy status of women. Since immunological pregnancy tests were not developed before the 1960s, women living a century ago relied on urine-based pregnancy tests using different animals, ranging from mice to frogs.

- A 39 year old woman who died of **St Anthony's Fire** – a toxic disease, ergotism, caused by ingesting the purple club-headed fungus in infected rye and other cereals – or Erysipelas, an acute skin infection, typically presenting with a skin rash.

- A 48-year-old woman who died of **'the turn of life'** – the menopause

- An old man who succumbed to **'general decay'.**

East Manchester

Gorton monastery: the polygonal apse with stained-glass windows by Ralph Bolton Edmundson

Phillips Park Cemetery

The oldest civic cemetery in Manchester, the last resting place of 300,000 souls, and most definitely full. It opened in 1866 and is named for the local MP Mark Phillips close to the river Medlock. Well, we say 'the last resting place' but torrential rain in July 1872 contrived with the flooding of the river to form what was effectively a dam. Said dam broke and torrents poured down Clayton Vale, sweeping all before it, including coffins and bodies. The press reported 50 corpses in various stages of decomposition, the locals nearer 500; the Government Enquiry settled on 76, all of which had been recovered.

Whatever, one thing is certain and that is that Phillips cemetery was the last resting place of two early VCs: Privates **George Stringer** and **William Jones**. Jones won his at Rorke's Drift in 1879 in the Anglo-Zulu War, as immortalised in the film 'Zulu'. Coincidently, the grave of **John Richardson** is also here (buried 1897): he was one of the 600 light cavalry men who charged the Russian guns at Balaclava in the Charge of the Light Brigade of 1854. Phillips Park was to be Richardson's second valley of death, as it was for his comrade Sgt Richard Brown.

Co-op Live Arena, Etihad Campus

Scenes from the Paul McCartney concert in December 2024

At 23.5K it boasts the biggest maximum capacity of any indoor arena in the United Kingdom and is bigger than Manchester Arena, which is less than 2 miles away. The estimated cost of the scheme exceeds £365 million. It includes 32 bars, restaurants and lounges as well as a nightclub.

After a series of embarrassing delays the opening act turned out to be Elbow in May 2024.

Co-op Live boasts the largest floor space of any indoor venue in the UK, a significantly lower ceiling, and tiered seating that brings fans closer to the artist. Cutting edge visual technology, outstanding acoustics and innovative sound bowl design mean the best audio experience imaginable whether standing or seated.

110. Gorton Monastery, Gorton Lane

The usual dilapidation and vandalism followed and, were it not for the supreme efforts of locals Elaine and Paul Griffiths, that would have been the end

In 1861 the then Bishop of Salford, Herbert Vaughan, invited a Belgian community of Recollects, a branch of the Franciscan Order of Friars Minor, to come to Manchester and found a new church. The Franciscans arrived in Gorton in December 1861 and began work on a new friary with construction lasting from 1863 to 1867, and most of the building work done by the friars themselves.

It was the largest church built in England since the Reformation; the architect was Edward Welby Pugin, the son of the celebrated architect Augustus Pugin. In 1901 there were 6,000 parishioners.

But the familiar story of industrial decline, unemployment and slum clearance intervened to force the closure of the monastery and the bankruptcy of the property developer while the Franciscans left the area. The usual dilapidation and vandalism followed and, were it not for the supreme efforts

The majesty that is Gorton

of locals Elaine and Paul Griffiths that would have been the end. Grants and funding came in and conservation returned the place to something very close to its former magnificence and beauty - Manchester's modern-day, multi-faith sanctuary.

In 1997, Gorton Monastery was placed on the World Monuments Fund Watch List of 100 Most Endangered Sites in the World rubbing shoulders with Pompeii, the Taj Mahal and the Valley of the Kings.

Clayton Hall Living History Museum, Ashton New Road

Clayton Hall is a 15th-century manor house in Clayton, Manchester; it is a Grade II* listed building, the mound on which it is built is a scheduled ancient monument, and a rare example of a medieval moated site. Part of the Hall has been converted into a hands-on Living History Museum. These six rooms, dressed in late Victorian style, depict the latest historical period in which the Hall was privately owned. There is also a Textiles Room devoted to vintage garments and sewing techniques, with several antique hand- and treadle-operated sewing machines. A Memories Room houses a large collection of local and British history materials.

Fairfield Moravian Settlement, Droylesdon

The authentic victorian kitchen

Cobbled streets and Georgian houses? The Fairfield Moravian Settlement opened in 1785. It was planned and built by Moravians and it functioned as a self-contained village with its own inn, shop, bakery, farm, laundry, fire-engine, night-watchman and its own doctor. There were separate houses for sisters and brethren. The single men operated a bakehouse, and the single Sisters had a farm, a laundry, and did beautiful needlework. During the nineteenth century, the Moravians ran seven Sunday schools, a Mechanics' Institute and a night school as well as their own library.

'Moravian woman and child' (2009); sculptor Peter Walker

South Manchester

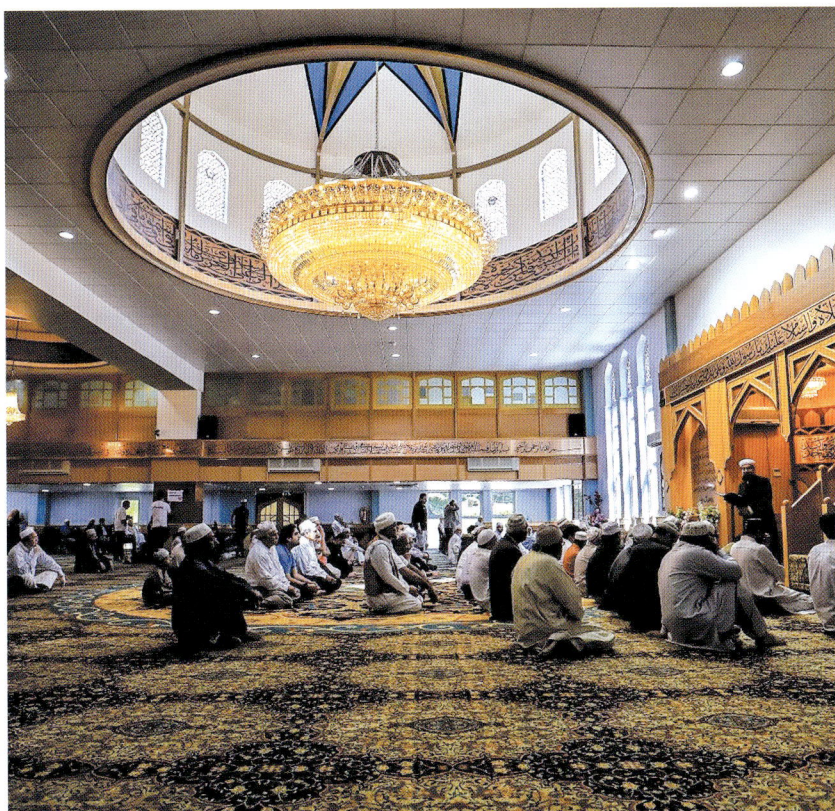

Muslim men pray for victims of the attack at Manchester Arena at a mosque in Manchester, 23 May 2017.

Fallowfield

Mention Fallowfield today and most people see droves of students plying back and forth to the city's universities, many from the University of Manchester's Fallowfield Campus – the Owens Park halls of residence, the Firs Botanical Grounds and Platt Fields Park, crowding the local bars and filling local restaurants and cafes – all very wonderful for the local economy and the ambience of the place. Indeed, these students help to make Fallowfield what it is today – a lively, leafy suburb benefitting from many cultures, diversity and entertainment.

Fallowfield has a rich and fertile history taking in the 8th century Nico Ditch earthwork; the Platts of Platt Hall and Platt's Field Park; and two of the country's leading independent schools – Manchester High School for Girls and Manchester Grammar School. Patricia Frederika Phoenix (née Manfield) better known as Coronation Street's Elsie Tanner – one of our first 'sex symbols' – was born at St. Mary's Hospital in Fallowfield in 1923 while the 1893 FA Cup Final kicked off here behind Owens Park (Wolves beat Everton 1-0); in 1986 the UK's first drive-through McDonald's opened in Fallowfield.

Judith Rosemary Locke Chalmers OBE (born 1935) is best known for presenting the travel programme 'Wish You Were Here…?' from 1974 to 2003; in the 1960s, she presented 'Family Favourites' and 'Woman's Hour' on the radio and 'Come dancing' on TV. She also appeared as the original Susan in 'The Clitheroe Kid', and worked with Ken Dodd on his radio show. Born in Stockport, she was educated at Withington Girls' School, an independent day school in Wellington Road, Fallowfield.

The 'Toast Rack', once known more prosaically as the Hollings Building or College, is a Modernist building completed in 1960 as the Domestic Trades College. On 1st January 1977 Hollings and Didsbury College of

Education were amalgamated with Manchester Polytechnic, later to become the Metropolitan University until closure of the "Hollings Campus" in 2013. Its striking architecture reflects its origins as a catering college. Nikolaus Pevsner described the building as "a perfect piece of pop architecture". English Heritage described the Grade II listed structure as, "a distinctive and memorable building which demonstrates this architect's [Leonard Cecil Howitt] love of structural gymnastics in a dramatic way". To others the building encapsulates the spirit of the 1951 Festival of Britain. It is highly practical: the tapering shape provides different sized teaching spaces for small or large classes, the tailoring workshops were kept separate to minimise noise from the sewing machines, and "The Fried Egg" – comprised a circular hall intended for catwalk shows, the library and two refectories.

Platt Hall, Platt Fields Park

Platt Hall was the home of the Worsley family for 300 years. The current hall, a listed Georgian building, was built by John and Deborah Carill-Worsley to the designs of John Carr of York, later modified by Timothy Lightoler, in 1746 at a cost of £10,000. It replaced a timbered black and white building that had been the home of Charles Worsley, one of Cromwell's lieutenants and Major General for Lancashire, Cheshire and Derbyshire during the interregnum. On Cromwell's bidding Charles took away 'that bauble' – meaning the Mace – from the House of Commons and kept it safe until the next sitting of Parliament.

The first record of the Platt Estate comes in 1150, when 'Matthew, Son of William' conveyed the "lands of Platt" to the Knights of St. John. In 1225 the estate was acquired by the Platt family who then occupied the lands for the next 400 years until it was taken over by the Worsley family in 1625. At this time, the Platt Hall Estate was a country park on the borders of the Cheshire Plain. In 1907 a resolution was passed recommending the Corporation buy

Platt Fields Park in elegant Edwardian days

Platt Fields site for public use and thereby save the park and house for future generations; this led to the purchase of the land from **Mrs. Elizabeth Tindal-Carill Worsley**, the last owner of the estate, for £59,975 in 1908. During the winter of 1908–09 over 700 unemployed men were given work on laying out the park, inverting the Gore Brook and planting banks with trees and shrubs. The main feature and centrepiece was the construction of a lake and island that covers just over 6 acres. Platt Fields Park was formally opened by the Lord Mayor of Manchester, Councillor Behrens, on 7th May 1910. Between 1919 and 1925 when unemployment was again high, the parks committee provided more work for local people, levelling the park and playing fields, forming the bowling greens, tennis courts and bathing pool. The part of the playing fields overlooked by Trinity Church was once a speaker's corner.

Manchester High School for Girls, Grangethorpe Road

Manchester High School for Girls was founded in 1874 by nine prominent men and women of Manchester: it was originally established in Chorlton-on Medlock; in 1881 a new school was built in Dover Street, now occupied by the University of Manchester School of Social Sciences.

Alumnae include **Clara Freeman**, the first woman to be appointed to the board of Marks & Spencer; **Merlyn Lowther**, the first female Chief Cashier of the Bank of England (1999–2004); **Libby Lane**, the Church of England's first female bishop; **Edith Hesling**, the first woman barrister called to the bar at Gray's Inn; **Catherine Chisholm** (1879–1952), Manchester High School doctor: 1908–44, GP and paediatrician, and the first woman to graduate from Manchester University Medical School in 1904. She was also founder of the

In this 1905 photo Miss Caroline Coignou is showing girls a toad, with mixed results

Senior girls in a 1900s secretarial class with Miss Kiero Moore, standing on the right. The school's association with the Pankhursts is particularly strong: Adela Pankhurst, Manchester High School pupil, 1893–1902, campaigner in the Australian suffragette movement; Christabel Pankhurst, 1893–97, the first woman to be awarded an LLB degree by Manchester University, founder member of the Women's Social and Political Union and leading campaigner in the British suffragette movement – sister of Sylvia Pankhurst, 1893–98.

Girls and teachers in 1899. At the outbreak of war in September 1939 the school was evacuated to Cheadle Hulme; by 1940 a new school building was being built at Fallowfield at the Grangethorpe Road site. The unfinished buildings were destroyed by bombing on 20th December 1940. In 1941 the school moved temporarily to Didsbury and by 1949 a new building at Grangethorpe Road was occupied. The move to the new school was complete by 1952.

Manchester Babies Hospital (later the Duchess of York Hospital) in 1914. In 1950 she became the first woman to be awarded an honorary Fellowship by the Royal College of Physicians; **Eileen Derbyshire**, played Emily Bishop in Coronation Street; and **Julia Bodmer**, née Pilkington, Manchester High School pupil: 1945–53, discovered the details of the human leukocyte antigen (HLA) with genetic different genetic differences causing transplant rejection.

Dressmaking in the 1900s.

Manchester High for Girls and staff had a very busy First World War. They worked in local Red Cross hospitals as nurses and ancillary staff, acted as interpreters for Belgian soldiers who were patients in Manchester hospitals and made prodigious amounts of jam and clothes for patients. One old girl worked as a doctor in Serbia, another member of staff worked with the Quakers in France but died of typhoid. Some scholarships were endowed for the daughters of sailors, one of the school magazines contains a letter from the officer on a torpedo boat destroyer who signed himself "Chevalier of the Legion of Sea Hun Strafers".

Manchester Grammar School

Manchester Grammar School is the largest UK independent day school for boys; founded in 1515 as a free grammar school – the Manchester Free Grammar School for Lancashire Boys – next to Manchester Cathedral (Manchester's Parish Church). By 1808 there were efforts to relocate the school; Engels, in his *The Condition of the Working Class in England*, said of the insalubrious area: 'Going from the Old Church to Long Millgate … one is in an almost undisguised

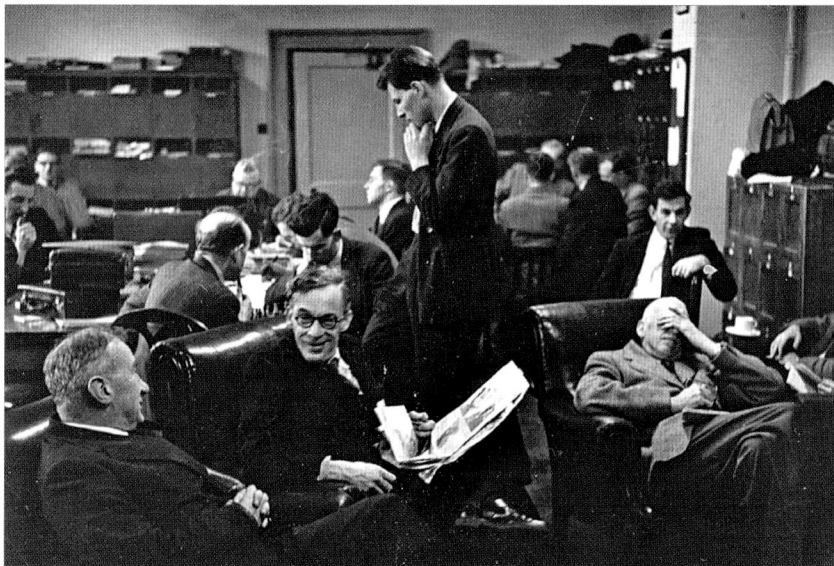

The common room in 1954. The 'master' on the right is having a particularly bad day. This is a rare photograph: staff rooms at this time were usually obscured in a fog of cigarette and pipe smoke making the clarity of this image all the more remarkable. The school's alumni are called Old Mancs, and include former England cricket captain Mike Atherton, Thomas de Quincey, playwright Robert Bolt, journalist and broadcaster Martin Sixsmith, actors Ben Kingsley and Robert Powell, and historian Michael Wood.

Free school milk started with the 1906 Education (Provision of Meals) Act, which allowed Local Education Authorities to deliver free school meals, including milk. Surprisingly, not all LEAs availed themselves of this even though milk had long been recognised as helping undernourished children – good nutrition having been identified as key to effective learning; by the end of the 1930s not even half were offering the free meals. In 1945 Ellen Wilkinson, the Minister of Education under Clement Atlee (the first woman to take the post and anti-poverty champion) was influential in having Parliament pass the Free School Milk Act which gave every school child under 18 the right to a third of a pint of milk each day.

A tuck shop typically sells confectionery, sandwiches, crisps, soft drinks and the like. More often than not we associate them with schools but they can refer to any small, food-selling retailer. The origin of tuck probably comes from the popular shops run by members of the Tuck family between 1780 and 1850. The earliest reference found is to Thomas Tuck whose "Tuck's Coffee House" in Norwich was popular among the city's literary circles in the late 18th century and which had a library for the use of customers.

Long Millgate workshop. Note the visionary eye protection. Many of the Upper School for the Latin and Greek pupils were boarders from surrounding counties. When Thomas De Quincy came as a boarder in 1800, classes were at 7.00am to 9.00, 9.30 to 12.00 and 3.00pm to 5.00.

working men's quarter, for even the shops and beer houses hardly take the trouble to exhibit a trifling degree of cleanliness … [The Irk, next to the school] is a narrow, coal black, foul smelling stream full of debris and refuse.' Long Millgate was the main route to reach the Collegiate Church from the north side of the town but even by 1817 it was seen as a dead end, physically and metaphorically. Procter, writing in his *Memorials of Manchester Streets,* said "For most useful and ornamental purposes, this street, ruthlessly cut into many pieces, has been virtually dead for many years, only requiring to be put decently out of sight". Richard Wright Procter (1816–1881) was an English barber, poet and author. The son of poor parents he was born in Paradise Vale, Salford. Apprenticed to a barber, he set up in business for himself in Long Millgate, where he also ran a circulating library. He remained there for the rest of his life.

The Edgar Wood Centre, formerly the First Church of Christ, Scientist, Daisy Bank Road, Victoria Park

> *"the only religious building in Lancashire that would be indispensable in a survey of twentieth century church design in all England".*
>
> *Nikolaus Pevsner, Hartwell, Clare (2002). Manchester. Pevsner Architectural Guides. London: p. 338*

Pevsner continued waxing lyrical on this Grade I listed building: "one of the most original buildings of that time in England, or indeed anywhere"[1]. Treasures include bronze lettering of sections of the Bible and works by Mary Baker Eddy[2], an Arabic organ screen, and chairs designed by architect Edgar Wood. Wood designed it in Expressionist style with Art Nouveau details in a Y-shaped plan, with a main range and two splayed wings, and with a cylindrical turret with a conical roof in an angle. It was the first purpose-built church in Britain for Christian Scientists and the

The Wonderful Edgar Wood Centre

second in Europe. At the time, Christian Scientists were just getting established in Manchester making great strides under the leadership of a striking and dynamic woman, Lady Victoria Alexandrina Murry, a daughter of the Earl and Countess of Dunmore and a godchild of Queen Victoria.

The Grade-II listed gateway, designed by Wood in Art Nouveau style, consists of a segmental arch with a steep gable containing a small semi-cylindrical oriel window. There is a blue plaque to Wood on the gateway. The Edgar Wood Centre in 1975 which closed in 2003, and the building was then used as a Universal Church of the Kingdom of God centre. The centre currently operates as a wedding and event venue under the name of Daisy Bank Manor.

'The relics of the stained glass are now in the Whitworth Gallery, and the church's ceremonial chairs from the rostrum have been placed there also. Another fine piece of furniture, a library display cabinet designed by J.H. Sellers, has been given to the John Rylands University Library'[3].

---

1 *Hartwell, Hyde & Pevsner 2004*, p. 469-71.
2 The *American religious leader and author who founded The Church of Christ, Scientist*
3 *John H. G. Archer, School of Architecture, University of Manchester, https:// manchesterhistory.net/manchester/churches/firstchurch.html*

By the way…Victoria Park Tolls

In April 1954 the gates that ensured tolls were paid and protected the Park were dismantled and Victoria Park officially ceased to be a private estate [4]. Tolls were introduced to stop non-residents from using the park to avoid a turnpike toll on Wilmslow Road[5]. Tolls were not the only ruse deployed to keep the riffraff out: pubs were *verboten* and the police had limited powers of arrest – a by-law which was allowed to prevail until 1935. Enter vigilantes, leading to the sort of criminal behaviour which the residents were so obsessed with curbing?

---

4 *https://rusholmearchive.org/victoria-park#*
5 *See https://manchesterhistory.net/LONGSIGHT/VICTORIA/foundation.html*

'Curry Mile', Rusholme

Proof that immigrants can truly enrich our culture with elements of their culture

The best road in Manchester (Wilmslow Road) with its plethora of curry houses, Pakistani sweet shops, garishly lit Asian grocery shops and Pakistani jewellers and vivid clothes shops. But it is the best road in Manchester for one other vital reason: the Pakistani and other communities living and working here symbolise and embody the (partial) acceptance in the city of those immigrants who came to the UK through the voucher system in response to the government's call for workers from the empire/commonwealth in the 1960s. Things were not made easy for those who responded, with racism and xenophobia both overt and insidious but if 'Curry Mile' shows one thing it is that immigrants can live side by side with the native population in this island nation of ours – and they can truly enrich our culture with elements of their culture[1].

Today this cosmopolitan part of Wilmslow Road is becoming even more cosmopolitan with the arrival of restaurants and other retail outlets from North Africa, Somalia, Iran, Kurdistan, Turkey, Syria and Afghanistan.

---

1 *See Qaisra Shahraz, 'Immigrant' in Paul Dobraszczyk, Manchester: Something Rich and Strange pp. 327–329, Manchester 2020*

Manchester: Secret & Strange Places to Visit

Manchester Central Mosque, Victoria Park

> *The doors are always open for Muslims and non-Muslims alike'*

Manchester Central Mosque (MCM) and Islamic Cultural Centre sometimes goes by the name of Jamia Mosque, and can be found resplendent in the middle of Victoria Park. See the chapter, 'Mosque', by Qaisra Shahraz in Paul Dobraszczyk, *Manchester: Something Rich and Strange* extolling the excellent multi-faith work the mosque does in the community, helping the homeless and other disadvantaged people[1]. 'The doors are always open for Muslims and non-Muslims alike', particularly during Ramadan.

MCM began as two adjacent houses, one owned by Syrian Textile Merchants operating in Manchester since the early 1900s, and the other in possession of the Indian community living in the nearby areas of Rusholme and Longsight.

By the way…

Qaisra Shahraz

"Then there was racism. At that time there was the National Front, you had name-calling and the use of the P-word and there were bricks into the window. That was part of that experience…I had some lovely teachers who welcomed me and taught me English. That made such a difference. People don't realise how much a language matters.

Qaisra is the Founder, Curator and Executive Director of MACFEST, Muslim Arts and Culture Festival. She is a Fellow of the Royal Society of Arts. In 2017, Qaisra was recognised by 'Lovin Manchester' as number 1 in a list of 50 Most Influential Women in Manchester, one of 100 influential Pakistani women in Pakistan Power 100 List and included in the Muslim Power 100 list (2018). On the 2019 International Women Day Qaisra featured in Manchester Metropolitan University's list of 11 Extraordinary Women From Manchester alongside Emmeline Pankhurst.

---

1 Paul Dobraszczyk, *Manchester: Something Rich and Strange* p. 323f , Manchester 2020

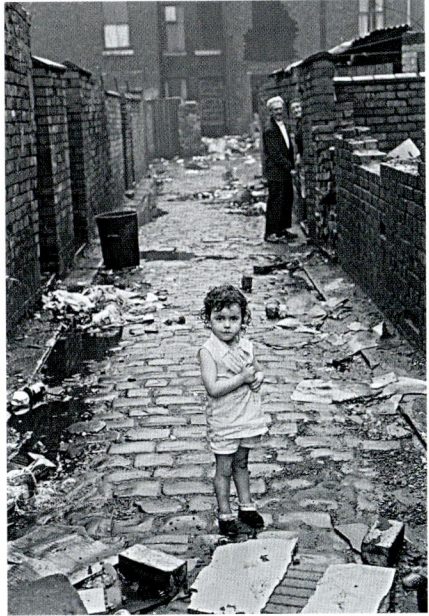

Leafy 4 Buckingham Crescent and a child at the end of a slum alleyway in 1972. Likes as not her life prospects ended at the end of that alleyway as well.

Richard Pankhurst, Victoria Park

[The House of Lords is]
"a public abattoir butchering the liberties of the people"

Richard Marsden Pankhurst (1834 – 5 1898) was an English *barrister* and socialist who was a fervent supporter of women's rights. He was born in Stoke but spent most of his life in Manchester and London; He was educated at Manchester Grammar School and Owens College. As a supporter of free secular education for all, he instigated evening classes for working class people at Owens College. As a Liberal he was a tireless campaigner for many causes, including free speech, universal free secular education, republicanism, home rule for the Irish, independence for India, nationalisation of land, the disestablishment of the Church of England and the abolition of the House of Lords. He established a National Society for Women's Suffrage, drafted the Women's Disabilities Removal Bill (the first women's suffrage bill in England) and was the original author of the bill which became the 'Married Women's Property Act 1882' which gave wives absolute control over their property and earnings.

He married Emmeline Goulden, Emmeline Pankhurst, who was some 24 years younger than he was, in 1878. With her, he helped establish a branch of the Independent Labour Party and together they formed the Women's Franchise League in 1889. They were part of a political circle which included Keir Hardie, Annie Besant, William Morris and George Bernard Shaw. Pankhurst had joined the Fabian Society and played a leading role in the protest against

Didsbury Wall Art 014 Phelgm – The Bird Towers, 171 Burton Road, West Didsbury.

One of Phelgm's popular monochrome works; Phelgm conjures up characters and scenes from an imaginary world he has imagined. Always black and white his detailed large scale murals can be found all over the UK. For West Didsbury he has created a series of 'Bird Towers' on the side of 'Folk'.

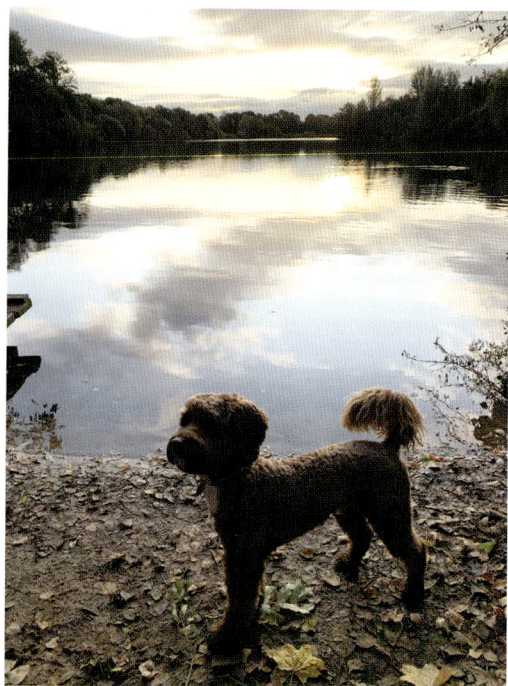

A resplendent Chorlton Water Park. The dog posing is called Buddy.

police behaviour during the events of Bloody Sunday in Trafalgar Square in 1887 at which he and Emmeline were present.

Known as the "Red Doctor", he stood for Parliament in 1883 as candidate for Manchester and in 1885 for Rotherhithe, Surrey, both times unsuccessfully. While his controversial views may not have won him many clients, he did earn great respect in the Independent Labour Party, even long after his sudden death at the age of 64 in his Victoria Park home.

With Emmeline, he was father to five children: Christabel Pankhurst (1880–1958), Sylvia Pankhurst (1882–1960), Francis Henry (1884–1888), Adela Pankhurst (1885–1961), and Henry Francis (1889–1910). His daughters, of course, all became suffragettes.

As a young girl Sylvia Pankhurst went with her father when he was campaigning for the Independent Labour Party seat in Gorton. Here is how she felt on one occasion:

> Often, I went on Sunday mornings with my father to the dingy streets of Ancoats, Gorton, Hulme, and other working-class districts. Standing on a chair or soapbox, pleading the cause of the people with passionate earnestness, he stirred me, as perhaps he stirred no other auditor, though I saw tears in the faces of the people about him. Those endless rows of smoke-begrimed little houses, with never a tree or a flower in sight, how bitterly their ugliness smote me! Many a time in spring, as I gazed upon them, those two red may trees in our garden at home would rise up in my mind, almost menacing in their beauty; and I would ask myself whether it could be just that I should live in Victoria Park, and go well fed and warmly clad, whilst the children of these grey slums were lacking the very necessities of life. The misery of the poor, as I heard my father plead for it, and saw it revealed in the pinched faces of his audiences, awoke in me a maddening sense of impotence; and there were moments when I had an impulse to dash my head against the dreary walls of those squalid streets.

Chorlton Water Park

A beautiful haven of a nature reserve for (dog) walkers and their dogs, runners and a few cyclists. Warmer days bring out picnics by the score, enjoyed until dusk. It boasts a serene central lake for all-night fishing with countless walking trails, many of which take you along the adjacent river Mersey with its kingfishers, geese and ducks. The park stands on the site of Barlow Hall Farm which is now Chorlton Golf Clubhouse.

Every winter the farmlands were flooded leaving a rich deposit of silt in the spring which produced abundant grasslands which were harvested for hay in the summer. These grasslands on both riverbanks still provide habitats for a wide variety of wildlife usually associated with ancient water meadows.

But where did that lake come from? Chorlton Water Park owes a lot to the M60. During the construction of the M60 motorway in the 1970s gravel was excavated from the site and the resulting gravel pit was subsequently flooded creating the lake that forms the centrepiece of the Water Park we enjoy today.

The park is home to at least 65 breeds of birds, including blue jays, cormorants, grebes, redwings, swans and herons while ever watchful buzzards and kestrels hover overhead.

Chorltonville

One of a number of garden suburbs in Greater Manchester – there are others at Burnage, Fairfield, Oldham and Alkrington. Arts and crafts influenced Chorltonville opened in autumn 1911 on 36 acres complete with 262 houses, in twelve roads, clustered around a "village green", The Meade. There were tennis courts, a children's playground and a bowling green.

In developing Chorltonville, Alderman James Herbert Dawson and William John Vowles aimed to lift the poorest Manchester people out of poverty and out of the slums they lived in; they would have been influenced by Ebenezer Howard's (1850–1928) vision of a kind of utopian city where citizens lived in harmony with nature, as expounded in his 1898 *Tomorrow: A Peaceful Path to Real Reform*, (retitled *Garden Cities of Tomorrow* in 1902.) Howard's towns were to be slum free and largely managed and financed by the residents who had a financial interest. They combined the best of town and country life. Equal opportunity, good wages, entertainment, low rents, beauty, fresh air were the objective. Examples included Cadbury's monumental achievements at Bournville and Robert Owen's and David Dale's 1786 village New Lanark; Saltaire – Titus Salt's 1851 model village – James Reckitt's Quaker garden village in Hull later in 1908, Joseph Rowntree's New Earswick largely for Rowntree's employees in York, and in later aspects of William Lever's Port Sunlight.

By the way…

There is, however, a sinister side to the story which may or may not have percolated down to Dawson and Vowles. Theodor Fritsch (1852 1933), German publisher, noted anti-Semite and writer, claimed to be the originator of the garden city concept, anticipating Howard in his 1896 *Die Stadt der Zukunft (The City of the Future)* – the 1912 second edition was subtitled *Gartenstad (Garden City)* – which became a blueprint of the German garden city movement as adopted by Völkisch circles. Völkisch was a German ethnic and nationalist movement active from the late nineteenth century until the Nazi era. In 1893, Fritsch published his most notorious work, *The Handbook of the Jewish Question,* which levelled a number of conspiratorial charges at European Jews and called upon Germans to stop intermingling with them. Hugely popular, the book was in its forty-ninth edition by 1944, having sold 330,000 copies, and counting Adolf Hitler among the many it influenced. Fritsch took a highly racist perspective – totally at odds with Howard's – which later became part of Nazi ideology and made Fritsch something of a Nazi prophet. His other work, largely published in his journal, *The Hammer: Pages for German Sense* (1902–1940), was anti-Semitic and supremacist. Even though German eugenicists were sitting on the board of the German Garden City Association in 1910, and the long tradition of town planning and architecture had been hijacked in the name of ethnic cleansing and eugenics, the association rejected Fritsch. This did not, however, stop their work leading to, for example, the establishment in Bremen of a *Siedlung* under the Third Reich: part garden city, part half-open prison, part eugenicistic selection centre.

Eugenics and Nazism apart Chorltonville was torpedoed anyway by the petty wrangling and small-minded procrastination so typical of British building policy, even today. A company was set up to manage the financials and lettings to tenants. This soon went bust and the houses were sold off to the sitting tenants. But it was a childish dispute over gas and electricity which bedevilled the garden suburb with the gas suppliers insisting the houses be lit by gas as well as providing gas for cooking and heating while the estate management company insisted on electric lighting.

By the way...
The Blues and Gospel Train, Wilbraham Road station

Neil Swift tells us that
'It was on this platform back on 7th May 1964 that a rather unique blues music event was staged by Granada TV under the stewardship of Producer John Hamp under the working title 'Blues and Gospel Train'. Famous US blues artists including Muddy Waters ... had travelled across the Atlantic to perform on a series of roadshows. Muddy was ably accompanied by Sister Rosetta Tharpe, Sonny Terry & Brownie McGhee, The Reverend Gary Davis and others on a miserably wet Manchester evening...Originally scheduled to be recorded at Granada Studios in Manchester, John Hamp's vision saw the show being switched to the railway platform transformed to a scene from the Wild West. Shutters were affixed to waiting room windows, a huge platform sign displaying the word 'Chorltonville' was erected, sacks, crates and 'Wanted' posters and even some farmyard animals were sourced to add to the effect. Blues enthusiasts lucky enough to have acquired one of the two hundred or so tickets initially arrived at Central Station in Manchester, and were then transported on a short train journey to Wilbraham Road station where they seated themselves on the platform.

https://pennyblackmusic.co.uk/Home/Details?id=26794

Sister Rosetta Tharpe on the Gospel Train TV Special

British Muslim Heritage Centre, College Road, Whalley Range

"There is much ignorance about the debt our own culture and civilisation owe to the Islamic world. It is a failure which stems, I think, from the straitjacket of history."

King Charles III

Many historians note the paucity of knowledge regarding the Islamic contribution to modern science and civilisation. In a speech to the Oxford Centre for Islamic Studies in 1993, King Charles III said when Prince of Wales
"There is much ignorance about the debt our own culture and civilisation owe to the Islamic world. It is a failure which stems, I think, from the straitjacket of history."

He is not wrong. Therefore, the BMHC aims 'to provide knowledge on the contribution Muslims have made and continue to make, to the progress of human civilisation. This is undertaken through pioneering initiatives that bring to light these historic achievements. In doing so we aim to create a unique atmosphere, bringing people together, not just at academic, professional and intellectual levels, but more crucially to the lay person living in a neighbourhood where harmony and cohesion need to be promoted'.

Built as the Lancashire Independent College its aim was to provide higher education for non-conformists who were barred from the Universities of Oxford and Cambridge until 1871. When the principal, John Fletcher in Roman, left for London the academy became the Lancashire Independent College and moved to Manchester; much later the college became known as the Northern Congregational College. No wonder the beautiful Grade II listed building could, ironically, easily be mistaken for an Oxbridge college.

During *World War II*, it was home to refugee academics, mainly from *Czecho-Slovakia*.

See also https://bmhc.org.uk/history/

Gita Bhavan Hindu Temple, 231 Withington Road

We love to take pictures and show them to the world.

The Gita Bhavan Hindu Temple is on the junction of Wilbraham Road and Withington Road, in Chorlton cum Hardy. Built in 1879, it was originally a Congregational Church which closed around 1987 when it was bought and restored as a temple for the Hindu Community. Part of the restoration includes this striking colourful frontage on to Wilbraham Road.

Dunham Massey

Dunham Massey is an Elizabethan country house with extensive gardens and an ancient walled deer park. The house has been inherited by generations of Earls of Stamford and Warrington. It served as a hospital during World War I.

Inside the house there are collections of silverware, artworks and furniture that the family amassed including portraits of family members.

Image courtesy of Simon J. Crossley

Stamford Military Hospital, Dunham Massey and The Carrel-Dakin Treatment

With the outbreak of the World War I the British Red Cross and the Order of St John of Jerusalem joined forces to create the Joint War Committee in which they pooled resources to provide services in support of the war effort. Auxiliary Hospitals were a major part of this provision: over 5,000 properties were offered involving private houses like Dunham and public buildings such as village halls and schools. The marvellous result was that 3,000 auxiliary hospital administered by the Red Cross county directors were established to help the growing numbers of war wounded.

*Dunham Massey Hall,
Richard Sparey from
Congleton*

The hospital as it was

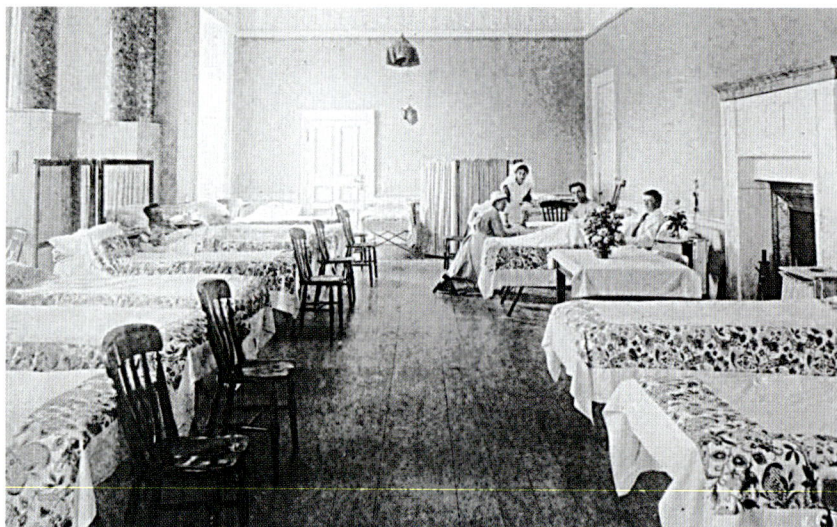

Penelope Grey, Countess of Stamford, wife of the 9th Earl of Stamford, made the house available to the Red Cross as a military hospital, becoming known as the Stamford Military Hospital from April 1917 to January 1919. In that time it looked after 182 injured soldiers with cases ranging from gas poisoning to those presenting with bullets in the brain. Lady Stamford was Commandant; the matron was Sister Catherine Bennett. Lady Stamford's daughter, the tireless Lady Jane Grey (later Turnbull), trained as a nurse at the hospital. The medical officers were a Dr Harry Gordon Cooper and Dr Percy Robert who used the foot of the Grand Staircase as an 'extremely unhygienic' operating theatre.

From 1 March 2014 until 11 November 2016, the main ward at Stamford Military Hospital (known as "Bagdad"), along with the operating theatre, nurses' station and the recreation room were brilliantly recreated to commemorate the 100-year anniversary of the start of World War I, along with actors playing the role of characters who worked, lived and recovered at the hospital.

Liz Webb, Dunham's Visitor Experience Manager said at the time:

"Everyone will be given (as the soldiers were) a hospital admission ticket on arrival. Each ticket will carry the name and short history of a particular soldier, whose progress they'll be able to follow as they journey through the hospital." "Apart from one original bed, each of the hospital beds in Bagdad Ward will represent a named soldier who illustrates a particular war injury – such as shell shock or trench foot. His story, the medical treatment he received and what happened to him when he left the hospital will be told through archive photographs, letters and records kept by nursing staff."

'One of the real soldiers to have been treated at Dunham Massey was Private William Johnstone, who arrived with two pieces of shrapnel in his brain. The doctor, assisted by Lady Jane, had to drill through his skull in the makeshift operating theatre under the great stairs. "Surgery was performed there because it was next to the billiards room, which had a toilet. Sadly, they managed to remove the first bit of shrapnel, but he died at Manchester Royal Infirmary before they could remove the second piece."'[1]

By the way…

The Carrel-Dakin Treatment

This groundbreaking infection control method in the fight against sepsis was developed by French surgeon Alexis Carrel (1873-1944): his approach consisted of removing debris from the wound and debriding the necrotic tissue. The surgeons would then irrigate the wound with Dakin's solution, developed by English chemist Henry Dakin (1880-1952). The treatment was used at Dunham Massey to good effect, saving many lives and avoiding amputations.

Alan J. Hawk goes on to tell us how

The diluted sodium hypochlorite solution chemically sterilizes the wound and acted as a solvent against remaining necrotic tissue and pus. Unlike iodine or carbolic acid, Dakin's solution does not damage healthy tissue. Under the Carrel-Dakin method, closure would only occur only after the bacterial count of the wound showed that it was sterile[2].

In short, 'the Carrel-Dakin technique was a major breakthrough for fighting infection. During the Battle of Champagne in 1915, 80% of the wounded were infected with gas gangrene bacteria. A year later, when surgeons applied the Carrel-Dakin technique during the Battle of the Somme, that number was 20%'.

Indeed, 'Despite deadlier weapons, as well as more severe and contaminated wounds, an injured soldier was less likely to undergo a limb amputation during WWI than during the U.S. Civil War. Only 35% of soldiers who sustained a femur fracture in WWI underwent amputation, compared with 56% of similarly injured combatants during the U.S. Civil War. A large part of this success can be credited to the Carrel-Dakin technique'.

---

1 https://www.independent.co.uk/life-style/history/first-world-war-centenary-dunham-massey-hall-reconverted-into-a-hospital-9169187.html

2 Clin Orthop Relat Res. 2019 Dec; 477(12): 2651–2652. Published online 2019 Oct 25.

Further reading

Sanctuary from the Trenches: The Stamford Hospital at Dunham Massey, National Trust, 2014

Gaydos J. History of Wound Care: A Solution to Sepsis: The Carrel-Dakin Method. *Today's Wound Clinic.* 2017;11:2.

Keen WW. *Treatment of War Wounds.* Philadelphia, 1918

Olive Shapley (1910–1999), Rose Hill, Didsbury

> *'hard-hitting and brutally eye-opening documentaries about real people and their lives'*

Some women have had the ability to pack much more than their fair share of achievements and professionalism into their lives, leading the way in what are often male bastions (such as the BBC here) and smashing glass ceilings. Olive Shapley was clearly one of those action women, who, in achieving what she did, paved the way and made things a bit easier for countless women who came after her in the media, in social care and in the support of less fortunate women.

Olive Shapley, Peckham born, is one of Manchester's significant women and a pioneer of social documentary in the North from the 1930s. She was one of the most well-known and radical voices on the airwaves

'and despite the predicable internal conservatism and workplace sexism Olive prevailed. From presenting *Woman's Hour* to creating a safe house for abused women, Olive's remained a voice not only known to millions of people, but as the voice who spoke out for them'[1].

When Shapley got that job as *Children's Hour* organiser in Manchester 'in 1934 it was a crucible of creative, radical programming, initiated by Archie

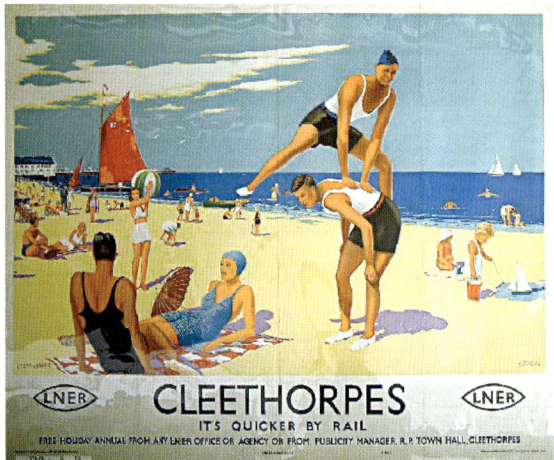

The poster that brought Olive to the North London & North Eastern Railway, 'Cleethorpes' by James Greig, 1941. Beach scene. Text: 'It's quicker by rail'. Science Museum Group Collection © The Board of Trustees of the Science Museum

Olive here on the left, winning hearts and minds

Harding, a Marxist intellectual whom Reith had banished from London to where he couldn't 'do so much damage'.

In an interview Shapley said: "As a Londoner, I wanted to live in the North. There was a lady trying to buy a hat for a wedding, and every one she tried on, the girl fell about saying, "Aye, love, you look terrible." I thought, "It was never like this in London," and I knew then it was the North for me."

Shapley was the first producer to routinely leave the studio behind. Using enormous mobile recording vans to travel across the region, she'd interview people in their own homes or workplaces, encouraging them to speak into the BBC microphone as naturally as possible[2].

On recording the first social documentaries in Manchester, Shapley said:

"This started because I was standing on a station platform one day – I can't remember which station – and there was a great [British Railways] advertisement for Cleethorpes, a great, big, colourful advertisement of a laughing, happy family with their buckets and spades. There they were, having the time of their lives, looking well fed and tanned, and on the other platform opposite were the real Mancunians, who might never get to Cleethorpes. It was a time of great distress up here, much more than it was in the South, and I felt I wanted to reflect this in some way. I remember going to County Durham for the first time and seeing miners sitting on their hunkers on the corners of streets, and thinking, "BBC should be doing something about this."

The Guardian obituary in 1999 said of her: 'Her private experiences - of two nervous breakdowns, of psychoanalysis, [of losing a child to cancer] as a socialist, professional woman and single parent - anticipated current concerns by 50 years.' She brought formerly taboo subjects, like menopause and women without men, onto the air. When domestic crises occurred, she brought her children into work with her; they learned to sit quietly and draw on the back of old scripts and became expert cutters of tape [3].

The obituary adds:
In 1950 she began working in television, presenting the Women of Today series, and narrating tales for very young children in Olive Shapley Tells a Story. In 1952 she married Manchester businessman Christopher Gorton, and the following year they moved back to Manchester, into Rose Hill, an enormous Victorian Gothic house in Didsbury. By the late 1950s Shapley decided to shift to TV production rather than presentation and devised an innovative books programme, Something to Read. She had to fight the BBC to get Guardian journalist Brian Redhead as the presenter - they objected to his supposedly incomprehensible Geordie accent.

More of Olive Shapley's great, pioneering achievements:

- When she recovered from a depression after the sudden death of her husband she went on to present the northern edition of Woman's Hour, as well as three series of The Shapley File on social issues, and contribute to many other programmes. She always felt privileged at being able to broadcast out of her own personal passions.

- In 1965, after her children had left home, Shapley moved into a small part of Rose Hill and turned the rest into accommodation for 'unsupported mothers' (Shapley preferred this term rather than the stigmatised 'unmarried mothers') and babies.

- At 63, Shapley went round the world alone, on the grounds that 'I've always liked to travel without much money'. By 1979, with the changed social climate, referrals to Rose Hill were drying up, and for two years until she sold it, Shapley turned it into a home for Vietnamese 'boat people'.

- Shapley never completely adjusted to living on her own, even in her beloved Didsbury, and depression returned. She tried to set up a communal living arrangement for older people *but she was too advanced for the times.*

See *Olive Shapley, Baroness Barbara Castle* (Foreword) *Broadcasting a Life: The Autobiography of Olive Shapley* (1996)

---

1 Antrobus p. 95
2 https://www.visitmanchester.com/ideas-and-inspiration/blog/post/listen-bbc-archive-releases-historic-interview-with-manchester-based-broadcasting-pioneer/
3 https://www.theguardian.com/news/1999/mar/15/guardianobituaries

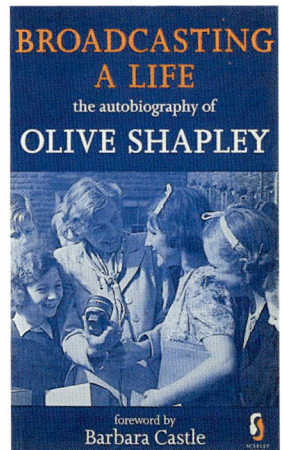

Fletcher Moss Park & Botanical Gardens, Didsbury

Beautiful. Peaceful. Colourful. Mindful. Enjoy the different ability walks, birds and birdsong. Dog friendly. Fletcher Moss Park once enjoyed status as a Botanical Garden, but cuts in Local Government funding mean that it can no longer officially be described as such. However, there are still many interesting and rare trees and plants to see, especially in the Rockery and heather gardens.

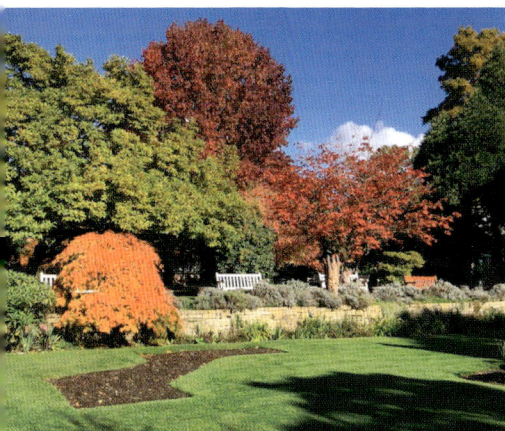

Autumn https://fletchermossgardens.org.uk/

The gardens and house, 'The Croft', were sold to Alderman Fletcher Moss in 1912. As described below, the Croft was the birthplace of the Royal Society for the Protection of Birds (RSPB). Alderman Moss subsequently donated Fletcher Moss Gardens to the people of Manchester in 1919.

By the way…

Fletcher Moss it was who in 1915 persuaded the philanthropist set Andrew Carnegie in Roman to fund the construction of a public library in Didsbury.

Emily Williamson, The Plumage League (RSPB), Didsbury

Emily Williamson is another significant woman who has been silently air-brushed out of the history books until quite recently. Her long-overdue statue was unveiled in Didsbury's Fletcher Moss Park on the anniversary of her birth on 17 April 2023.

You have to take your hat off to Emily Williamson (1855–1936), not only was she a fervent suffragist but she was also opposed to the use of feathers in ladies' hats which were all the rage at the time and reaching ever-outrageously

About 12,000 people voted after four shortlisted designs were shown at RSPB reserves, before the winner was announced at Manchester Art Gallery.

The sculpture, designed by Eve Shepherd, also shows Mrs Williamson holding a copy of the 1921 Act. She died in 1936.

silly proportions. Emily was determined to put an end to this, mindful of the death toll in birds which was the collateral damage required to sport such pointless plumage, all in the name of one-up(wo)manship and vanity.

What was the trigger? Emily was given to watching one of her favourite species, the Great Crested Grebe, being hunted to extinction; she implored the British Ornithologists' Union to take a stand against 'murderous millinery', but they ignored her letters.

Emily set the ball rolling when she shared her disgust at this appalling trade in birds with some like-minded friends at her home, the Croft, in Fletcher Moss Gardens. She launched a campaign to put an end to it all when she invited them to sign a pledge to wear no feathers. And so, the Plumage League was hatched, later to become the revered Society for the Protection of Birds in 1889 with 20,000 members in the first ten years made up of over 150 branches and doubling by 1898. Queen Victoria became an early member, which may well have given pause for thought to the inevitable largely male scoffers. In 1891 she joined forces with another all-female group – the Fur, Fin and Feather Folk of Croydon. Disaffected milliners, bird killers and posh women were outraged, dubbing the RSPB 'feather faddists'. Explicit exceptions included birds killed for food and the ostrich, because the harvesting of its tail feathers was not painful.

Initially, all members were women. It took thirty years for The Plumage Importation (Prohibition) Act to be passed, bringing an end to the trade in exotic bird skins - and endangered species began to recover.

But Emily didn't stop there: in 1891 she founded the Gentlewomen's Employment Association in Manchester, which in turn spawned first the Princess Christian Training College for Nurses pioneering the use of real living infants instead of dolls. Another first followed in 1898 with the Loan Training Fund, which subsidised further education costs for young women, the first in the UK.

Southern Cemetery

> *A memorial to the victims of the Katyn massacre - the slaughter of 22,000 Polish nationals by the Soviet NKVD in 1940 - is located next to Princess Parkway.*

Opened in 1879, Southern Cemetery is the largest municipal cemetery in the UK and the second largest in Europe. Graves significant in the social and political history of Manchester include: L. S. Lowry buried next to his parents in 1976; former Manchester United Manager, Sir Matt Busby, and his wife Jean; Rob Gretton (manager of Joy Division and New Order) and Tony Wilson, co-founder of Factory Records.

A memorial to the victims of the Katyn massacre - the slaughter of 22,000 Polish nationals by the Soviet NKVD in 1940 - is located next to Princess Parkway. Among other special sections, there is a Jewish section and a Muslim section.

The ideal place to let sleeping dogs lie.

Withington Baths, Burton Road

it daringly hosted the first ever mixed bathing in Manchester

Saved from the brink of wrecking ball oblivion by determined and perceptive locals in 2015 (a petition to save the Baths attracted over 8,000 signatures) this magnificent tiled and stain-glassed palace of a pool is the only Edwardian era baths to survive in Manchester. It is also famous for shocking the shockable Edwardians in 1914 when it daringly hosted the first ever mixed bathing in Manchester as introduced on a trial basis. Bathers (particularly the women?) were advised to proceed "with great caution" according to records at the time. Whatever next?

Madge Addy, Rusholme

> *After a career in hairdressing Madge went on to nurse for the International Brigade fighting fascism in the Spanish Civil War*

Madge Addy was an extraordinary woman, and not quite the sort of woman you would expect to encounter in Chorlton working in a hairdressers. In between the shampoos and perms Madge and her family lived with their widowed mother in Rusholme Grove, Rusholme.

And here's the interesting bit: after the pink rinses she went on to nurse for the International Brigade fighting fascism in the Spanish Civil War; Madge arrived in Spain in 1937 and became a head nurse at a hospital in a monastery at Uclès in Castile and was taken prisoner at the war's end. When Franco released her, she went on to work for the 'Special Operations Executive' in France with MI9 in World War 2 where she played a key role in setting up one of the largest escape and evasion networks for Allied troops in western Europe. Apart from the OBE, Madge is honoured with an International Brigade memorial plaque which decorates the outside of the hairdressing salon. Madge also married three times – we take this in our stride today but in the 1940s this was unusual to say the least, particularly when two of the marriages were to foreign men.

Quarry Bank, Styal Rd, Styal, Wilmslow

> *'Jane Greg… the most violent creature possible'*

Quarry Bank is near Styal just south of Manchester – one of the first cotton factories to be built following the lapse of the patent on Richard Arkwright's water-powered spinning machine. Samuel Greg (1758–1834) was one of the pioneers of the factory system at the dawn of the Industrial Revolution; on his retirement Quarry Bank was the largest textile mill in the country. Samuel and his wife, Hannah, took on responsibilities for the welfare of their employees, many of whom were children recruited from the local workhouse, building a model village alongside the factory.

But it was not all good works: at the same time, Greg inherited and operated a slave plantation in the West Indies. His sister, Jane Greg, was described by the British commander General Lake in suppressing the Society of United Irishmen in advance of their rising in 1798, as 'the most violent creature possible' and as someone who had caused 'very great [political] mischief' in her native Belfast.

Samuel Greg invested his wife's £10,000 dowry in building the Quarry Bank Mill. That was the easy bit: the difficulty in such a rural setting was attracting labour and building a workforce. This is where Hannah Greg's influence came

Education – without this you are nothing. You may possess all other things, and yet without this one

The importance of education for young quarry mill workers.

to the fore with the decision to develop a 'model village'. Each family (average of eight people per family) had a cottage built which could boast a parlour, a kitchen, two bedrooms, a cistern, a backyard and a good-sized vegetable garden. The village was expanded to include two chapels, a school, a shop, a farm, and a pub. Hannah was probably responsible for setting up the Sick Club and The Woman's Club as well as the Styal Infants School.

By 1790, operations were up and running: by 1816, pauper and orphan children made up 36 per cent of the workforce for which Greg was paid between £2 and £4 for each workhouse child employed. Once the children had passed a medical examination, they were contractually bound to the Gregs by an indenture. On average, children completed their contract at 18 years of age, although some girls did stay until they were 21. The children were accommodated in Apprentice House designed to house ninety children who were cared for by husband-and-wife superintendents. The Apprentice House has a chequered history: runaways, accidents and punishments were common, but there were success stories and a reputation for providing a higher standard of care than other mills of the time. The children received their board and lodging, and 2d a week. Overtime, for which they earned 1d per hour was available; this went some way to pay for any fines which were incurred for errors. Any savings were kept for them by the mill as a pot of money waiting for them when they finished as apprentices.

The working day started early at 6 a.m. and lasted until about 7 p.m., with a ten-minute break for breakfast at 8.30 a.m. when they were served porridge so thick it apparently could be eaten out of their hands. There was an hour for lunch.

Christie Hospital, Wilmslow Road, Didsbury

We start with hope. Hospitals make a rare appearance in local interest and travel books, but the Christie Hospital is such a beacon of hope that it needs to be included because from this all else follows. Unlike the other 150 or so entries the hospital is not a place you will be visiting unless, of course, it is to see in-patient relatives, or attend for a diagnostic procedure, observation, therapy or for an operation - and, hopefully, recuperation. However, the contribution this state-of-the art facility makes to Manchester and the wider north west is inestimable, relevant and valid so it is rewarding to see how it fits into the history and life-blood of Manchester.

Radium Street in Ancoats gives us a hint of what was to come: it was originally called German St until WW1 when, for obvious reasons, the name was changed: a reflection of Rutherford's experiments with radium at Manchester University.

It all started at Stanley House, Lorne Street off Oxford Road for 19 patients in 1892 - now occupied by Manchester Royal Infirmary. The hospital was established by a committee under the chairmanship of Richard Christie, a lawyer and academic, as the Cancer Pavilion and Home for Incurables funded with a legacy from Sir Joseph Whitworth. The hopelessly stigmatic 'Incurables' was soon ditched as inconsistent with the aims, scope and ethos of the hospital so it was named after Richard and Mary Christie in 1901 after Christie himself had died. In 1929 it was then the only provincial hospital solely for cancer treatment. It had close links with the Holt Radium Institute founded in 1914, which moved to Lister House on Nelson Street in 1921. In 1928, the hospital had 14 beds, 374 in-patients and over 7,000 out-patients who were administered radium treatment (see below).

A driving force in the nascent fight against cancer were the industrial diseases which were rife in industrial cities like Manchester; research was being carried out on occupational conditions such as mule spinners' cancer and chimney

The Paterson building at the Christie Hospital

sweep's cancer with scientists and doctors looking for possible links to machine oils and airborne soot.

The two institutions then moved from Stanley House to a new purpose-built facility in Withington, where Christie's main site remains to this day. About the same time Dr Ralston Paterson was building a team of physicists and clinicians who turned the hospital into a world recognised centre for the treatment of cancer by radiation and allowing the Christie to set the first international standards for radiation treatment in 1932. To celebrate Paterson's achievements and the Holt-Paterson legacy in nuclear medicine the local Holt brewery formulated a Paterson Ale.

Mary Christie, wife of Richard Christie, is one of the many forgotten women in our nation's history of medicine who did inestimably valuable work in many fields.

Dr Paterson's wife, Dr Edith Paterson was another; she started research work at the Christie in 1938 - initially alone, unpaid and having to provide her own equipment - becoming a world-renowned pioneer in biological dosimetry, childhood cancers and anti-cancer drug treatment methods.

'Think like a proton: stay positive'.

Further reading

Alexis-Martin, Becky, 'Radium', in Paul Dobraszczyk, *Manchester: Something Rich and Strange* pp. 238ff, Manchester 2020

Chrystal, Paul, *Factory Girls and Climbing Boys: Women and Children at Work*, Barnsley 2023

Fox, Brian, W. *Christie's: Christie Hospital and Holt Radium Institute, A brief history of a world-famous cancer hospital*, Christie Hospital NHS Trust, Manchester 1996

The Holt Radium Institute

It owes its origins, not just to surgeons at the MRI, but from funding from the Holts brewing family

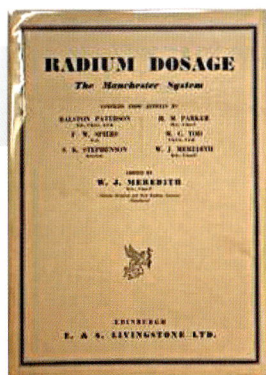

RADIUM DOSAGE
The Manchester System

COMPILED FROM ARTICLES BY
RALSTON PATERSON   H. M. PARKER
F. W. SPIERS   W. C. TOD
S. K. STEPHENSON   W. J. MEREDITH

EDITED BY
W. J. MEREDITH

EDINBURGH
E. & S. LIVINGSTONE LTD.

The Manchester and District Radium Institute was founded in 1914. It owes its origins, not just to surgeons at the MRI, but from funding from the Holts brewing family; between them they decided to use their own resources, and to develop the use of radium. Prominent among them was Sir William Milligan, an ENT specialist at the MRI who was exploring the use of radium to treat cancer of the larynx. When Sir Edward Holt then pledged £4,000, the Manchester and District Radium Fund was born.

Radium Dosage: The Manchester System by Meredith, W. J.; Ralston Paterson; H. M. Parker; Et. Al (1947)

It's aim was to buy radium and set up a small laboratory in the basement of MRI. Professor Ernest Rutherford was a member of the Technical and Scientific subcommittee of the Fund; it was agreed that the fund needed to raise £25,000. Local 'radium' days were arranged and collections made in the workplaces, public houses and clubs. By August 1914, a total of £31,000 had been raised leading to the creation of the Manchester and District Radium Institute from the proceeds in 1914. In 1920 the Institute moved to Lister House, a former nursing home on Nelson Street.

The supply of radium could not keep up with demand and while Manchester could boast the second largest supply of radium in the country, producers were cynically limiting supply in order to maintain high margins. In 1930, the government set up the National Radium Commission to supply radium to National Centres and the Northern Radium Centre was established at the Manchester Radium Institute with Dr Ralston Paterson as director.

Tatton Park

During World War II Tatton played a major role in the training of all allied paratroops by No.1 Parachute Training School RAF based at nearby RAF Ringway.

The Japanese Garden – one of the many spectacular things to see

Tatton Park is an expansive and beautiful historic estate in Cheshire, north of Knutsford. Amongst its delights it contains a mansion, Tatton Hall; a medieval manor house, Tatton Old Hall; Tatton Park Gardens, a farm and a deer park of 2,000 acres (8.1 km²). It hosts over a hundred events annually including, since 1999, North West England's annual Royal Horticultural Society flower show.

The settlement is now a deserted medieval village but its buildings and roadways can still be seen as imprints within the estate's parkland. We learn from Alan Scholefield that

'During World War II Lord Egerton's parkland played a major role in the training of all allied paratroops by No.1 Parachute Training School RAF based at nearby RAF Ringway. On 6 July 1940, Squadron Leader Louis Strange approached his pre-World War I fellow aviator and friend Maurice Egerton to ask for his co-operation in granting permission for the Royal Air Force to use his estate for this most important wartime purpose. Lord Egerton readily agreed to the proposal and the first live test jumps from aircraft were made on 13 July by RAF parachuting instructors'.

Scholefield, R.A. (1998), Manchester Airport, Stroud, pp. 19–21

Cuckooland, Tabley

One of the aims is to contribute to the appreciation and estimation of this timepiece through its importance in horology and historic significance in the Western culture

Close to Tatton Park on the A566 Chester Road, this is a little piece of southern Germany in Cheshire. Celebrated as the best collection of cuckoo clocks in the world, the 700 or so Black Forest clocks have been brought together by brothers Roman and Max Piekarski who started to learn the skills of clock-making in Manchester from age 15.

The astonishing collection comprises 300 years of cuckoo clock-making history, stretching from 1850 to the 21st century. It has saved the ancient craft of cuckoo-clock making from extinction.

Highlights:

- They have a "cuckoo and echo" clock that emulates the whistles and bellows the bird makes in the wild and is thought to be one of only six in the world.

- The museum also displays many timepieces made by Johann Baptist Beha, one of the most reputed, innovative and creative Black Forest clockmaker of all times.

- Examples in Art Nouveau, Arts and Crafts and other unusual styles.

- Other rarities include; picture frame cuckoo clocks, several timepieces with a life size automaton cuckoo bird on top of the case, models combined with paintings of people or animals with blinking or flirty eyes, etc.

Photo by Kirsty Davies

- Designer cuckoo clocks, a series of avant-garde 21st-century creations autographed by foremost international designers such as (in alphabetical order): Christie Bassil, Lorenzo Damiani, Mattia Cimadoro, Raffaele Darra and Riccardo Paolino & Matteo Fusi.

One of the main aims of the museum is 'to restore and preserve the most unusual, outstanding and unusual examples to be enjoyed by future generations, as well as to contribute to the appreciation and estimation of this timepiece through its importance in horology and historic significance in the Western culture.

Open as a guided tour.

White Nancy, Windmill Lane, Bollington

How strange? But wonderful all the same. A circular, 18 feet sugar loaf sandstone shape with a ball finial at the apex, 'White Nancy' was built in 1817 by patriotic John Gaskell junior of North End Farm to commemorate the victory at the Battle of Waterloo. It was originally intended to be a summerhouse with a stone table and benches.

Unsurprisingly, vandals apart, it has attracted much attention and at Christmas has been painted up as a pudding or as Father Christmas; at

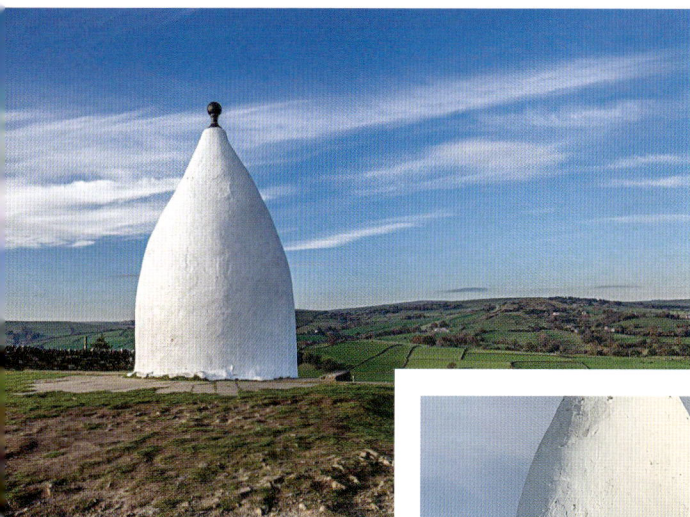

Courtesy of Margaret Lawless and the Copyright and Licensing Team at Art UK.

The people posing (Rachael C and Jacqui E) and the dogs (Buddy and Poppy) help to give an idea of the size of White Nancy.

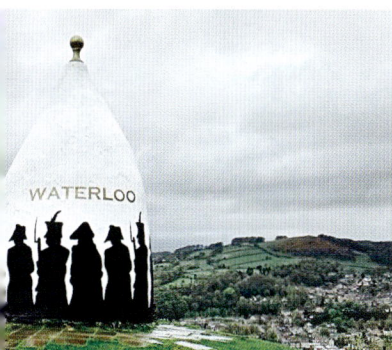

Reliving the victory at Waterloo in 2015

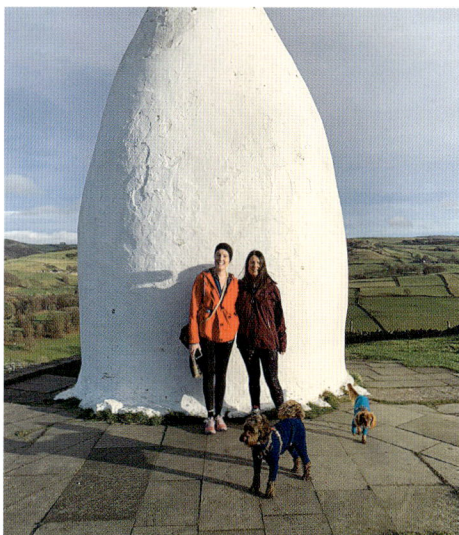

Easter it has doubled as an Easter egg. In 2012 a Jubilee crown and the dates 1952–2012 were added to the north-west face and in 2012 Olympic rings graced the south-east face with the number 29 which was added later to mark Team GB's 29 gold medals. It has also been painted with a large red remembrance poppy.

In 2015, to recognise the reason for its construction, Nancy was painted with a '200th Anniversary of the Battle of Waterloo' motif, and the silhouettes of soldiers in traditional military uniform from the time.

For the most part it has been white, except during World War II when it was painted green, black and khaki to camouflage it from enemy pilots and thereby reduce its benefit as a landmark.

Jodrell Bank, Bomish Lane, Macclesfield

Here is an example of just one of the main events here in 2024: 'join us in celebrating Pink Floyd's 50th anniversary of 'The Dark Side of the Moon' with an unforgettable experience at Jodrell Bank!'

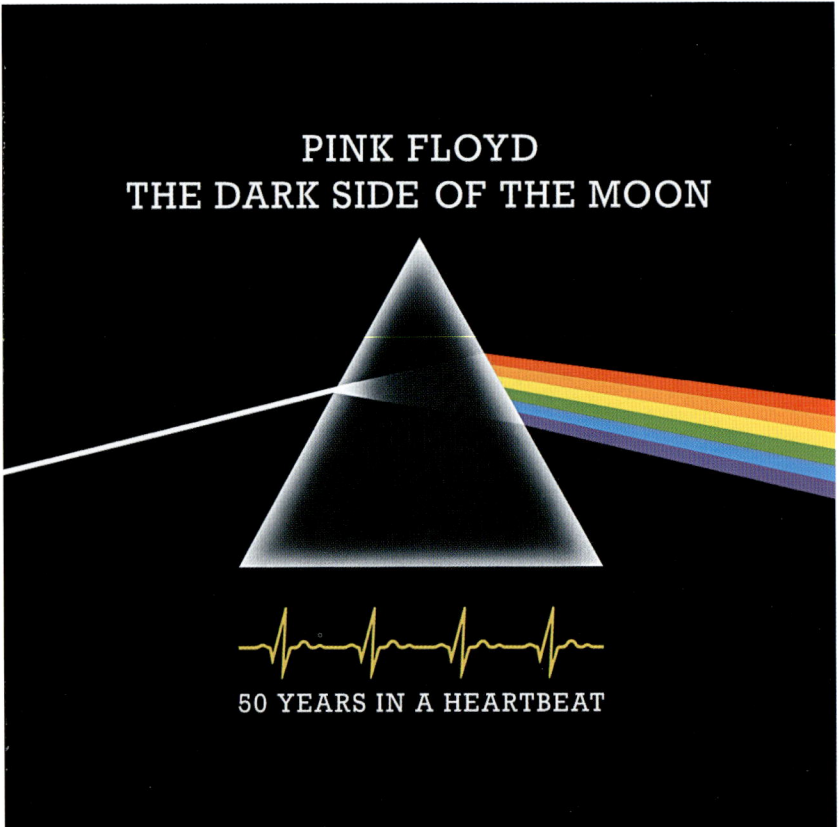

https://www.jodrellbank.net/events/pink-floyds-50th-anniversary-of-the-dark-side-of-the-moon/

Get ready to be amazed as the magic of the album comes alive in a ground-breaking Planetarium spectacular. Immerse yourself in a mesmerizing fusion of captivating visuals and surround sound, taking you on a journey through time and space. This one-of-a-kind event combines cutting-edge technology with the heart of Pink Floyd's music. Step into an immersive 3D world that will transport you beyond imagination. Don't miss out on this incredible opportunity to dive into the cosmic depths and feel the music like never before.

Jodrell Bank Observatory is owned and managed by the University of Manchester and is a world-leading science research institute, with its scientists working at the cutting edge of modern astrophysics. The observatory was established in 1945 by Bernard Lovell, a radio astronomer at the university, to investigate cosmic rays after his work on radar in World War II. It has since played an important role in the research of meteoroids, quasars, pulsars, masers, and gravitational lenses, and was heavily involved with the tracking of space probes at the dawn of the Space Age.

The main telescope at the observatory is the Lovell Telescope with a diameter of 250 ft (76 m) making it the third largest steerable radio telescope in the world. There are three other active telescopes at the observatory; the Mark II and 42 ft (13 m) and 7 m diameter radio telescopes.

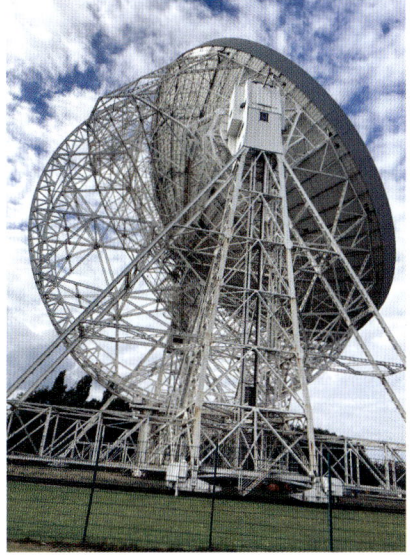

Stockport

Hat Works – the Museum of Hatting, Wellington Mill, Wellington Rd South

You've got to take your hat off to this superb museum

If you've always liked hats, you'll love them when you come out of this fascinating recently extensively refurbished museum. If, so far in life, you can take a hat or leave it, then when you leave Hat Works you'll emerge astonished by the variety of styles, the dazzling range of colours - bright and more

subdued – and the extraordinary uses hats have been put to in the past. The museum invites us to 'be inspired by the array of colours, shapes, patterns and textures of the hats on display'. It's hard not to. You can try on and buy hats from the hat shop.

Hats and headwear apart, there is a factory floor showing the history of millinery, especially in the region around Stockport - centre of hat making in the UK. Tours are available.

The restoration of the machines has been funded by a grant from the Association for Industrial Archaeology which promotes the study, preservation and presentation of Britain's industrial heritage.

The website reveals

Wellington Mill has been a hat factory, bicycle factory, snooker hall and bike shop. It was built to spin cotton in 1828, however, it's better known as the home of We Make Hats, part of the Ward family's business empire.

Sarah Ward was a key figure in building the retail side of the enterprise. She took sole control of their shop in Stockport Market Place at the age of 29 whilst raising 3 small children. She expanded the business to Lower Hillgate and opened a warehouse on High Street. When Sarah retired, she passed a thriving business to her sons, William and Edwin whose company became Ward Bros. They purchased Wellington Mill in 1895 and continued the hatting and outfitting business.

Robinsons Brewery Visitors Centre, Apsley St, Stockport

Don't forget the three 1/3 pint samples of Robinsons beers the brewery throws in for good measure

The one hour-long tours of the brewery showing its operation and history are the centrepiece of any visit to this superb spotlight on an important part of Stockport's social and industrial history – and, of course, there are the three 1/3 pint samples of Robinsons beers the brewery throws in for good measure.

Founded in 1849 at the Unicorn Inn, *Stockport*, Robinsons has ever since been a significant player in the production and provision of beer in the north west; it can boast a heritage stretching back over 184 years, from humble beginnings to becoming one of the UK's largest independent family brewers, with around 250 pubs across the North West and Wales.

A visit enables you to observe 'the magic of the brewing process, admire new and original brewing equipment, create your own perfect pub guide, find an ideal pub to run, and visit the Shire horses'.

The website gives us some facts about the stunning Shires, still working after 100 years:

Mojo and Challenger have their breakfast at 6.30am and their supper at 8.30pm each day. Each Shire can eat for up to 18 hours a day.

The Shires see the dentist every 6 months to check on the health of their 42 teeth.

Mojo's favourite treat is Polos... he can devour a whole packet in seconds.

The Shires' average walking speed is 4 miles per hour.

Stockport Air Raid Shelters, 65 Chestergate, Stockport

The Chestergate Hotel: you can check out but you can never leave

There are some truly atmospheric and evocative places to visit featured in this book. The Stockport Air Raid Shelters, however, remain one of the most powerful and poignant places to go in Stockport and Mnchester, and are well worth the short trip from Manchester city centre.

The Shelters are a system made up of almost one mile of underground air-raid shelters dug under Stockport during World War II to offer protection to local inhabitants during air raids while German bombers thundered overhead and their high explosive bombs and incendiaries crashed down on homes and factories causing death and destruction all around.

Hewn out of the natural red sandstone cliffs, the fascinating network of underground tunnels offers visitors an unparalleled insight into life in blacked-out wartime Britain in the 1940's. Visitors can learn what this subterranean life was like for local people during the war by wandering through the tunnels or from the displays in the tunnels and from the state-of-the-art audio-guides. Guided tours are available.

The doors opened in 1939 and were the largest purpose-built civilian air raid shelters in the country. They were originally designed to provide shelter for up to 3,850 people. Due to demand, they were extended to accommodate as many as 6,500 during the course of the war.

In 1996, the shelters were ingeniously repurposed as a visitor attraction to give visitors a realistic feel of the ambience of the times: the anxieties, the camaraderie and neighbourliness and the facilities, and the hope the tunnels evoked.

Some facts:

- the shelters had basic amenities: electric lights, benches and bunk beds, flushing toilets, first aid post and sick bay, not forgetting facilities for nursing mothers
- in the war the shelters were nicknamed the 'Chestergate Hotel' because of the 'luxurious' standard of accommodation they offered. The shelters also boast 16-seater toilets
- everyone had to possess a gas mask and carry it with them at all times

Stockport Viaduct

Don't look up...or down

The adjective 'awesome' has come to describe anything, no matter how ordinary and mediocre. However, by definition almost, a good number of the locations and constructions in this book can claim to be described as inspiring real awe. Stockport Viaduct, is one of those constructions. You see it above as you speed down the M60, it's often visible below as you come in to land at Manchester Airport and it seems to loom everywhere you look in Stockport itself.

Stretching majestically just north of Stockport station, Stockport Viaduct carries the West Coast Main Line across the River Mersey and is one of the largest brick structures in the world. It is redolent of the early railway age and a true icon (another one of those increasingly redundant words) of the Industrial Revolution.

Work began in March 1839 and despite its sheer immensity and flooding courtesy of the Mersey, the viaduct was completed in December 1840 with services starting for the Manchester and Birmingham Railway the same month. Around 600 workers were employed in shifts, working day and night. It took 21 months to complete using around 11 million common bricks and 400,000 cu ft of stone and cost £72,000; it is 111.1 ft high above the bed of the Mersey. In the late 1880s it was widened to accommodate four tracks by the London and North Western Railway. In the 1960s, overhead catenary lines were installed by British Rail for the West Coast Main Line electrification scheme.

The viaduct is mentioned in the introduction to the Northern Mill Towns in Elizabeth Gaskell's North and South. It has been portrayed in several works by L.S. Lowry.

Courtesy of Max *Wieland, Communications Team at Stockport Council*

Winter's Clockhouse, Little Underbank

a unique hydraulically operated device lowered the entire window display into the relative safety of the shop cellar at close of business every day

What better way to promote your clockmaking business? Old Father Time, a Victorian guardsman and a sailor have stood sentinel above the Winter's clock since 1859, striking every 15 minutes. The striking (in every sense of the word) mechanism was sensitively restored in 2021.

Security has always been a priority at Winter's: a unique hydraulically operated device lowered the entire window display into the relative safety of the shop cellar at close of business every day.

Great Underbank Hall

Underbank Hall is an early 16th-century town house which became a Grade II* listed building on 13 May 1952. Attempts to make it Stockport's Town Hall came to nothing. The District Bank Ltd bought it in 1829 as one of its early branches; Nat West swallowed this up years later. Highlights include the oak panelled rooms, two 15th century fireplaces and the huge banking hall at the rear from 1915.

The Plaza, Mersey Square

> *The last word in cinema opulence with its stunning art deco design, plush blue and gold seats and the heavenly Compton organ transporting you into another world.*

Built 1932–1933 it originally seated around 1,873, and in its current restored state has 614 seats in the stalls, 318 in the front circle and 254 in the rear circle. After 30 years of bingo it closed in 1999 but not before English Heritage had listed it Grade II* and saved it for locals to find a trust to buy and preserve it. English Heritage rightly gushed "a remarkably lavish exercise in the Art Deco style", and an "exceptionally complete example of a 1930s 'super' cinema, which survives little altered and retains its Compton organ".

During World War II the fact that it was cut into the rock face led to the Plaza being considered one of the safest places to shelter during an air raid, even though the Stockport Shelters were nearby. According to Lauren Livesey, as well as screening films, it staged variety acts, hosted acrobatic troupes, offered stand-up comedy, concerts and during Christmas 1960, staged its first pantomime.[1]

---

[1]   Livesey, Lauren (31 December 2020). *"The Plaza: the North's Finest Super Cinema". Art Deco Society UK.*

The auditorium, restored to its original state as it was in 1932 with exact replica seating.

Manchester...
in so many words

Many, from Daniel Defoe to Tony Wilson, have taken it upon themselves to praise or lambast Manchester, to satirise or romanticise this city and its inhabitants. Here is a short selection of some of their wise, or otherwise, words. We start with a perspicacious Daniel Defoe

Manchester, one of the greatest, if not really the greatest mere village in England. It is neither a wall'd town, city, or corporation; they send no members to Parliament; and the highest magistrate they have is a constable or headborough[1]; and yet it has a collegiate church, several parishes, takes up a large space of ground, and, including the suburb, or that part of the town called – over the bridge; it is said to contain above fifty thousand people;...I must not quit *Manchester* without giving some account of the college there, which has been very famous for learning and learned men... *Manchester* boasts of four extraordinary foundations, viz. a college, an hospital, a free-school, and a library, all very well supported...By the bounty of the said founder [Humphrey Cheetham], is also erected a very fair and spacious library, already furnished with a competent stock of choice and valuable books, to the number of near four thousand, and daily increasing with the income of...settled upon the same by the said worthy benefactor, to buy books for ever, and to afford a competent salary for a library keeper. There is also a large school for the hospital boys, where they are daily instructed, and taught to read and write. I cannot doubt but this increasing town will, some time or other, obtain some better face of government, and be incorporated, as it very well deserves to be...

- **Daniel Defoe,** *A Tour Through the Whole Island of Great Britain* (1727)

Manchester...the largest, most rich, populous, and busy village in England having about 2,400 families...they have looms which work 24 laces at once, which were stolen from the Dutch.

- **William Stukely,** *Itinerarium Curiosum* (1724)

'The dwellings of the labouring manufacturers are in narrow streets and lanes, blocked up from light and air… crowded together because every inch of land is of such value, that room for light and air cannot be afforded them.'

Robert Southey describing what he saw when he visited Manchester in 1808.

After visiting Manchester in 1835, the French social critic **Alexis de Tocqueville** wrote:

From this foul drain the greatest stream of human industry flows out to fertilize the whole world. From this filthy sewer pure gold flows. Here humanity attains its most complete development and its most brutish, here civilization works its miracles and civilized man is turned almost into a savage.

Manchester is as great a human exploit as Athens…It is the philosopher alone who can conceive the grandeur of Manchester and the immensity of its future.

From early morn to the late twilight, our Coningsby for several days devoted himself to the comprehension of Manchester. It was to him a new world, pregnant with new ideas, and suggestive of new trains of thought and feeling. In this unprecedented partnership between capital and science, working on a spot which Nature had indicated as the fitting theatre of their exploits, he beheld a great source of the wealth of nations which had been reserved for these times, and he perceived that this wealth was rapidly developing classes whose power was imperfectly recognised in the constitutional scheme, and whose duties in the social system seemed altogether omitted.

- Henry Coningsby Esq in *Coningsby by* Benjamin Disraeli (1844)

"I have never seen so demoralised a class as the English middle classes. Their sole happiness is derived from gaining a quick profit. They feel pain only if they suffer a financial loss. Every single human quality with which they are endowed is grossly debased by selfish greed and love of gain…"

- Frederick Engels, 1845

I would like to live in Manchester. The transition between Manchester and death would be unnoticeable.

- Mark Twain, 1846

Far, far away in the distance, on that flat plain, you might see the motionless cloud of smoke hanging over a great town, and that was Manchester – ugly, smoky Manchester; dear, busy, earnest, noble-working Manchester…

- Elizabeth Gaskell, *Libbie Marsh's Three Eras*, 1847

Manchester is a city which has witnessed a great many stirring episodes, especially of a political character. Generally speaking, its citizens have been liberal in their sentiments, defenders of free speech and liberty of opinion.

- **Emmeline Pankhurst**, *My Own Story*, 1914

I will not praise Manchester. I will agree with you that it rains there every day, that it is the ugliest city in Britain, that it is cocksure and conceited. I will, I say, agree to all this. You may say anything disagreeable you like about Manchester, and I will not care. Nevertheless...I have stayed in Athens, and Athens is a marvellous city; I know my Paris, and Paris is not without fascination; I have been to Cairo, and bazaars of Cairo seemed to me so wonderful that I held my breath as I passed through them. But these places are not Manchester. They are not so glorious as Manchester, not so vital, not so romantic, not so adventurous...But already I have broken my word: I have begun to praise Manchester in my second paragraph. Let me begin a third.

- **Gerald Cumberland (pseudonym for Charles Frederick Kenyon),**
Set Down in Malice, a Book of Reminiscences, 1919

Manchester and Liverpool have a strange relationship. You can tell a joke in Liverpool and they won't understand it in Manchester. That's because they can't hear it.

- **Ken Dodd**

As for the Town Hall in Albert Square, once you have seen its silver plate and paintings and busts, its marble columns and mosaic floors, its stone staircase climbing past a blaze of stained glass, all other town halls fade into insignificance. What a world it represented – cotton and shipping and commerce, the like of which we shall never see again. It's a wonder they didn't use gold bars instead of bricks and stone.

- **Beryl Bainbridge**, *English Journey, or, The Road to Milton Keynes*, 1984

In those days, for a Mancunian to visit the capital was an exercise in condescension. London was a day behind Manchester in the arts, in commercial cunning, in economic philosophy. True, it had the monarch and the government and was gratuitously big. It had more history than Manchester, but history was no more than a tourist frippery. When foreigners came to Manchester, they came to learn, not to feed ravens and snap beefeaters. Manchester was generous and London was not. London had something of the air of Chorlton-cum-Hardy.

- **Anthony Burgess**, *Little Wilson and Big God*, 1986

If proximity to great sporting events, an excellent reference library, a fine art gallery, the best curry houses in the Western world and some of the unlikeliest looking transvestites on the planet are considered pertinent, then Manchester deserves its ranking.

- Howard Jacobson, writer, winner of Man Booker prize, in 2011 as Manchester makes *Conde Nast*'s best cities list.

"This is Manchester, we do things differently here."

Tony Wilson, Factory Records co-founder, Haçienda manager and radio and television presenter

"Manchester kids have the best record collections."

- Tony Wilson

"Manchester is in the south of the north of England. Its spirit has a contrariness in it – a south and north bound up together – at once untamed and unmetropolitan; at the same time, connected and wordly."

- Jeanette Winterson from her *Why Be Happy When You Could Be Normal?*

"Manchester's got everything except a beach."

- Ian Brown - lead singer of the Stone Roses

For good or ill, communism transformed the globe, but how many of us realise the crucial role played by a Manchester public library - Chethams, the oldest library in the English-speaking world - in the honing of that ideology?

- Michael Portillo

"If it stopped banging on about its football teams and its bands and its shops and its attitude, Manchester has something that it can be genuinely, enormously proud of, something that it should shout from the rooftops.

Manchester changed the world's politics: from vegetarianism to feminism to trade unionism to communism, every upstart notion that ever got ideas above its station, every snotty street-fighter of a radical philosophy, was fostered brawling in Manchester's streets, mills, pubs, churches and debating halls."

- Stuart Maconie from his *Pies and Prejudice: In Search of the North.*

"A city that thinks a table is for dancing on."

- Mark Radcliffe

---

1   In English law, the term headborough referred historically to the head of the legal, administrative, and territorial unit known as a tithing, which sometimes was known as a   borough.

Manchester Music

Many places in the UK rightly claim an association with a specific, identifiable musical output: Liverpool, Sheffield, Newcastle, Glasgow and London are obvious musical Meccas. But Manchester is also high on the list with memorable music stretching from the Hollies in the 60s and 70s to the Madchester scene in the 80s and 90s. Here are just a few of the acts which are still on repeat and resonate today.

Friedrich and his Dreamers in 1964

Number 51 Keppel Road in Chorlton was where the Gibb family lived before they emigrated to Australia. Their front doorstep was where they rehearsed their impressive harmonies in their first group, the 1950s skiffle band the Rattlesnakes. As the **Bee Gees** Barry, Maurice and Robin went on to enjoy unparalleled success in the following decades, penning and recording some of the most popular songs in modern music – selling over 120 million records to date. Their first gig in 1957 was at the nearby Gaumont.

Freddie and the Dreamers. Freddie came together with his Dreamers in 1962 in West Didsbury; Freddie was a milkman. In the 1980 Rolling Stone History of Rock & Roll, Lester Bangs wrote:

> Freddie and the Dreamers [had] no masterpiece but a plenitude of talentless idiocy and enough persistence to get four albums and one film soundtrack released... the Dreamers looked as thuggish as Freddie looked dippy... Freddie and the Dreamers represented a triumph of rock as cretinous swill, and as such should be not only respected, but given their place in history.

Hollies Allan Clarke and Graham Nash are two of the 22,500 lads who have passed through the doors of Salford Lads' Club; the Hollies regularly practised there. Clarke grew up on Hulton Street near Ordsall Park now behind St Clement's Drive; he and Nash (No 1 Skinner Avenue, now James Henry Avenue) were best friends from primary school and came together during the skiffle craze of the late 1950s, developing into a vocal-and-guitar duo modelled on the Everly Brothers, working as "Ricky and Dane Young" and then the Two Teens; they teamed up with a local band, the Fourtones which they quit and joined another Manchester band, the Deltas which had lost two members including Eric Stewart (later 10cc with Graham Gouldman), who left to join a "professional" band, the Mindbenders. The Hollies broke in North America with an original song from Manchester's Graham Gouldman. Look Through Any Window.

Davy Jones of the **Monkees** signed his life changing contract in 1964 after leaving Varna Street School in Openshaw.

An 18-year-old Glyn Geoffrey Ellis lived at 272 Mount Road in Levenshulme; as Wayne Fontana and his Mindbenders, he scored a 1965 number 1 The Game of Love.

The Free Trade Hall is, of course, where **Bob Dylan** was demonised as Judas by an old school folkie for having the temerity to plug his guitar into an amp, thus helping change the course of popular music for ever. May 17, 1966 was the date. Dylan was not the only cause for controversy here: in 1956 **Paul Robeson** was booked to play but the prejudicious and racist US Government had seized his passport thus confining him to the US; the concert went ahead with recorded Robeson music. Vulgar plugging in had a precedent too when **Muddy Waters** showed up in 1958 with a lively and loud electric band; this elicited boos from the morally superior element of the audience who seemed not to have known that Waters had not played folk blues since the 1940s.

BBC's Top of the Pops made its debut on January 1, 1964, in a former Wesleyan Chapel in Dickenson Road, Rusholme, opposite Moon Grove. Top of the bill were the **Rolling Stones** moodily miming *I Wanna Be Your Man*. Others on stage that afternoon were **Dusty Springfield** wishin' and hopin', the **Swinging Blue Jeans** shaking their hips, and the **Dave Clark Five** who were glad all over. Top of the Pops was a Manchester institution until 1967.

The Rolling Stones Riot at Kurhaus, Netherlands

When it comes to using Manchester lyrics, in 1968 **Herman's Hermits** brought it all home and got the ball rolling when they released *It's Nice to be Out in the Morning* which name-checked seven Manchester suburbs, extolling them as home even though they can't compete with the sights of Rome[1]:

Adwick Green where the grass is grey/Beswick Hulme, and Harpurhey/Whalley Range where the tomcats roam/They're not the sights of Rome/But it's home

Boggart Hole Clough in Blackley and Besses o' th' Barns where the brass bands blow, are the others. Old Trafford gets the inevitable name check:

United's ground where the champions score/ A hundred goals to the reds stand's roar/ And Bobby Charlton, Best and Law/It's a most fantastic day/When they play

Whalley Range gets a mention in **Morrisey's** *Miserable Life* [2]:

What do we get for our trouble and pain? Just a rented room in Whalley Range What do we get for our trouble and pain? ...Whalley Range! Into the depths of the criminal world I followed her ...

Eighties band **James** too hailed from this reputed 'criminal world'. They were previously known as FM unfriendly *Venereal and the Diseases* and *Volume Distortion*. Moss Side was where **Barry Adamson** grew up, he of Magazine in the late 70s before he worked with Visage, Depeche Mode and Nick Cave and the Bad Seeds. Adams first solo album was Moss Side Story – an imaginary soundtrack to a non-existent film-noir set locally. **Joy Division's** Best of album cover was shot on Epping Walk Bridge on January 6, 1979; they practiced in a rehearsal studio next to the bridge, used in the promotional video for *Love Will Tear us Apart*.

Hulme was no more salubrious, particularly the Crescent estate in the 70s. it was here that **Nico**, singer with the Velvet Underground, found a home

Ian Curtis *(1956–1980) of Joy Division. Artist Simon James Crossley; www.simonjamescrossley.com*

while getting clean off heroin, warming to the bohemian and punk environment which was left after the depredation and desperation moved on. Hulme too saw the first flowering of the Madchester movement when in May 78 **Tony Wilson** established a post-punk night club called the Russell Club on the corner of the Crescent estate: seeds for the New York inspired 'The Factory' had been sown. Elaine Bookbinder, or **Elkie Brooks** to you and me, was born in Salford in 1945 to a Jewish baker; as a child Brooks began singing at bar mitzvahs and weddings; according to Brooks, her unofficial debut was a gig at a club called the Laronde on Cheetham Hill Road, when she was 13 years old. Dubbed 'the British Queen of the Blues' her band was Vinegar Joe with Pete Gage and Robert Palmer. but she went solo in 1974 and turned out some classic songs as Chris Rea's *'Fool If You Think it's Over'*, *'Pearl's A Singer'* and *'Lilac Wine'*.

Elkie as Pearl, the singer

It was a low budget EP by two Bolton boys who renamed themselves Howard Devoto and Pete Shelley and formed the punk **Buzzcocks** in 1976 which really formed the template for Manchester music of the years that followed. The four songs on *Spiral Scratch* were recorded in Stockport and released on their own label New Hormones. They waxed unlyrically but memorably about lazing late in bed, navigating the supermarket and other mundanities which crowd into all our lives. None of that glam rock and progressiveness - and zero involvement of the pernicious established music business - with the Buzzcocks.

The Fall were formed in 1976 in Prestwich. They underwent numerous line-up changes, with vocalist and founder Mark E. Smith as the only constant member. The band was named after the 1956 philosophical novel by Albert Camus, *La Chute*, or *The Fall* in English.

Ian Brown of the **Stone Roses** (before that the Waterfront) and pursuer of a long solo career lived in Timperley from around 1970 and attended Altrincham Grammar School for Boys. He drew his influences from the Sex Pistols, the Clash, and Manchester-based Slaughter & the Dogs.

Brown did time in Strangeways when arrested after a gig in Paris and later sentenced to four months for using threatening behaviour towards an airline stewardess and captain, a charge he denied. He had threatened to cut off the hands of the stewardess and then hammered on the cockpit door, as the plane came in to land. A few weeks before, he had treated a magazine critic, who had given his album a one-star review, to a "good kicking". Look out Amazon reviewers – he knows where you live.

Martin Fry of **ABC** was born in Stretford and grew up in leafy Bramhall. Lexicon of Love, their debut album, was probably their high point along with the six top 20 hits.

The reason why Ed Simons applied and was accepted by Manchester University to study Medieval History in 1989 was nothing to do with the academic reputation of or destinations resulting from this course; it was quite simply because **New Order** and the **Smiths** were from Manchester. Tom Rowlands likewise, keen as he was to immerse himself in the Haçienda night club. Fate brought Ed and Tom together as aficionados of hip-hop, techno and acid house and they ended up DJ-ing as the 237 Turbo Nutters, later the Dust brothers, then the **Chemical Brothers**.

More seeds were sown to the rear of Deansgate station in Little Peter Street; this is the site of the Boardwalk night club, all the rage in the '80s and '90s where Verve, James, the Charlatans and Rage Against the Machine played. Also (at the bottom of the bill) in August 1991 was an 18-year-old from Burnage heading up a band called Rain; he had a brother in the audience who he teamed up with to form **Oasis**. Tim Burgess of the **Charlatans** was born in Salford's Linkfield Drive. Later he moved to Cheshire but then returned to a flat in Nine Acre Court, Ordsall Park.

Speaking of Burnage, the Dickensian-sounding Fogg Lane Park is that park where the young Gallagher brothers played football as shown on the video for their second single *Shakermaker*.

Paul 'Bonehead' Arthurs, Oasis guitarist, lived at 8 Stratford Avenue off West Didsbury's Burton Avenue in the 1990s. The cover photo of *Definitely Maybe* was shot in his living room. The *Shakermaker* video also features the back yard.

The Palace theatre is not far from an underground toilet converted into a bar called the Temple – the very place name-checked by Guy Garvey of **Elbow** fame in his 2008 *Grounds for Divorce* (There's a hole in my neighbourhood Down which of late I cannot help but fall).

The Northenden Campus of Manchester College (closed 2022) can lay claim to two former students who graduated to become guitar legends. First is Billy Duffy of the **Cult** (formerly Death Cult). He is personally responsible for persuading **Johnny Marr** to take up performing as a guitarist, and encouraging **Morrissey** to make his first foray out front with punk-rock band the Nosebleeds.

Cemetry Gates (sic) was released as a B-side to the Smiths' 1986 single "*Ask*" and on the band's 1986 third album The Queen Is Dead. It was inspired by the strolls he took with his friend, Linder Sterling, around the Southern Cemetery in Chorlton. The album cover photo was taken in front of the Salford Lads Club and now hangs in the National Portrait Gallery. The Smith's Room in the Lads Club is a treasure trove of Smiths' memorabilia.

Paul Young (not the one with the home-loving hat but the one for whom everyday hurts by **Sad Café**) was brought up in Wythenshawe. The band **Doves** win no prizes for geography: their 2002 B-side *The M62 Song* was recorded under a motorway flyover they thought was the M62 in Northenden, only to learn that it was actually the M60 they were under.

Simply Red is a soul and pop band formed in Manchester in 1985. Band leader, singer and songwriter Mick Hucknall, was the only original member left when the band initially disbanded in 2010. Their 1991 album Stars is one of the best-selling albums in the United Kingdom. Originally, Hucknall was in a punk group called The Frantic Elevators, whose seven-year run ended in 1984 with critical acclaim for their final single, "*Holding Back the Years*".

Those cemetery gates

M People, V Festival 2014, Chelmsford. Photo Drew de F. Fawkes

M People is a Manchester dance music band formed in 1990 with success throughout most of the 1990s. The name M People is taken from the first letter of the first name of band member Mike Pickering, who formed the group. Heather Small became the distinctive vocalist of the group. She had been in the English soul band Hot House, which had released a number of critically acclaimed records without registering any real success.

Diamond Skulls are a Manchester band featuring Simon Crossley from Chorlton, and Olly Watkins. Their debut album was *Revelator*; their latest *80s Kid*, was released in January 2025. https://diamondskulls. co.uk/

Watkins on the left; Crossley on the right

We know James Henry Miller better by his stage name **Ewan MacColl**, the eminent English folk singer-songwriter, folk song collector, labour activist and actor. MacColl (1915 –1989), he is known as one of the instigators of the 1960s folk revival as well as for writing such classic songs as "*The First Time Ever I Saw Your Face*" and "*Dirty Old Town*".

MacColl collected hundreds of traditional folk songs, including the version of "*Scarborough Fair*" later brought to global popularity by Simon & Garfunkel, and released dozens of albums with other folk legends such as Peggy Seeger and others, mostly of traditional folk songs. He also wrote many left-wing political songs, remained a lifelong communist and engaged in political activism.

MacColl and Peggy Seeger

MacColl was born at 4 Andrew Street, in Broughton, Salford to Scottish parents, William Miller and Betsy (née Henry), both socialists. He attended North Grecian Street Junior School in Broughton which he left in 1930 with a basic education, during the Depression and, joining the ranks of the unemployed, began a lifelong programme of self-education whilst keeping warm in Manchester Central Library. William Miller was an iron moulder and trade unionist who had moved to Salford with his wife, a charwoman, to look for work after being blacklisted in almost every foundry in Scotland. Betsy Miller knew many traditional folk songs such as "*Lord Randall*" and "*My Bonnie Laddie's Lang A-Growing*",of which her son later created written and audio recordings; he later recorded an album of traditional songs with her.

Ben Harker tells us that he was an activist in the unemployed workers' campaigns and the mass trespasses of the early 1930s. One of his best-known songs, "*The Manchester Rambler*", was written just before the mass trespass of Kinder Scout in the Peak District and starting point of the Pennine Way. He was responsible for publicity in the planning of the trespass [3].

Interestingly, Dominic Casciani has written how in 1932 MI5, opened a file on MacColl, after local police asserted that he was "a communist with very extreme views" who needed "special attention". For a time the Special Branch kept a watch on the Manchester home that he shared with his first wife, Joan Littlewood. MI5 caused some of MacColl's songs to be banned by the BBC, and prevented the employment of Littlewood as a BBC children's programme presenter[4]. A BBC presenter for 'Children's Hour' and Communist Party member, Littlewood also came under the scrutiny of MI5. A letter in the file, marked 'SECRET' (dated March 1939) and sent to W.H. Smith Esq., the Chief Constable for Hyde, tells him that Miller (MacColl) – known to the writer to be a Communist Party member - lives with his parents and wife at Oak Cottage and concludes by saying Miller and Littlewood seem to have no known association with communists in Hyde, but "at weekends, and more particularly when Miller's parents are away from home, a number of young men who have the appearance of communist Jews are known to visit Oak Cottage. It is thought they come from Manchester. What exactly does a communist Jewish person look like?

The letter also informs him that Miller works for the BBC in Manchester and that his wife, Joan Miller – another communist – broadcasts under the name 'Joan Littlewood' and is "said to be 'Aunty Muriel' of Children's Hour."

Pattison continues: after being called up in July 1940, Private James H. Miller was placed on the 'Special Observation List' "to see whether he is trying to carry on propaganda." He was declared a deserter on 18th December 1940 and remained AWOL for the rest of the war. This is when he changed his name to Ewan MacColl. Military reports suggest he was popular with his fellow soldiers and exerted influence over them owing to his greater intelligence. He was a member of the Regimental Concert Party and produced 'several songs and skits'. One of his songs was a particular favourite with the men:

"The medical inspection boy's is just a bleedin' farce. He gropes around your penis and noses up your arse. For even a Private's privates, enjoy no privacy, you sacrifice all that to save democracy. Oh, I was browned off, browned off, as could be [5]."

Kirsty McColl, his daughter from his second marriage to Peggy Seeger, successfully followed him into music.

The music room at Afflecks. Courtesy John Mee.
https://www.johnmeephotography.com/return-to-afflecks-palace/

See also The British Pop Culture Archive, John Rylands Library
The British Pop Archive (BPA), is a unique collection of national significance dedicated to the preservation and research of popular music, popular culture, counter-culture, and youth culture.

---

1   *Graham Gouldman, ©Schubert Music Publishing Inc. (Graham Gouldman)*

2   *Johnny Marr / Steven Morrissey, Universal Music Publishing Group, Warner Chappell Music, Inc 1984*

3   *Harker, Ben (2005). "'The Manchester Rambler': Ewan MacColl and the 1932 Mass Trespass". History Workshop Journal. Spring (59): 219–228.*

4   *Dominic Casciani (5 March 2006). "Why MI5 monitored singer Ewan MacColl". BBC News.*

5   *Pattison, Derek, How Hyde 'Spymasters' looked for Commies on BBC Children's Hour, November 30, 2013 See https://radicalmanchester.wordpress.com/*

Literary Manchester
& Stockport

'Home to 4 historic libraries, 23 public libraries plus many more independents. 2 Universities in the City Centre with a student population of 98,000, plus 2 writing schools. More than 40 arts and culture festivals, including Manchester Literature Festival. More than 10 independent publishers such as Carcanet and Comma Press. The home of writers and radicals such as Anthony Burgess, Emmeline Pankhurst, Lemn Sissay, Carol Ann Duffy, John Cooper Clarke, Elizabeth Gaskell, Jeanette Winterson. Manchester: A UNESCO City of Literature'.
- www.manchestercityofliterature.com/

Reading this, it is hardly surprising that Manchester-cum-Salford has attracted a very unfair and disproportionate share of literary excellence. Here is a brief account of why the city has become one of the great cities of the written word, and a city of the book in whatever form it may take.

To **Charles Dickens** in *Hard Times* (1858) Manchester is Coketown

a town of red brick, or of brick that would have been red if the smoke and ashes had allowed it; but as matters stood, it was a town of unnatural red and black like the painted face of a savage.

It was a town of machinery and tall chimneys, out of which interminable serpents of smoke trailed themselves for ever and ever, and never got uncoiled.

It had a black canal in it, and a river that ran purple with ill-smelling dye

- Hard Times, (Chapter 5)

Maria Jane Jewsbury and *Phantasmagoria*

Maria Jane Jewsbury (later Fletcher; 1800–1833) was a writer, poet and reviewer who also wrote for the Manchester Gazette and the Athenaeum - all fitted in while bringing up her younger siblings for 12 years. Her *Phantasmagoria* of poetry and prose (1825), *The Three Histories* (1830) and *Letters to the Young* (1837) were her most popular works and are the most enduring. Her literary circle of friends included William Wordsworth and Dorothy, Sara Coleridge and Thomas De Quincey. In 1832 she married Rev. William Kew Fletcher (died 1867); the couple sailed for India where she kept a journal and had poetry printed in the *The Athenaeum* as *"The Oceanides"*.

Jewsbury's father was the master of a cotton factory, but as a consequence of the War of 1812 with America which impacted on the cotton business, the family had to move to George Street; in 1818, when the business failed. Jewsbury's mother died one month after giving birth. It was then that aged 19, Jewsbury took on the mother's role for the household, so that her father could continue working.

Jewsbury became ill in June 1833 and died of cholera at Poona on 4 October 1833; many of her papers reside in the library of Manchester University.

The Ritz is where **John Cooper Clarke** met, and created, Salome Maloney:

I was walking down oxford road
Dressed in what they call
the mode I could hear them
spinning all their smash hits
At the mecca of the modern
dance, the Ritz

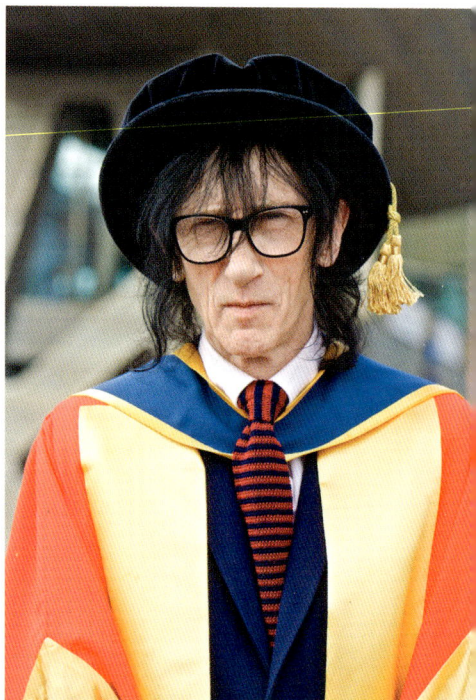

Cooper's work had done much to increase the accessibility of poetry, opening it up to a wide audience, not least Alex Turner of the Arctic Monkeys who recorded *'I Wanna Be Yours'* on their fifth album *AM* (2013). The poem was on the GCSE English syllabus in the '90s as part of an anthology and to date has clocked up a staggering billion + views on Tik Tok[1].

John Cooper Clarke, *The Bard of Salford became a doctor in July 2013 after receiving an honorary degree in his home city. The University of Salford awarded the Punk Poet a Doctor of Arts for bringing poetry to non-traditional audiences for over three decades.*

The adaptation, produced by James Ford and Ross Orton, contains additional lyrics written by Alex Turner. By 3 April 2024 the recitation had received over two billion streams on Spotify.

In March 2023 *The Guardian* noted that "if it was previously Britain's favourite wedding poem, it's now quantifiably the world's favourite British poem, full stop."

I wanna be your vacuum cleaner
Breathing in your dust
I wanna be your Ford Cortina
I will never rust...

The **International Anthony Burgess Foundation**, obviously pays homage to the Manchester-born author, and is home to a collection of possessions, including the original manuscript of *A Clockwork Orange*, with doodles by the author, and letters to Stanley Kubrick, who directed the film of the book.

Chetham's Library, which was founded in 1653 and claims to be the oldest public library in the English-speaking world, traces Manchester's literary legacy back to Tudor times. **Marx** and **Engels** worked here, and their desk in an alcove of the wood-panelled reading room can still be seen.

Elizabeth Gaskell's *House*, home to the author of Cranford, North and South and other classics look, according to The Guardian 'as if the family had just popped out and left the table set for dinner'.

Gaskell documented Manchester's industrial and social revolution from her kitchen desk after the family moved to the house in 1850. Her Milton in North and South is our Manchester. First impressions were not good, and a world away from the comfortable luxury of airy Cheyne Walk (number 93) in posh Chelsea:

Nearer to the town, the air had a faint taste and smell of smoke; perhaps, after all, more a loss of the fragrance of grass and herbage than any positive taste or smell. Quick they were whirled over long, straight, hopeless streets of regularly built houses, all small and of brick. Here and there a great oblong many-windowed factory stood up, like a hen among her chickens, puffing out black 'unparliamentary' smoke, and sufficiently accounting for the cloud which Margaret had taken to foretell rain.

Her controversial views contrasted starkly with the norms of the Victorian age: "Few female voices were as courageous as hers," says Janet Allan of the Gaskell Society. "Her greatest skill was to use storytelling to address the social issues of the era."

By the way:
To give an idea of how salubrious Cheyne Walk was, and still is, Keith Richards of the Rolling Stones bought a house there (number 3) in 1967 with Anita Pallenberg, the actress. George Eliot (Mary Anne Evans) lived at number 4. At number 14, we find the former home of philosopher Bertrand

Russell. Meanwhile, number 16 was home to both Dante Gabriel Rossetti, and Victorian poet Algernon Charles Swinburne. Bram Stoker spent time at number 27, Mick Jagger and Marianne Faithfull lived in number 48 while at number 119 Ronnie Wood owns the house that JMW Turner died in. Number 120 is where **Sylvia Pankhurst** briefly lived, while at number 122, a block of flats, was home to T.S. Eliot, Henry James, W. Somerset Maugham, and Ian Fleming who all lived here at one time or another. Meanwhile, Laurence Olivier, George Best, and Mick Fleetwood have all resided along Cheyne Walk.

Lemn Sissay's poem "Hardy's Well" on the side of the pub it is named after on Wilmslow Road, Rusholme. Credit: Google Street View

Born in Wigan in 1967, **Lemn Sissay** is a poet, playwright and has been chancellor of the University of Manchester. He was also the official poet for the London 2012 Olympics and the 2015 FA Cup. His poetry collections include *Rebel Without Applause*, *Morning Breaks in the Elevator* and *The Emperor's Watchmaker*.

Frances Hodgson Burnett (1849 –1924) the author of '*A Little Princess*', '*Little Lord Fauntleroy*' and '*The Secret Garden*' was raised in Manchester's York Street, Cheetham Hill, and Salford.

Dame Carol Ann Duffy (born 1955) the Scottish poet and playwright is professor of contemporary poetry at Manchester Metropolitan University and creative director of its Writing School. She was appointed Poet Laureate in 2009 holding the position until 2019. She was the first female poet, the first Scottish-born poet and the first openly lesbian poet to hold the post of Poet Laureate.

Richmal Crompton Lamburn

Richmal Crompton is, best known for her *Just William* series of books, humorous short stories. She was born in Bury, 1890, and went to school in Warrington.

Sophie Hannah was born in Manchester and attended Beaver Road Primary School in Didsbury and the University of Manchester. From 1997 to 1999 she was Fellow Commoner in Creative Arts at Trinity College, Cambridge. Hannah published her first book of poems, *The Hero and the Girl Next Door*, at the age of 24. Her poems have been studied at GCSE (including *"Rubbish at Adultery"* and *"Your Dad Did What?"*), A-level, and degree level across the UK. She is even better known for her psychological crime novels her first of which, *Little Face,* was published in 2006, and her latest contemporary crime novel, 'The Couple at the Table', was published in 2022. Hannah also founded and is CEO of, and coach at, Dream Author Coaching Ltd, a coaching programme for writers and/or anyone who aspires to write.

Howard Jacobson (b. 25 August 1942) is a British novelist and journalist who writes comic novels often concerning the dilemmas faced by British Jewish characters. He is a Man Booker Prize winner, for his novel *The Finkler Question*.

Jacobson was born in Manchester to parents of Russian-Jewish heritage (his father's parents came from Kamianets-Podilskyi in what is now Ukraine, and his mother's family from Lithuania). He was brought up in Prestwich, and educated at Stand Grammar School before going on to study English at Downing College, Cambridge, under F. R. Leavis.

"I am living in a town where the sole and universal object of pursuit is precisely that which I hold most in abhorrence. In this place trade is the religion, and money is the god. Every object I see reminds me of those occupations which run counter to the bent of my nature, every sentiment I hear sounds a discord to my own. I cannot stir out of doors but I am nosed by a factory, a cotton-bag, a cotton-dealer, or something else allied to that most detestable commerce."

So thundered the Romantic **Thomas De Quincey** who was born into a rich family in 1785 at the Princes' Tavern, 86 Cross Street, at what is now the corner of Cross and John Dalton streets. His father was a successful merchant with an interest in literature. Soon after Thomas' birth, the family moved to The Farm and then later to Greenheys, a larger country house in Chorlton-on-Medlock. He was an essayist, literary critic and journalist. He is most famous for his *Confessions of an Opium Eater*. The first version appeared anonymously in the London Magazine in 1821 and details his early years in Manchester. One of the best accounts, which was only fully realised in a later edition, takes him to the Portico Library.

From the review of Guilty Thing: A Life of Thomas De Quincey by Frances Wilson in The Times April 9, 2016 by Daisy Goodwin

In 1800, De Quincey, aged 15, was ready to go up to Oxford, his scholarship being far in advance of his years. "That boy could harangue an Athenian mob better than you or I could address an English one," his master at St Edward School Bath said. He was sent to Manchester Grammar School, in order that after three years he might win a scholarship to Brasenose College, Oxford, but he fled after 19 months. De Quincey inaugurated the tradition of addiction literature in the West.

Jack Rosenthal CBE (1931–2004) was an English playwright who wrote 129 early episodes of Coronation Street and over 150 screenplays, including many original television plays, feature films, and adaptations. He was born in Cheetham Hill; his parents were married in 1927 in Manchester, and were children of Russian Jewish immigrants. During the 1960s, he contributed material for various television comedy shows, including the satirical *That Was The Week That Was*. Rosenthal won three BAFTA awards for *Bar Mitzvah Boy*. Rosenthal met actress Maureen Lipman in 1969 in a pub in Manchester while Rosenthal was writing for Coronation Street. He was a lifelong Manchester United fan, listing his recreations in Who's Who as "checking Manchester United's score, minute by minute, on teletext".

Paul Taylor – Trombone Poetry no less

Paul Taylor was born in and grew up in Oldham. He attended the University of Hull and then took up a career in music (trombone) with bands such as The Bureau and the Yiddish Twist Orchestra. At the same time he was cultivating his poetry-writing with a special brand of verse that is at once innovative, humorous and thought-provoking – indeed, everything Aristotle demanded in poetry. His latest compilation is called *Better Late than Sorry* (2021) and features such gems as:

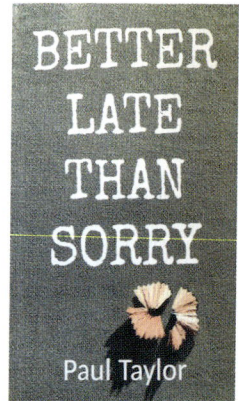

BETTER LATE THAN SORRY

Paul Taylor

how to use a pencil
how to look on the bright side
what use is a trombone
how to measure wind
what spoons can do for you
what those insects are doing

He writes and performs as a solo artist in a project known as Trombone Poetry [https://trombonepoetry.com/]

Paul Taylor writes and performs as a solo artist in a project known as Trombone Poetry.

He works as a freelance musician and runs two irresistible and affordable trios: Click Beetle, which plays his many compositions,

and The Blowpipes Trombone Trio, which plays classical and folk music, jazz and whatnot. He has spent many happy years playing in the best Latin bands in Europe and pretending to be Colombian.

News of all these musical and literary activities are chronicled in The Trombonicle.

He hails from Oldham and pines for Hull.

The wonderful William Shakespeare window in Manchester Central Library
See pp. 277 for details of Rosa Grindon's involvement in the window.

Jeanette Winterson CBE FRSL is a writer, journalist and a professor at the University of Manchester. She broadcasts and teaches creative writing.

Her first book, *Oranges Are Not the Only Fruit*, was a semi-autobiographical novel about a lesbian growing up in an English Pentecostal community. Other novels explore gender polarities and sexual identity and later ones the relations between humans and technology.

"Book collection is an OBSESSION, an OCCUPATION, a DISEASE, an ADDICTION, a FASCINATION, an ABSURDITY, a FATE. It is not a hobby. Those who do it must do it."

- Jeanette Winterson

This is how she prescriptively and piercingly defines Manchester:

"Manchester is in the south of the north of England," she writes. "Its spirit has a contrariness… at once untamed and unmetropolitan; at the same time, connected and wordly."

Elizabeth Raffald

Before Mrs Beeton there was Manchester's Elizabeth Raffald

Elizabeth Raffald (née Whitaker; 1733 – 1781) was author, innovator and entrepreneur. Born and raised in Doncaster, Raffald went into domestic service for fifteen years, ending as the housekeeper to the Warburton baronets at Arley Hall, Cheshire. She left her position when she married John, the estate's head gardener. The couple moved to Manchester where Raffald enterprisingly opened a register office to introduce domestic workers to employers – a kind of hiring fair in an office, or an early recruitment agency; she also ran a cookery school and sold food from the premises. In 1769 she published her blockbuster cookery book *The Experienced English Housekeeper*, which contains the first recipe for a "Bride Cake" - the modern wedding cake. She is also probably the inventor of the Eccles cake.

To go with her recruitment office in August 1772 she published *The Manchester Directory*, a listing of 1,505 traders and civic leaders in Manchester — the first such listing for the up-and-coming town and one of the early forerunners of the business and trade directories which appeared at the end of the 19th century and to the end of the 20th.

The Raffalds went on to run two important post houses in Manchester and Salford before being hit by financial problems, not helped by John's heavy drinking. Elizabeth died suddenly in 1781, just after publishing the third edition of her directory and while still updating the eighth edition of her cookery book.

After her death there were fifteen official editions of her cookery book, and twenty-three pirated ones (plus ça change). Her recipes were ruthlessly plagiarised by other authors, notably by Isabella Beeton in her bestselling Mrs Beeton's

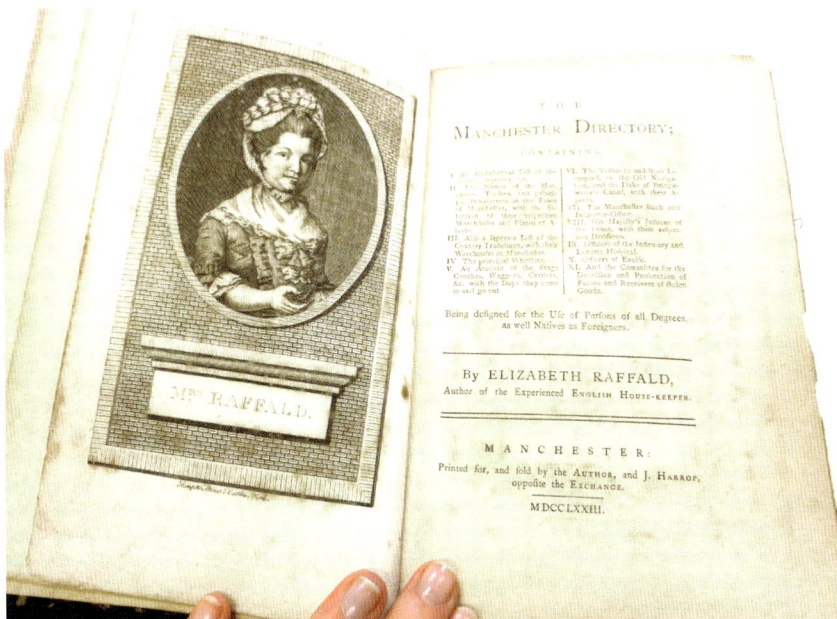

Book of Household Management (1861). Nevertheless Raffald's recipes have been admired by several modern cooks and food writers, including Elizabeth David and Jane Grigson.

By the way…

Raffald was by no means the only victim of plagiarism

Beeton's modern biographer Kathryn Hughes talks of her "lifting" and "brazenly copying" recipes from others, and says that this was "the way that cookery books had been put together from time immemorial ..." The New York Times said, "Isabella [Beeton] plagiarised only the best". This led to the comment that "Mrs Beeton couldn't cook but she could copy".[2] Hughes recounts that Beeton's "first recipe for Victoria sponge was so inept that she left out the eggs" and that her work was "brazenly copied ... almost word for word, from books as far back as the Restoration". The influential 20th-century food writer Elizabeth David dismissed her as "a plagiarist" and later wrote: "I wonder if I would have ever learned to cook at all if I had been given a routine Mrs. Beeton to learn from".[3]

1   "GCSE Poetry: 'I Wanna be Yours' by John Cooper-Clarke". TES.
2   Brown, Mark (2006-06-02). "Mrs Beeton couldn't cook but she could copy, reveals historian". The Guardian.
3   Cooper, Artemis (2000). Writing at the Kitchen Table – The Authorized Biography of Elizabeth David. Michael Joseph. p. 45.

Still from A Taste of Honey, 1961. Northern life in a nutshell

Shelagh Delaney

Set in Salford, her *A Taste of Honey* was initially written to be published as a novel but later turned into a play; this and the subsequent film are both classics. According to Adam O'Riordan writing in the Guardian (5 April, 2017) 'this is a work in which drabness and desire walk arm in arm, through the story of Jo and her mother Helen and some very difficult love life. It was later adapted for the screen by Tony Richardson and became a classic of British New Wave cinema. Manchester's arts have always cross-pollinated, and it would go on to influence a young Steven Patrick Morrissey, who references Delaney and her work in a number of his songs'. These songs include: *'What Difference Does it Make (I'll Probably Never See you Again)';'Asleep (Sing Me to Sleep)' 'Reel Around the Fountain';* and *'The Night Has Opened My Eyes'.*

George Orwell, *The Road to Wigan Pier*

In January 1936 Orwell was commissioned by publisher Victor Gollancz to make a study of unemployment in the depressed areas of the north of England and to write about what he had seen. The deal was that the book resulting from the journey would not only be published by Gollancz but would also be considered as a selection of the Left Book Club, which the publisher was planning to form in the spring of that year.

Travelling partly on foot and partly by public transport his journey took him to Coventry, Birmingham, Wolverhampton, the Potteries, Macclesfield, Manchester (where he stayed five days), Wigan (two weeks), Liverpool (one week), Sheffield (four days), Leeds (one week), and Barnsley (two weeks) [1].

So, he set off from London buoyed up with a small advance from his publisher, to investigate the "distressed areas" of northern England.

"I do not believe that there is anything inherently and unavoidably ugly about industrialism. A factory or even a gasworks is not obliged of its own nature to be ugly, any more than a palace or a dog-kennel or a cathedral. It all depends on the architectural tradition of the period. The industrial towns of the North are ugly because they happen to have been built at a time when modem methods of steel-construction and smoke-abatement were unknown, and when everyone was too busy making money to think about anything else. They go on being ugly largely because the Northerners have got used to that kind of thing and do not notice it. Many of the people in Sheffield or Manchester, if they smelled the air along the Cornish cliffs, would probably declare that it had no taste in it [2]."

Robert Roberts

The Classic Slum: Salford life in the First Quarter of the Century
A Ragged Schooling, Growing Up in the Classic Slum

Robert Roberts (15 June 1905 – 17 September 1974) was an English teacher, writer and social historian, who wrote two evocative accounts of his working-class childhood in *The Classic Slum* (1971) and *A Ragged Schooling* (1976).

Born and raised above his parents' corner shop at 1 Waterloo Street in a deprived district of Salford, Roberts left school at 14 to undertake a seven-year apprenticeship as a brass finisher. Used as a form of cheap labour to carry out menial tasks, he was, predictably, dismissed when the apprenticeship ended in 1926. Roberts inherited his mother's love of reading and socialist politics; while he spent the next three years unemployed, he attended evening classes to study foreign languages and social history.

In 1929, he was hired as a teacher at a commercial college. After a short period teaching in Liverpool, he spent most of the 1940s and the 1950s working on a relative's farm in Yorkshire while teaching adult education classes and writing for the radio and newspapers. In 1957, he was hired as an education officer at Strangeways where he taught illiterate prisoners to read and write, experiences on which he based his first book, *Imprisoned Tongues* (1968).

Jack Hilton, Rochdale *'Caliban Shrieks'*

> *This brilliant book has been the focus of my life for 2 years. One of the best English works of the last century - forced from print, for 7 decades, by snobbery.*
>
> *- Jack Chadwick*

Some very determined literary investigation has led to the publication of Jack Hilton's *Caliban Shrieks* after 20 years of languishing in nowhere in particular. Jack Chadwick, the indefatigable investigator says:

Thrilled to publish this investigative profile of Jack Hilton with @ManchesterMill. A man whose life and work to me makes him an absolute legend — of Manchester, of the labour movement, of working-class creativity[4].

Ian Youngs, BBC Entertainment & Arts reporter, told us in July 2023 that a 1930s novel that was acclaimed by George Orwell and WH Auden before being forgotten for decades is to be republished after a Manchester bartender rediscovered it and solved a mystery about the author's last wishes. Jack Chadwick chanced upon an old copy of Jack Hilton's semi-autobiographical *Caliban Shrieks* in 2021 in Salford's Working Class Movement Library.

Youngs continues that academics had previously failed to find who inherited the rights to the book after Hilton died in 1983. But Chadwick succeeded by appealing for information in pubs near the writer's last home. He put up posters asking "Do you remember Jack Hilton?", which eventually led him to track down the widow of a friend, who was unaware she had inherited the author's estate[5].

Chadwick then launched a campaign to get the book back into print, and it has now been signed by Vintage, an imprint of Penguin, the UK's largest publishing house.

Jack Chadwick discusses Jack Hilton on BBC Radio 4 Front Row

'Hilton was a plasterer from Rochdale who based the vivid and groundbreaking book on his own experiences growing up in slums, living in workhouses after World War One, and suffering unemployment and hardship after the Great Depression at the end of the 1920s.

Auden hailed his "magnificent Moby Dick rhetoric", while Orwell said Hilton's voice was "exceedingly rare and correspondingly important" and declared he had a "considerable literary gift".

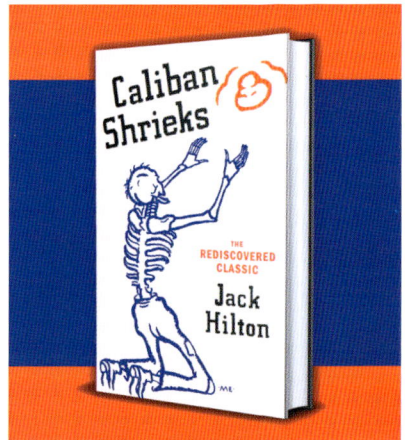

Orwell even asked to come and stay with Hilton in Rochdale to write his own account of English working-class life. Hilton didn't have room, but suggested a friend in Wigan instead. That led Orwell to write his landmark The Road To Wigan Pier, which was published two years after Caliban Shrieks.

Chadwick said Hilton was "a writer of great talent who came from nowhere to blow wide open the parameters of literary modernism".

Vintage described *Caliban Shrieks* as "a masterpiece of both modernist and working class literature, [which] continues to speak as angrily and impassioned today as it did on its first rave publication in 1935".

The BBC programme continues by revealing the denouement:

Chadwick put up the appeal posters in pubs near Hilton's last address. In one, before he had finished his pint, a woman approached him and gave him the names of the writer's two best friends.

The friends too had passed away, but Chadwick tracked down the widow of one and put a letter through her door.

Through another stroke of luck, during further research, he found a document that said Hilton had left his copyrights, along with all his other possessions, to the same friend, and they had passed to his widow when the friend died in 2021.

The woman, who had been unaware that she owned Hilton's estate, donated the rights to Chadwick on the condition that he must do his utmost to breathe life back into his work.

Asa Briggs, *Victorian Cities: Manchester, Leeds, Birmingham, Middlesbrough, Melbourne, London (1990)*

Briggs called Manchester, a "shock city of the industrial age" and goes on: 'If the new industrial city was a triumph for tough, pushing, millowners, it was also torn by the class struggle. Manchester forced to the surface problems of class, of the relations between rich and poor' thus shaping, according to Gordon Rimmer[3], the national image of the industrial North. Catastrophe was forecast on the basis of divided communities, with a wide gap between the few rich and the poor masses and with working-class hostility to the Liberal politics of the business community.

Evelyn Waugh's *Vile Bodies* has a brief section based in Manchester when in chapter seven, Adam and Nina are at the horse races in Manchester, watching Indian Runner canter home unexpectedly in first place, when Adam spots in the crowd the drunk Major (who had promised to put £1,000 on 'Indian Runner' on Adam's behalf, money that Adam had won on the toss of a coin). Adam tries to track him down, in vain.

Robert Oxton Bolt *CBE* (1924–1995)

Bolt was an English playwright and a two-time Oscar-winning screenwriter, known for writing the screenplays for Lawrence of Arabia, Doctor Zhivago, and A Man for All Seasons, the latter two of which won him the Oscar for Best Adapted Screenplay.

He was born in *Sale*, Cheshire but it was at Manchester Grammar School where his affinity for Sir Thomas More took root. After leaving school aged sixteen, he worked unenthusiastically in an insurance office, but after studying in the evening for five weeks he passed three A-levels and went on to the University of Manchester, from which, after a year, he undertook wartime service as a pilot officer candidate in the RAF (air-sickness preventing him from continuing past training) from 1943 to 1946. He returned to the University of Manchester graduating with an honours degree in history. For many years he taught English and history at Millfield School and only became a full-time writer at the age of 33 when his play *The Flowering Cherry* was staged in London in 1958, starring Celia Johnson and Ralph Richardson.

He first earned notice for his original, award-winning play *A Man for All Seasons* – a depiction of Sir Thomas More's clash with Henry VIII over his divorce from first wife Catherine of Aragon.

After *Lawrence of Arabia* Bolt fell foul of the law, and as part of the Committee of 100 he was arrested and imprisoned for protesting against nuclear proliferation. He refused to be "bound over" (i.e., to sign a declaration that he would not engage in such activities again) and was sentenced to one month in prison as a result.

1 Hammond, J.R. (1982). The Road to Wigan Pier. In: A George Orwell Companion. Literary Companions. Palgrave Macmillan, London

2 Orwell, George, The Road to Wigan Pier, chapter 7

3 Rimmer, G. (1964). [Review of Victorian Cities, by A. Briggs]. Social and Economic Studies, 13(3), 405–408

4 https://manchestermill.co.uk/p/he-captured-the-imagination-of-orwell

5 https://www.bbc.co.uk/news/entertainment-arts-66131911

See main entries above for

Fredrich Engels - *The Conditions of the Working Class in England*
Elizabeth Gaskell - *Mary Barton* and others

Walter Greenwood - *Love on the Dole*

Isabella Banks - *The Manchester Man*

See also https://www.manchestercityofliterature.com/about/writers-in-manchester/

Manchester Women Who Have Made a Difference

'recognition for those who have made a real difference in what is still largely a man's world'

First in the Fight – the book of 20 redoubtable and significant women who made a difference to the making of Manchester - does a splendid job in responding to that question so often asked: 'Where Are All the Women'? When we see a statue of a man, this question may present itself and provoke the need for an explanation or answer, as do other forms of political, scientific, academic and cultural celebration – books, paintings, murals - when observing (usually male) civic leaders and benefactors of the past and present.

Rosa Leo Grindon, the Suffragist Shakespearean Scholar

From humble beginnings as a daughter of an agricultural labourer in a rural Derbyshire village Rosa (1848–1923) attended Cheltenham Ladies College. We learn from http://www.johncassidy.org.uk/grindon.html

By 1871 she had made her own way in life and was living, aged 22 in Stafford, as a 'companion' to an 88-year-old widow… By 1881 Rosa was living in the Stockport area, employed as housekeeper at Torkington Lodge, home of the wealthy landowning Barlow family. While working in domestic roles, Rosa studied for a diploma awarded by the University of St Andrews and known as the Lady Literate in Arts (L.L.A.) which was considered the equivalent of a Master's degree and could be earned by what today is know as 'Distance Learning.) In 1883 she gained a diploma in botany, political economy, and physiology.

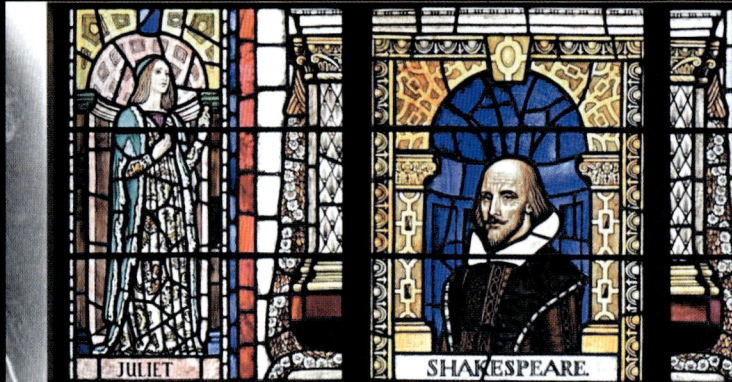

Detail of the Shakespeare Window

She became a leading light in Manchester's literary and theatrical circles, an authoritative Shakespearean scholar and, as a Suffragist, an outspoken champion of women's rights. As an example her response to women being precluded from membership of some of the city's august societies was to resurrect Lydia Becker's Manchester Ladies' Literary Society, to which she invited the leading Shakespearean actors Henry Irving and Ellen Terry to speak.

The website gaskellsociety.co.uk/event/rosa-grindon/ tells that she 'challenged the largely male-dominated interpretations of female figures in Shakespeare's plays.... Such was her standing that she was the first woman to be invited to speak at the Shakespeare Festival in Stratford-in-Avon. Later, she led the preparations for Manchester's Shakespeare Tercentenary Celebrations in 1916 and funded the Shakespeare Window in the bequest in her will.

Emmeline Pankhurst it was who won the poll set up to elect the woman most deserving of a statue in Manchester's St Peter's Square; in her victory she polled more votes than 19 other women who have also contributed enormously in one way or another to Manchester women's lives, improving and amplifying the lot of Manchester (indeed British) women generally in so many ways, from the right to vote, equality in education, the freedom to excel as entrepreneurs, legal protection in the workplace and in the domestic setting, and so on... her steely presence exudes determination and influence as she carries a mighty responsibility for her 19 companions, winners all. **Emmeline Pankhurst** becomes a fitting and powerful blend of all their virtues and achievements too; for example, she represents the women who marched to St Peter's Fields flying the flag for electoral reform and social change. While many of the 19 might be called radicals, the Peterloo women were for the most part – despite the jaundiced male gaze fixed on them, ordinary, rational and reasonable women asking for an equally reasonable deal in life for them and for their children. The blurb for *First in the Fight* adds:

> 'For the centenary of some women being able to vote in 2018, the journey began for a statue to be erected, symbolising the incredible lives and achievements of Manchester's radical women. This book provides a glimpse at the lives of the twenty women who were long-listed in the campaign, who all made Manchester first in the fight for freedom, and feminism'.

One way of gauging and comprehending the sheer range of their collective achievements and vision is to understand that these twenty women not only brought women for the first time into the national consciousness as achievers, succeeders and influencers, they actually changed the very complexion and future of our country's health care, our workplaces, education system, political and voting systems as well as issues of birth control and abortion. They successfully pushed back against institutional and laddish sexism, misogyny and social and professional prejudice.

The other 19 winners include:
Born in Withington, **Margaret Ashton** (19 January 1856–15 October 1937) was an English non-militant suffragist, local politician, pacifist and philanthropist, and the first woman city councillor for Manchester when she was elected Councillor for Manchester Withington. She worked relentlessly for the peace movement nationally and internationally and was a well-known speaker on public platforms across the country. She was a signatory to the Open Letter, a call for peace addressed in sisterhood "To the Women of Germany and Austria", which was published in *Jus Suffragii* in January 1915. She started a Manchester branch of the Women's International League for Peace and Freedom

Her entry in *British National Biography* informs us that 'as a member of Manchester's public health committee and chair of the maternity and child welfare subcommittee, Ashton endorsed municipal mother and baby clinics and promoted free milk for babies and new mothers. In 1914 she founded the Manchester Babies Hospital with Dr Catherine Chisholm (1878–1952).

Manchester Archives tells us that she resigned her position as executive committee member of the National Union of Women's Suffrage Societies in 1915 in protest at their decision not to send delegates to the International Congress of Women at The Hague. She was elected as a delegate to the Congress although she could not attend as the English Channel was closed to shipping. She became a founder member of the Women's International League and worked for the organisation until her death.

Her mighty efforts and determination would, in the normal course of events, have ensured Margaret a place in women's history and in the political and social history of the UK. However, a dispute with the local council led them to impose a spiteful and petulant form of modern day *damnatio memoriae* thus ensuring the virtual erasing of her name from the city's history. Was the council made up of men, I wonder…

How such petulance?

Tradition had it that Manchester councillors were honoured with having their portrait hang in the town hall, and so it was that a portrait was commissioned by C.P. Snow, *Manchester Guardian* editor. Margaret's portrait was rejected – a great opportunity lost to have a woman's likeness on show to balance out all those men. The councillors of Manchester believed Margaret to be a traitor on account of her stand on World War I so no portrait was going up on their wall; furthermore, she was removed from the Education Committee in 1917.

22 March 2023 saw Cavendish Primary School in Didsbury mark International Women's Day on 8 March with a mural of Margaret Ashton (1856–1937), the celebrated Unitarian women's rights campaigner.

Thanks largely to the efforts of Alison Ronan at Manchester Metropolitan University, Margaret is now up there with her peers, salvaged from the storerooms of Manchester Art Gallery before going on display there and in the People's History Museum.

Nonetheless, Margaret's legacy remains impressive. In 1938, some friends and admirers of Ashton formed a memorial committee which funded two activities:

- A seat in the Manchester Town Hall for the use of the Lady Mayoress and other guests. On the reverse of the seat was a table recording her accomplishments.

- A bi-annual memorial lecture series, organised by the University of Manchester, alternating between the university and the Corporation of Manchester.

In 1982, the Harpurhey High School for Girls was re-opened as Margaret Ashton Sixth Form College.

Her name and picture (and those of 58 other women's suffrage supporters) are on the plinth of the statue of Millicent Fawcett in Parliament Square, London; it was unveiled in 2018.

In 2022, a mural depicting Ashton, by artist Emma Bowen, was painted on a wall at Cavendish Community Primary School in West Didsbury. Ashton had laid the school's foundation stone in 1904.

---

1. *By Helen Antrobus and Andrew Simcock, 2019*

This banner was presented to the Women's Trade Union Delegation to Russia, April-July 1925 which was led by Mary Quaile of the Transport and General Workers' Union.

The slogan on this banner reads 'Workers of the world unite. United Struggle of Russian and English men and women workers will ensure world victory of the proletariat'. The banner portrays 2 women against a backdrop of factories and Lenin's tomb.

The slogan on the reverse of the banner reads 'To English women delegates of the General council of Trade Unions Long Live the unity of the Trade Union Movement. The women trade unionists of Tvet, May 1925.

Mary Quaile

the fight for equality and the fight for the vote were never the same thing

Mary T. Quaile (1886–1958) was born in Dublin but grew up in Manchester from 1890, leaving school at the age of 12 and working at first in service and then in the famous Clarion Café. Hers was a radical thinking household – James, her father, was active in the Ancient Guild of Incorporated Brick and Stone Layers.

According to the census in April 1911, the family were living at 1 Pimlott Street in Longsight. In addition to Mary, who was the eldest, the census listed four sons – John, William, Charles and James – and two daughters – Kathleen and Isabella.

Mary left England and worked in the French port of Brest where she learnt French, a skill that no doubt later proved very useful at her future international trade union meetings.

The usual bigotry and prejudice followed Irish immigrants like the Quailes, but, inspired by a visit by Margaret Bondfield, Quaile began persuading catering workers in the city to join a union[1]. As a result, in 1911, she was appointed as Assistant Organiser of the Manchester Women's Trade Union Council (WTUC), then later as its Organising Secretary.

In 1908 the Clarion Café had opened at 50a Market Street; the *Clarion* being Robert Blatchford' socialist newspaper in 1890. Mary was involved in the formation of a Manchester branch of the National Café Workers' Union, founded in Liverpool by a Mrs Billinge, who was a member of the local Fabian Society. The branch gathered a number of members in Manchester and consequently, on 8 November 1909, a meeting took place in the MWTUC offices at 9 Albert Square to set up a Manchester branch.

In 1919, the WTUC became part of Manchester Trades Council, and Quaile became the National Woman Officer of the Dock, Wharf, Riverside and General Labourers' Union, which later became part of the Transport and General Workers' Union. She was also active at the Trades Union Congress (TUC), and served on the General Council of the TUC from 1923 to 1926.

In 1925, Quaile led a women's TUC delegation to the Soviet Union visiting, and impressed by, schools and factories and the treatment of girls and women therein[2]. She was also appointed to the Women's Advisory Committee of the International Federation of Trade Unions. Due to poor health from Parkinson's, she resigned from all her national posts in 1933[3].

Ellen Wilkinson (1891–1947): MP and mental health campaigner

> *she played a prominent role in the 1936 Jarrow March to London to petition for the right to work*

Born at 41 Coral Street in Chorlton-on-Medlock, Ellen Cicely Wilkinson saw that teaching was one of the few careers then open to educated working-class girls, and so in 1906 for half the week she attended the Manchester Day Training College, and during the other half taught at Oswald Road Elementary School. Her classroom approach — she sought to interest her pupils, rather than impose learning by rote — led to frequent clashes with her superiors, and convinced her that her future did not lie in teaching. In 1910 Wilkinson won the Jones Open History Scholarship, which gave her a place at Manchester University. There she joined the university's branch of the Fabian Society, and eventually became its joint secretary. She continued her suffragist work by joining the Manchester Society for Women's Suffrage, where she impressed Margaret Ashton. Later she was a British Labour Party politician who served as Minister of Education from July 1945 until her untimely death in 1947; she was also Parliamentary Secretary to the Minister for Pensions of the United Kingdom (1940–1940). as the MP for Jarrow, she became a national figure when she played a prominent role in the 1936 Jarrow March of the town's unemployed to London to petition for the right to work.

Inspired by the Russian Revolution of 1917, Wilkinson joined the British Communist Party, and preached revolutionary socialism while seeking constitutional routes to political power through the Labour Party. She was elected Labour MP for Middlesbrough East in 1924, and supported the 1926 General Strike. In the 1929–31 Labour government, she served as PPS to the junior Health Minister. She made a connection with a young female member and activist

Wilkinson marching with the Jarrow marchers

Jennie Lee. Following her defeat at Middlesbrough in 1931, Wilkinson became a prolific journalist and writer, before returning to parliament as Jarrow's MP in

1935. She was a strong advocate for the Republican government in the Spanish Civil War, and made several visits to the battle zones.

In October 2016, Wilkinson was chosen in a public vote to be the subject of the first female statue in Middlesbrough.

Esther Roper (1868–1938): suffragist and trade unionist

Life that is love is God
- Sappho

Esther Roper (1868–1938) was a suffragist and social justice campaigner who championed the fight for equal employment and voting rights for working-class women. Although she conducted most of her education and subsequent work in Manchester, she was born near Chorley, the daughter of Edward Roper, a factory hand who later became a missionary, and Annie Roper, the daughter of Irish immigrants. She was educated by the Church Missionary Society.

Esther was one of the first women to study for a degree at Owens College and, according to Sonja Tiernan, was in 1886 admitted as part of a trial to establish whether females could study without harm to their mental or physical health[4]. In 1897 with fellow student Marion Ledward, she founded and edited *Iris*, a newsletter for female students which highlighted issues impacting on women's education, and encouraged networking between current and former students[5].

In 1891 Roper graduated from Owen's College with a First in Latin, English Literature and Political Economy. She kept in touch with the college, becoming a leading member of its women-only Social Debating Society. In 1895 she helped establish the Manchester University Settlement in Ancoats to offer education and cultural opportunities to the local working poor.

In 1896 she met Irish poet and aristocrat Eva Gore-Booth in Italy who gave up a life of privilege to move in with Roper in a terraced house in Rusholme, Manchester. Roper and Gore-Booth were vegetarians. In the late 1800s and early 1900s they helped to organize groups of female flower-sellers, circus performers, barmaids and coal pit-brow workers when their right to work was threatened by new legislation.

They argued that women's livelihoods were at stake, that women were capable of making their own decisions about how they were employed, and working women's lack of vote left them disempowered in the workplace. In 1900 they founded and edited the *Women's Labour News*, aimed at uniting women workers.

In 1903, the couple helped to found the Lancashire and Cheshire Women's Textile and Other Workers Representation Committee, which organized the campaign of the first women's suffrage candidate to stand in a general election. In 1905, Roper became secretary of the National Industrial & Professional Women's Suffrage Society. From 1906 Roper and Gore-Booth distanced themselves from Pankhurst's Women's Social and Political Union. They disagreed with the use of militant tactics and Emmeline Pankhurst's disinterest in campaigning for working-class women's rights.

They were prominent pacifists during the First World War, working in the International Committee of Women for Permanent Peace. Among other things they helped support the wives and children of imprisoned conscientious objectors. After the war they became members of the Committee for the Abolition of Capital Punishment and worked for prison reform.

Shena Simon, Baroness Simon of Wythenshawe (1883–1972)

Shena Simon was clearly a high achiever committed to improving education for working class women and achieving a higher degree of social equality for them and decent housing with decent facilities

In 1911 Shena Simon became secretary of a committee for safeguarding women's rights under David Lloyd George's National Insurance Act 1911. Her husband was Lord Mayor of Manchester from 1921 to 1922. As Lady Mayoress, Simon upset the apple cart by refusing to attend a function at St Mary's Hospital for Women because there were no women on the Board or among the medical staff.

In 1926, Shena and Ernest Simon bought from the Tattons and then donated Wythenshawe Park to the city of Manchester for use of the people living on the Wythenshawe estate. The couple stipulated that the park 'be forever kept as an open space for the people of Manchester'. She was a firm advocate of parks for the people and observed that there was a severe shortage of such open space in Manchester. Nowadays Wythenshawe has twelve parks and 18 woodland areas including Wythenshawe Park, which was designated a Local Nature Reserve in 2011. It covers over 270 acres of green space and is home to Manchester's only community farm, Wythenshawe Community Farm. At the centre of the park is the historic Wythenshawe Hall with its Civil War and Tatton heritage. The park also has riding stables, a horticulture centre, children's play area, athletics track, football pitches, tennis courts, bowls and golfing facilities.

In 1931, Wythenshawe was transferred to the City of Manchester, which had begun building a large new housing estate there in the 1920s with an area of approximately 11 square miles making it the largest council estate in Europe. Shena Simon devoted much energy to planning the Wythenshawe housing estate. It was intended as a "garden city", where people could be rehoused away from the insufferable and insanitary conditions prevailing in industrial Manchester. The estate was initially built without many shops, amenities or services, and there was very little employment available in the area. Although Northenden already had a shopping area on Palatine Road, the earliest new shops were built in the 1930s. It took decades for some areas of Wythenshawe to get their own neighbourhood shops, which meant residents had to travel or visit a mobile shop van.

Shena Simon was clearly a high achiever committed to improving education for working class women and achieving a higher degree of social equality for them and decent housing with decent facilities; here are some of the high points in the work she was able to do for Manchester and the people of Manchester:

- She joined Margaret MacDonald in the National Union for Women Workers
- She was an active member of the WPSU
- She founded the Manchester & Salford Women's Citizen Association
- Once on the Manchester Council Education Committee she fought against cuts, for the abolition of school fees, for comprehensive schools and for married women to be able to remain in post as teachers.

Kathleen Ollerenshaw, Withington

Dame Kathleen Mary Ollerenshaw, DBE (née Timpson (1912 – 2014) was a prominent British mathematician and politician who was Lord Mayor of Manchester from 1975 to 1976. She was born at 1 Parkgate Avenue in Withington, where she attended the Montessori Lady Barn House School (1918–26). She was a grandchild of the founder of the Timpson shoe repair business, who had moved to Manchester from Kettering and established the business there by 1870.

Ollerenshaw became completely deaf at age 12 and was taught to lip read by the expert Professor Alexander Ewing at the University of Manchester, determined to overcome the prejudice and lack of provision. Kathleen had caught a cold while on holiday when aged eight and this aggravated a family genetic disorder, otosclerosis.

She gravitated toward the study of mathematics because it requires no dependence on hearing, as she herself says:

Nearly all mathematic equations and diagrams are found in books or are shown on a blackboard as the teacher speaks. Answers are written down. Learning mathematics is rarely dependent on the spoken word.

Maths apart she also was an able hockey player and rose to captain at Somerville College, Oxford. Dancing too was very much on her social agenda.

Kathleen took a First and started work at the Shirley Institute in Manchester, a prominent textile research centre, using her skills in statistics in work on the waterproofing of military equipment.

After World War II, the Ollerenshaws moved to Manchester, where Kathleen worked as a part-time lecturer in the mathematics department at Manchester University while raising her children and continuing her work on lattices. In 1949, at the age of 37, she received her first effective hearing aid.

When not being a mother and/or an academic, Ollerenshaw served as a Conservative Councillor for Rusholme for twenty-five years (1954–79), a member of the city council's finance committee (1968–71), a chairman of the education committee of the Association of Municipal Corporations (1967–71), Lord Mayor of Manchester (1975–76), High Sheriff of Greater Manchester from 1978 to 1979, and the prime motivator in the creation of the Royal Northern College of Music. She was made a Freeman of the City of Manchester.

An avid amateur astronomer, Ollerenshaw donated her telescope to Lancaster University, and an observatory there bears her name. She was an honorary member of the Manchester Astronomical Society and held the post of vice-president for many years.

Kathleen Ollerenshaw died 10 August 2014 (aged 101) at Didsbury.

Dame Kathleen heading for the stars

Louise Da-Cocodia MBE, BEM, JP (1934 – 2008)

"deep in my mind is my commitment to bridge the gap which has led to the blacks being treated as inferior".

Born in Saint Catherine, Jamaica, Louise Da-Cocodia moved to Britain in 1955 to train as a nurse, invited as part of a government overseas recruitment drive to staff the recently established National Health Service. As a nurse-in-training, she often encountered odious racism from colleagues and patients but in

1958 she rose above the barbaric behaviour and qualified as a prestigious Staff Registered Nurse, and so began a nursing career spanning 31 years[6].

In 1966 she was appointed as Assistant Superintendent of District Nurses, the first black senior nursing officer in Manchester when even as a manager she had to put up with racist remarks from colleagues along the lines of "Those black [so and so's] coming here and giving us orders!" These experiences of prejudice inspired Louise to dedicate herself to tackling race equality issues: "deep in my mind is my commitment to bridge the gap which has led to the blacks being treated as inferior"[7].

In the 1960s and 1970s, she served on regional Race Relations Board committees (later known as the Commission for Racial Equality, handling complaints brought under new anti-discrimination laws such as the Race Relations Act 1965. In 1981 she helped transport victims of the Moss Side riots to hospital, and later sat on the Hytner Inquiry Panel investigating the causes of the unrest[8]. In 1984 she published a paper in the *International Journal of Social Psychiatry* exploring the effects of racism in nursing.

From 1984, Louise served three terms as Chair of the West Indian Organisation Co-ordinating Committee. Here are more of Louise's seemingly endless list of achievements:

- Served on a number of governing boards and committees, including Manchester Health Authority, Voluntary Action Manchester, and Manchester Metropolitan University.
- She was also a lay inspector at the Crown Prosecution Service, and also a Justice of the Peace.
- In 1990 she was nominated to the Manchester Magistrates' Bench, where she served for 14 years.
- In 1999 she was appointed Deputy Lieutenant of Manchester.
- She co-founded and steered a number of community enterprise schemes, including the Cariocca Education Trust and Arawak Walton Housing Association.
- She was also a founder member of Moss Side and Hulme Women's Action Forum, the Agency for Economic Development in Manchester[9].

Louise Da-Cocodia always strove to promote equality of opportunity for Manchester's inner-city residents in housing, education and employment, stating that she was inspired by an aim

"…to help young Black people understand that this is their home, this is the society they live in, and that they have a part to play in developing it. Young Black people need role models around, not necessarily high-profile ones…"[10]

By the way…
Racism and prejudice were faced by the many Louise da-Cocodias of the Windrush generation.

One such woman who answered the call was Louise Da-Cocodia (1934–2008). She arrived in Britain in 1955 to begin her training as a nurse at St. Olave's hospital in London. The Ahmed Iqbal Ullah Race Relations Resource Centre, the collections of which are held in Manchester's Central Library, holds the transcripts of an oral history project called 'Roots Family History'. For this project, post-war first- and second-generation Caribbean immigrants, then living in Manchester, were interviewed about their experiences and how they adapted to life from one island to another. Louise discusses her experience as one of only a few black women at the time training to be nurses in the NHS, by then only in its seventh year, the difficulties and discrimination she and her peers faced, but also the pride that she took in her work.

The article goes on to tell us how Louise always took pride in her work and strove to expand her knowledge and training, but nevertheless, she was, unfortunately, one of the many black women who was subjected to discrimination based on the colour of her skin; this was not recognised as racism at the time, and was accepted as the norm. Black women were expected to "take a lot on the chin"; Louise also recalled how the white nurses she worked with often got preferential treatment, in that they were given the easier jobs, while black nurses like herself would typically be asked to do the 'worst' work, such as cleaning soiled sheets and emptying bedpans. But to complain about this treatment would be "telling tales".

The article concludes that the prejudice that black nurses received came also from the patients; typically coming from older patients, racial slurs and ignorance were often regular features in the work; some would object to their treatment being given by black nurses, while others became hysterical that they had merely been touched by black hands (keep your dirty hands off me), or often they just carried the ignorant belief that Jamaica and the West Indies were in Africa. We can add instances of faeces being hurled at black nurses and white doctors shunning black nurses when it came to delegation.

Sunny Lowry MBE (1911–2008)

> *Sunny was unable to compete against the men. But it wasn't just the men: men and women from different social classes were segregated as well*

Sunny Lowry MBE (1911–2008) was born in Longsight, daughter of a fish wholesaler from Levenshulme, and was the seventh British woman to swim the English Channel, in 1933[11]. Sunny was raised with her four brothers and sisters on Kirkmanshulme Lane.

Lowry, while a student at Manchester High School for Girls, joined the Victoria Ladies Swimming Club at Victoria Baths (also known as Hathersage

Sunny and Jabez training

Baths) around 1920, but it only offered single-sex swimming sessions so she trained with her sister at Levenshulme baths so that she could attempt distance swimming competitions on Windermere. She also practised distance swimming in the sea at her parents' holiday home in Rhos-on-Sea in North Wales. On one occasion she swam from her home to Colwyn Bay and back again.

Her father suggested that she train to swim the Channel. This she did, choosing Westgate on Sea near Margate in Kent as a good venue.

Sunny's trainer in Kent was Jabez Wolffe who had put her on a high protein diet (including eating 40 eggs a week in omelettes).[12] She trained for 3 or 4 hours a day in the build up to her first attempt.

Her first attempt was from England to France and took place on 10 August 1932. She got quite close to the French coast but eventually the strong east–west currents from France prevented her from finishing.

Making her third attempt on 28 August 1933, Sunny, then aged 22, successfully swam from Cap Gris Nez to St Margaret's Bay, Dover; the swim took her 15 hours 41 minutes. The flag she made to accompany her swim featured the Manchester bee, the red rose of Lancashire and the initials LSC, Levenshulme Swimming Club.

Lowry was a determined and strong-minded woman as demonstrated by her rejection of the customary heavy wool one-piece swimsuit in favour of a, at the time risqué, lighter crimson two-piece suit. For this she was berated as being a "harlot" for baring her knees.[3] Sunny recalls the reaction her daring outfit provoked:

"We were training once at Margate and I kept having to come out of the water and I was showing about an inch of flesh all the way round. A lady came to me and she said 'I'll report you to the police, you are indecent!'"

This outrageous swimsuit is now on display at the Dover Museum "Swimming The Channel" exhibition.

Elizabeth Wolstenholme-Elmy (1833 - 1918)
Manchester's Free Love Advocate and Feminist

> *Elizabeth was especially keen to expose marital rape for what it was: a legal inequality and a form of sex slavery.*

Wolstenholme-Elmy spent the best part of her life as a campaigner and organiser, significant in the history of women's suffrage in the United Kingdom. She published essays and some poetry, using the pseudonyms 'E' and 'Ignota'; she was born in Cheetham Hill and grew up in Eccles. While her elder brother Joseph (1829–1891), received a good education and became a professor of mathematics at Cambridge University, Elizabeth had to make do with two years at Fulneck Moravian School but, not to be deterred, she continued learning what she could, and became headmistress of a private girls' boarding school in Boothstown near Worsely. She stayed there until May 1867, when she moved school to Congleton, Cheshire.

Sarah Irving tells that as an advocate of 'free love', a pacifist and more controversially a secularist, the Victorian feminist Elizabeth Wolstenholme-Elmy did not lead a conventional life. Born in Eccles in 1833 and self-educated, she went on to become a significant pioneer of the British women's emancipation movement. She was at the heart of almost every Victorian feminist campaign ranging from the demand for better education, the right to vote and the rights of prostitutes to the sensitive issue of marital rape[13].

The result of this unconventionality, and of operating outside the social norms of the day, was that

Emmeline Pankhurst and Elizabeth Wolstenholme-Elmy in 1908

Unfortunately, her rather forthright nature as well as the scandal surrounding her pregnancy out of wedlock meant that she was marginalised in official histories. In accounts by the Pankhurst family, she is unfairly portrayed as a bad mother, a scandalous 'free love' secularist; her partner Ben Elmy is painted as a cruel and unfaithful man. Maureen Wright, who teaches history at the University of Portsmouth, wanted to challenge that misrepresentation with a more balanced look at Wolstenholme-Elmy's life[14].

Maureen Wright identifies a life-changing moment in Elizabeth's young life:

But Elizabeth defied her guardian and studied privately, preparing herself to be a governess and, latterly, headmistress of her own girls' school. She had no desire to remain in the domestic realm. She placed her commitment to feminism from the moment when, acting as a bridesmaid aged 17, she fully realised what marriage meant for women – a "lifelong sentence of pauperism and dependence" with no control over their actions or autonomy over their own bodies[15].

Wright makes the significant point that regarding her work at The Grange, it's clear too that the curriculum she taught was not one only of female "accomplishments" (such as singing, dancing and drawing) but included political economy, mathematics and other skills thought to be to 'masculine' in nature for a girls' school. Elizabeth sought to fit her girls for not only the world of marriage and motherhood, but for the world of work, and many of them went on to become headmistresses of schools.

Here are more of Elizabeth's many contributions to female emancipation and empowerment:

- Member of the Manchester National Society for Women's Suffrage, the Manchester Branch of the Society for the Employment of Women and the Northern Counties League for the Repeal of the Contagious Diseases Acts.
- Formed the Manchester branch of the Society for Promoting the Employment of Women in 1865
- Founded the Manchester Committee for the Enfranchisement of Women in 1866
- She was a founder member of the Married Women's Property Committee (MWPC), established in 1867/8 to campaign for the rights of women in marriage and was its Secretary until the passage of the Married Women's Property Act, 1882.
- In 1867, Wolstenholme represented Manchester on the newly formed North of England Council for Promoting the Higher Education of Women.
- Executive Committee member of the Ladies' National Association for the Repeal of the Contagious Diseases Acts (LNA) from 1870.
- From 1871–74 she was Secretary of the Vigilance Association for the Defence of Personal Rights (VADPR).

It was, however, Elizabeth's secularism that caused the greatest challenges for many of her contemporaries: as a secularist she was an advocate of 'free love', a concept which became particularly problematic when she fell pregnant. Living together while un-wed obviously subverted the staid moral structures of mid-Victorian society.

We have seen how Elizabeth was especially keen to expose marital rape for what it was: a legal inequality and a form of sex slavery. Why did she feel so strongly about this issue? Maureen Wright explains:

Elizabeth's abhorrence of marital rape became clear in 1880, when she stood on the platform of the London Dialectical Society to declare her desire to see the practice criminalised. Her opposition was in part built on personal reasons and a desire to see a legal inequality quashed.

Wives were often beaten or starved for non-compliance or, as evidence from one notable legal case of 1891 shows, imprisoned against their will. Elizabeth saw the crime of marital rape as one common to women of all classes, and thus a cause of unity. At a moment when even polite society was concerned with the ever-increasing rise in sexually transmitted diseases she found a receptive audience, in some quarters, for her views…

Print of the Peterloo massacre published by Richard Carlile 1819 showing Mary Fildes in full flow.

Of all the disadvantages married women faced Elizabeth believed this 'sex slavery', as she termed it, to be the worst. For all her efforts, Elizabeth did not see a law passed against it in her lifetime – in fact this did not pass the Statute Book for another 100 years, in 1991.

Mary Fildes

how ironic when Corruption did all the trampling on Justice that day

People wonder when they look at contemporary images of the Peterloo atrocity who that brave and committed woman was up there on the stage passionately waving her banner and encouraging the crowd? Standing with the main act, speaker Henry 'Orator' Hunt, 27-year-old Mary Fildes is up there dressed in Sunday-best white, gripping her banner pole, and sporting a red Cap of Liberty, with her banner depicting Justice triumphant with Corruption underfoot: how ironic when Corruption did all the trampling on Justice that day. Fildes was president of the Manchester Female Reform Union and mother of five children. Her prominent position on the platform and her exhortations would make her a target of violence.

Katherine Connelly, in her article *The Women of Peterloo*, explains how the special constables, who arrived to arrest the speakers, beat her with their truncheons. When she tried to escape from the platform her dress caught on a nail and, whilst trapped, suspended above the ground, she was slashed with a sabre by a soldier who seized her banner as a trophy.

'To Henry Hunt, Esq., as chairman of the meeting assembled in St. Peter's Field, Manchester, sixteenth day of August, 1819, and to the female Reformers of Manchester and the adjacent towns who were exposed to and suffered from the wanton and fiendish attack made on them by that brutal armed force, the Manchester and Cheshire Yeomanry Cavalry, this plate is dedicated by their fellow labourer, Richard Carlile.'

A coloured engraving that depicts the Peterloo Massacre (military suppression of a demonstration in Manchester, England by cavalry charge on August 16, 1819 with loss of life) in Manchester, England. All the poles from which banners are flying have Phrygian caps or liberty caps on top. Not all the details strictly accord with contemporary descriptions; the banner the woman is holding should read: Female Reformers of Roynton — "Let us die like men and not be sold like slaves".

Mary Fildes' obtrusiveness on the platform, and the way she was targeted by the authorities, testified to the vital role that women played in this struggle for democracy.[16]

1. *Bondfield was the first woman cabinet minister in the first Labour Government in 1924*
2. *See Antrobus p. 20–21*
3. *See the highly informative and detailed https://maryquaileclub.wordpress.com/who-was-mary-quaile/ for full details of Mary's trade union career.*
4. *Tiernan, Sonja (2012). 'Eva Gore-Booth: An Image of Such Politics. Manchester University Press. pp. 33–34.*
5. *"Iris, University of Manchester Publications Collection, ref GB 133 UMP/2/5; GB 133 Former reference: UA/73". Archives Hub*
6. *Mrs Louise Adassa Da-Cocodia: CV" (PDF). Cariocca.com.*
7. *Roots Oral History Project, Rude Awakening: African-Caribbean Settlers in Manchester, An Account*
8. *Taylor, Paul (6 July 2006). "News Special: Moss Side Riots 25 years on". Manchester Evening News.*
9. *"The Bright Star", Eulogy by Sarah Da-Cocodia; see also transcript of Louise Da-Cocodia's speech "West Indians in Manchester" at Manchester Literary & Philosophical Society April 1996 in Manchester Memoirs, Volumes 134–135, Page 72.*
10. *"Jamaicans in UK Pay Respects to Social Activist – Jamaica Information Service". Jis.gov.jm. 2 April 2008.*
11. *The Channel Swimming Association record her as the 15th person, and the 7th woman to swim the channel.*
12. *Elizabeth's two years of secondary education drew to a close when she was just 16, her uncle having declared that by then she had 'learnt everything it was necessary for a woman to know'.*
13. *Irving, Sarah, Elizabeth Wolstenholme-Elmy: Manchester's Free Love Advocate and Secular Feminist (April 8, 2012). – Manchester's Radical History (wordpress.com)*
14. *In her Elizabeth Wolstenholme Elmy and the Victorian Feminist Movement – The biography of an insurgent woman, Wright portrays the complex and also contradictory nature of her subject. The book is broken down into eight chapters which chart Elizabeth Wolstenholme Elmy's life from her birth to her death at the age of 84 in March 1918 – just days after hearing the good news that women had been granted the right to vote.*
15. *Arwa Aburawa interviewed Maureen Wright for Manchester Radical History: 'Elizabeth established precisely such a school, at The Grange in Boothstown Road, which catered for between 12–16 teenage pupils. In the spring of 1867 she moved her school to Moody Hall, a substantial Georgian residence in the town of Congleton where she continued in her role of Headmistress for another 4 years. Before her move to Cheshire Elizabeth founded the Manchester Schoolmistresses Association in 1865, and her pupils were among the first to sit the Cambridge Local Examination'.*
16. *https://www.counterfire.org/article/the-women-of-peterloo/#:~:text=The%20woman's%20name%20was%20Mary,beat%20her%20with%20their%20truncheons.*

EPILOGUE:
Gone...but never forgotten

Pierre Adolphe Valette (1876–1942)

Just as Lowry is synonymous with life in and around Salford, so Valette is with industrial, wet and smoggy Manchester.

In 1905 Salford artist L. S. Lowry secured a place at the Manchester Municipal College of Art, where he studied under the newly-arrived French Impressionist artist Adolphe Vallette. Valette arrived in England in 1904 and studied at the Birkbeck Institute, now part of the University of London. In 1905 he travelled to the North West where he designed greetings cards and calendars for a Manchester printing company. He attended evening classes at Manchester Municipal School of Art and in 1907 he joined the staff as a teacher. The Manchester Municipal College of Art is today part of the Manchester Metropolitan University and on the outside of the Grosvenor Building on Cavendish Street is a blue plaque commemorating Valette. Just as Lowry is synonymous with life in and around Salford, so Valette is with industrial, wet and smoggy Manchester.

One of its many treasures, Manchester Art Gallery has a room devoted to Valette where the viewer may compare some of his paintings with some of Lowry's, and judge to what extent Lowry's own style was influenced by him and by French Impressionism generally.

Albert Square' by Valette in Manchester Art Gallery

The Rialto, Broughton

For the most part of the 20th Century, The Rialto was the centre of everything in North Manchester and Salford – both for good and bad, light and dark…

The art deco Rialto which opened in 1927 is on the corner of Bury New Road and Great Cheetham Road; it boasts a heritage second to none with its 1,400 seats, nine shops, billiard hall, dance hall and assembly rooms. Its many incarnations included a spell as Potters Snooker Club where Alex Higgins, Jimmy White and John Virgo practiced, sometimes (un) ably assisted by George Best.

John Cooper Clarke lived originally above Friedman's chemist on the corner of Bury New Road and Great Cheetham Street East, opposite the Rialto cinema. Later, he lived on Camp Street and St Paul's Road, and was often seen walking his mum's dog along Bury New Road.

For the full hilarious story of John's early-ish years read his brilliant autobiography, *I Wanna Be Yours*, which includes the quote of all time from John's mum… 'You can't have everything – where would you put it?' and loads about Higher Broughton – an area that "seemed to house a disproportionately large number of the criminally insane".

Valette's 'York Street Leading to Charles Street'

'You can't have everything – where would you put it?'

John reckons the Graham Gouldman-written Hollies smash hit, Bus Stop, was written about the one outside his parent's flat, and that Roger Moore rented digs across the road[1].

Mike Leigh, in accepting the Freedom of Salford in 2019, cited The Rialto cinema as a major influence…"or as it was known the Riot Alto" he recalled "This was my alma mater. Here I savoured and cherished and was inspired by all manner of movies… This was when I would sit in the dark and think 'Wouldn't it be great if you could have a film where actors were like real people'."

"I've discovered over and over that he makes films at the centre of which he puts the sort of people who most other people are thankful not to be", states actor Timothy Spall in the book Mike Leigh on Mike Leigh "He gives them nobility. Nobody makes the mundane more poetic than Mike."

In 1963, Elkie Brooks worked as a singer at the Whisky A Go-Go Club at the Rialto, owned by Billy Charvin, beating fifty other girls in an audition, and there met Michael Parkinson, a news reader at the time, who got her on Granada TV…

"I was able to work at the Whisky pretty much every night" she wrote in her autobiography, *Finding My Voice*…the other guys would come over to Mum and Dad's on Sunday, and some evenings after work, and we would learn about fifteen new songs a week which, thinking back, was quite an achievement."

Originally from Castleton Road, Elkie lived at 119 Cavendish Road, just off Bury New Road on the Prestwich/Salford border during her childhood.

At the back of The Rialto was the Hilton Street rehearsal space, where Joy Division and A Certain Ratio shared a room…

Sadly the Rialto went the way of many other treasures and cultural beacons; after passing through the age of bingo it was demolished to make way for a MacDonalds. There you go…that's progress for you.

Joy Division

---

1. *https://www.burynewroad.org/salford/john-cooper-clarke/.*

The Athenaeum, Princess Street

> *a society for the "advancement and diffusion of knowledge". As such it is part of that great tradition the city enjoys for the spreading of knowledge to all strata of society.*

The Athenaeum was on Princess Street but has now been subsumed by and connected to Manchester Art Gallery. The club was built for the Manchester Athenaeum, a society for the "advancement and diffusion of knowledge", in 1837. As such it is part of that great tradition the city enjoys for the spreading of knowledge to all strata of society. The University and the Mechanics' Institute (later UMIST) are part of that tradition with the latter catering more for the knowledge hungry working man eager to better himself while the Athenaeum was more for the middle classes – merchants, professionals and intellectuals. The society, founded in 1835, first met in the Royal Manchester Institution next door until funds had been raised for a purpose-built building, the aim of which was to provide 'a facility for intellectual cultivation'. Dickens and Disraeli spoke there while Richard Cobden was a member.

Membership probably peaked at 1,400 in the 1840s; they could access a library of 6,000 volumes and learn languages or enjoy musical events, poetry readings and readings by notable authors.

The Clarion Café, 50c Market Street

> *the Tenants' Defence Association met here on 27 January 1916 to discuss the issue of ever rising rents – an issue which still plagues us today*

From October 31, 1908 if you ventured upstairs at 50c Market Street you would find yourself in the Clarion Café, with as many as 150 other diners, tea or coffee drinkers and like-minded people engaged in conversation about working class and socialist politics and life. As well as a place to eat and drink (including vegetarian meals), the Clarion Café also offered a venue for political meetings and social events, for example, the Tenants' Defence Association met here on 27 January 1916 to discuss the issue of rising rents – an issue which still plagues us today.

The Clarion movement emerged in 1891 with the publication of the Clarion newspaper by Robert Blatchford, a paper which promoted socialism and led to the formation of a number of social organisations including the famous Cycling Club but also rambling clubs and choirs, which came together as the Clarion Vocal Union and held its first united concert at Manchester's Free Trade Hall in May 1899.

The Clarion Cafés were opened in various northern towns and cities. The distinctive decoration owed much to the design ideas of William Morris and an illustrated frieze around the upper part of the walls was created by the Birmingham artist Bernard Sleigh to illustrate Morris's story "The King's Lesson".

The Clarion Café Morris Room

John Marsden, writing in the Manchester and Lancashire family History Society website in January 20123 tells that

On the floor above the restaurant was the Clarion Club's club room. Here, Clarion members, who paid a subscription between 5s and 10s ((25p to 50p) per annum could enjoy a comfortable lounge with similarly impressive decor, including murals by the well-known artist Walter Crane. While access to the club room was limited to Clarion members, guests could be admitted... including, on 26 March 1911 Keir Hardie, the (then) former Labour Party leader [https://mlfhs.uk/blog/the-clarion-café].

Marsden adds that 'many Clarion members and early socialists were vegetarian or "fruitarian" (perhaps "vegan") and the restaurant proudly announced "Vegetarian dishes a speciality" in its newspaper advertisements.

But it was by no means all politics and two veg.

The Manchester Evening News of 10 October 1910 announced "Play in the Manchester v City match will commence at 6:30 p.m., at the Clarion Cafe, Market-street. Visitors are cordially invited." This was not, however, a football derby but an opening fixture in the Lancashire Draughts League's programme. On Christmas eve the same year, the cafe hosted a meeting of some 70 members of the Dickens Fellowship and served them a potato pie supper. The Manchester Shakespeare Society also met there in April 1914.

The Manchester Clarion Cafe closed around 1936 and was demolished. The name, however, lives on, appropriately, in the Clarion Cafe at the People's History Museum in Manchester.

All is not lost, however:
the Pendle Clarion House was built in 1912 for Nelson Independent Labour Party and is the last remaining house of many across the country. These houses provided a place in the countryside for people to enjoy fresh air and comradeship, a tradition that continues to this day as it attracts

many walkers and cyclists. Set on Jinny Lane near Newchurch in Pendle …the house is open on Sundays throughout the year from 10.30 to 4.00. For more information visit www.clarionhouse.org.uk

Further reading

Denis Pye, "Fellowship Is Life: the Bolton Clarion Cycling Club and the Clarion Movement 1896–1914", North West Labour History Journal 10

Denis Pye, "Charlie Reekie's Dream, the story of the Manchester Clarion Clubhouses 1897–1951", North West Labour History Journal 17

Denis Pye, Socialism, Fellowship and Food, the Manchester Clarion Café 1908–1936, North West Labour History Journal 21

John Motson OBE (KO 1945 – FT 2023)

When Martin Buchan of Manchester United climbed the steps of Wembley Stadium to receive the trophy, Motson commented that it was "fitting that a man called Buchan should be the first to climb the 39 steps". Say no more…

10 February 2008 Manchester United V Manchester City gordonflood

It is a little-known fact – and one that 'Motty Mastermind' John Motson would surely have delighted in – that 'Motty' was born in Salford. Kicking off as a television commentator with the BBC in 1971, he commentated on over 2000 games on television and radio. His trademark 'Motty' coat is on display in the Museum of Football.

Motson's first FA Cup Final was the 1977 match between Manchester United and Liverpool. Motson was drafted in as a late replacement for David Coleman, who was in a contractual dispute with the BBC. When Martin Buchan of Manchester United climbed the steps of Wembley Stadium to receive the trophy, Motson commented that it was "fitting that a man called Buchan should be the first to climb the 39 steps". Say no more…

By the way…

Where's Kenneth Wolstenholme when you need him?

That other great commentator, Kenneth Wolstenholme, was born in Salford's Worsely, in Light Oaks Road to be precise. Before football, Wolstenholme (1920–2002) was a pilot in World War 2 flying over 100 sorties over Nazi Germany in Bristol Blenheims and Mosquitos, earning a DFC and Bar for his troubles. He will, of course, be remembered for those unforgettable words he delivered in the last minute of the 1966 World Cup Final which West Ham (sorry, England) won 4-2 against West Germany:

Some people are on the pitch… they think it's all over [Geofff Hurst slams the ball into the back of the net]… it is now !

The Tib Street Horn

The Big Horn or the Tib Street Horn was a trombone-shaped public sculpture. According to Terry Wyke, the sculpture resembles a trombone or some such other serpent-like musical instrument, with attached objects.[1] It was designed by David Kemp, a Cornish artist, and constructed near a former Victorian hat factory. Built from welded steel and galvanised ducting, it was 33 ft tall and 49 ft long, intended as a gateway sculpture to symbolise the growth of the city's Northern Quarter.

Tib Street Horn. On top of the remains of an old Victorian hat factory, opposite Afflecks. Photograph by Mike Peel (www.mikepeel.net).

1. Wyke, Terry (2004). *Public sculpture of Greater Manchester*. Liverpool, p. 64.

The Haçienda

Downstairs was a cocktail bar called The Gay Traitor, which referred to Anthony Blunt, a British art historian who spied for the Soviet Union.

The Haçienda was a nightclub and music venue which became famous during the Madchester years of the 1980s and early 1990s. The club was at 11–13, Whitworth Street West on the south side of the Rochdale Canal: before it was a club, the Haçienda was a yacht builder's shop and warehouse. Upstairs consisted of a stage, dance area, bar, cloakroom, cafeteria area and balcony with a DJ booth. Downstairs was a cocktail bar called The Gay Traitor, which referred to Anthony Blunt, a British art historian who spied for the Soviet Union. The two other bars, The Kim Philby and Hicks, were named after Blunt's fellow spies. From 1995, the lower cellar areas of the venue were converted to create the 5th Man, a smaller music venue.

The venue was instrumental in the careers of New Order, Happy Mondays, Oasis, The Stone Roses, 808 State, Chemical Brothers and Sub Sub. New Order provided much financial support, along with Tony Wilson at Factory Records, during the club's existence. Following a number of years of growing dereliction, the site was purchased from the receivers by Crosby Homes. They demolished the nightclub, and built the bland Haçienda Apartments. In 2010, Peter Hook had six bass guitars made using wood from The Haçienda's dancefloor. The fret boards have been made from dancefloor planks, so they have "stiletto marks and cigarette burns". Behind the flats and next to the Rochdale Canal a timeline depicts some of the bands that helped make the club, and themselves, famous - along with salient events in the club's history.

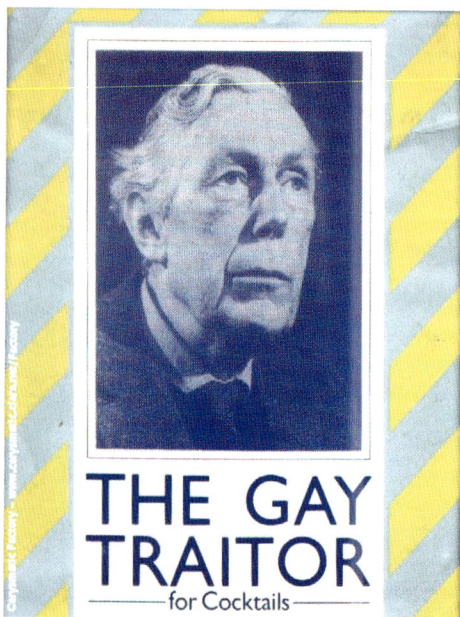

THE GAY TRAITOR COCKTAIL BAR. COCKTAIL LIST includes such delights as Death in the Afternoon (Pernod, Jim Beam and Sparkling Wine), Zero Hour (Brandy, Apricot Brandy, Creme-de-Menthe, Pernod), Jumping Jack Flash (Amphetamines and Barbiturates) and Molotov (Petrol, Rag, Milk Bottle) https://factoryrecords.org/cerysmatic/fac51gaytraitor.php

THE GAY TRAITOR
for Cocktails

St John's Gardens

Why did football games used to begin at 3pm on a Saturday?

St John's Gardens is between Lower Byrom Street, Byrom Street and Quay Street. Previously occupied by St John's Church and its graveyard between 1769 and 1931, the site was redeveloped into a formal garden in 1932. It contains a central memorial to the church and the 22,000 people buried in its graveyard, whose tombstones have been covered over by 18 inches of soil except for that of John Owens, founder of Owen's College.

William Marsden is also buried there: we have him to thank for successfully campaigning for the introduction of a half-day holiday from midday for workers on Saturdays, and that's why football games used to begin at 3pm, giving workers time to clock off, get home, have dinner and a pint before the football.

The web site "Cotton Town" says of Marsden: "Manchester man William Marsden began a campaign for an early finish on Saturdays in the 1840s. It was stoutly resisted by mill owners, horrified at the thought of machinery lying idle. The campaign succeeded and Manchester operatives were the first to finish at noon on Saturday."

Lewis' Department Store, Market Street

Innovative they certainly were, pioneering a number of retail techniques

Established as a drapers in Liverpool in 1856, Lewis's Manchester 1877 store was followed by Birmingham and Sheffield; and the chain gained a reputation for innovative retailing techniques such as self-service and the world's first Christmas grotto. Promotions were ground-breaking, with one offering to 'pay the railway fare of visitors from a distance whose purchases amount to £2 and upwards'. The store can claim the first escalator in Manchester and the biggest soda fountain in the British Empire. You could walk round the place without being pressurised into a purchase; there was no credit – cash only and unusually the ground-breaking newspaper adverts quoted prices. It was not just retail either: the store employed 300 tailors and 300 cobblers. Lewis's ceased trading in Manchester in 2002 with the store becoming a Primark.

But in the old days, everything was by no means what it seemed on the surface, on the shop floor. Underground attractions were extremely popular with the sub-basement offering penny-in-the-slot machines, distorting mirrors and an Edison's phonograph. They were the first to organise concerts in department stores at 1d for 30 minutes or so, a by-product of these was the training ground they offered aspiring artists. It did not stop there: one particularly sensational production was an immersive Venetian theme in which shoppers were carried along a two-foot-deep version of the Grand Canal in a gondola, ducking under a

Manchester: Secret & Strange Places to Visit   303

A display in Lewis' department store. Manchester, 1947

Mancunian Bridge of Sighs and taking in the magnificent sights of Venice. The basement was flooded with two feet of water for the event.

Trafford Park was the first industrial estate in the world, designed to service the trade on the nearby Manchester Ship Canal. At its height it provided work for 70,000 people. The first mural was erected in 1982, replaced by the second in November 1993.

Let's let artist Walter Kershaw describe the story of his wonderful For *Walls with Tongues*:

"I was approached by a Trafford town planner; he said would I be interested in designing and painting a mural on the first big building in Trafford Park? I said, yes, and told him it would best be painted on eight by four, six mil. plywood sheets. I went down and measured it up: sixty-four feet wide and seventy-five feet high, eleven layers of scaffolding, pulleys and racks. So, I painted it in my studio helped by Brigitte Curtis and one or two other friends; they would do the blocking in and I'd do all the finished work, often with a sable brush. We used household gloss and it took four years to paint, and when it was finished it was nailed up on the

Walls with Tongues, Trafford Park 1978-1982.

wall by joiners. And then when the scaffolding was taken down it was unveiled by Denis Law in 1982. And it was fantastic!" The mural, the largest ever made in Britain, was paid for by the businesses in Trafford Park supplemented by Trafford Council and lasted the full shelf life that Walter estimated. There was a huge response by local people; the opening by Denis Law, just transferred to United from Turin, headlined national news – which he shared – to his huge delight – "with the Raising of the Mary Rose!"

Maine Road Football Stadium

> *Maine Road gets its name from a renaming of Dog Kennel Lane by members of the Temperance Movement, inspired by their 1853 Maine law.*

Originally known as the Hyde Road Ground, the ground is named after the road that formed its western boundary. Why Maine Road? Under the incendiary leadership of Portland's Neal Dow - known internationally as the "Father of Prohibition" – the state of Maine approved a total ban on the manufacture and sale of liquor in 1851. This so-called "Maine Law" remained in effect, in one form or another, until the repeal of National Prohibition in 1934. In 1853, this US Maine law inspired the United Kingdom Alliance - hard-line group of prohibitionists - to advocate, divisively, a similar law prohibiting the sale of alcohol in the UK. This was opposed by less radical temperance organisations who preferred moral persuasion to a legal ban. The impotence of legislation in this field became all too clear when the Sale of Beer Act 1854 which restricted Sunday opening hours had to be repealed, following widespread rioting. In 1859 a prototype prohibition bill was overwhelmingly defeated in the House of Commons. The former Manchester City FC football stadium, Maine Road, gets its name from a renaming of Dog Kennel Lane by members of the Temperance Movement, inspired by the 1853 Maine law.

Ena Sharples

One of the great TV characters of the 1960s. Ena (Violet Carson) struck fear into the hearts of the other characters (except maybe Elsie Tanner) in every episode. Cross her at your peril. Here is Ena in full flow with Minnie Caldwell and Martha Longhurst. Some quotes:

- "Modern is a word for whitewashing muck with modern morals, modern marriage, modern society." - Ena
- "If I had my way, I'd like to go like me mother did; she just sat up, broke wind, and died" - Ena
- 'Annie Walker doesn't have a muriel' - Hilda Ogden

Violet Carson as Ena Sharples. Coronation Street in black and white December 9, 1960 7pm – November 3, 1969. And then it went colour.

Maxine Peake, actress

Maxine Peake (b. 1974) Peake was born in Bolton; she joined the Octagon Youth Theatre in Bolton age 13, before the youth theatre of the Royal Exchange in Manchester. She later completed a two-year performing arts course at the Salford College of Technology. Peake was a member of the Communist Party of Britain Salford branch in her youth; as a teenager Peake played for Wigan Ladies rugby league team.

At 21, she obtained a place at (RADA). Peake has appeared in numerous television and stage productions, including Victoria Wood' *Dinnerladies*, Channel 4's *Shameless*, in the lead role of barrister Martha Costello in the BBC's legal drama *Silk*. In 2013, Peake was appointed an Associate Artist of the Royal Exchange Theatre in Manchester and starred as Nellie in Mike Leigh's 2018 film, *Peterloo*.

Peake is a feminist and socialist. In 2014 Peake won the first Bolton Socialist Club Outstanding Contribution to Socialism Award for using her work to oppose the government's "crippling austerity measures".

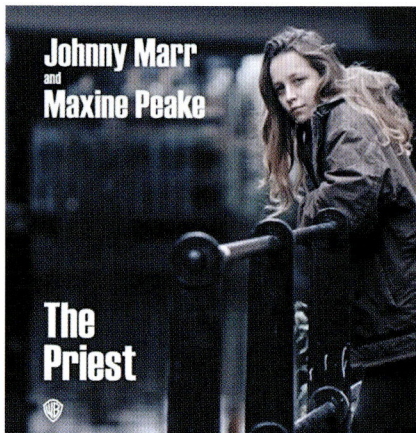

Single released in 2017, classified as poetry, indie rock, trip hop

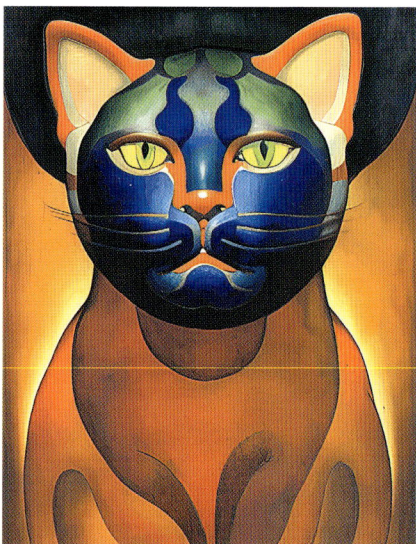

Cloisonne Cat Head Sculpture by Annie Swynnerton and Diego Rivera and Nicholas Roerich and Jean Delville - Creative Fabrica

Annie Swynnerton (1844–1933), Artist

Annie Louisa Swynnerton, ARA studied at Manchester School of Art and at the Académie Julian. **John Singer Sargent** admired her work and helped her to become the first elected woman member at the Royal Academy of Arts in 1922. Her main public collection of works are in Manchester Art Gallery; Annie was a close friend of leading suffragists of the day, not least the Pankhursts. **Susan Isabel Dacre** and Swynnerton shared a studio and in 1879, the two women founded the Manchester Society of Women Painters, which offered art education and exhibitions. **Emily Robinson** was also a member.

Louise Jane Jopling (1843 – 1933) was born in Manchester, the fifth of the

…in Lady Lever Art Gallery, Port Sunlight.

nine children of railway contractor **Thomas Smith "T.S." Goode** and his wife **Frances**. **Clara Clement** tells us that Jopling's *Five O'Clock Tea* was sold for £400 in 1874. Her *Five Sisters of York* was shown at the Philadelphia Exposition in 1876, and her The Modern Cinderella at the Paris Exposition of 1878[2]. 'she was not immune to the gender discrimination of her time: in 1883 she sought a portrait commission for 150 guineas, but lost it to **Sir John Everett Millais**, who was paid 1000 guineas for the same project[3].

Her social circle included James McNeill Whistler, Oscar Wilde, Kate Perugini (née Dickens) and Ellen Terry.

Louise Jopling was a long-term supporter of the National Union of Women's Suffrage Societies, and active in feminist causes. She served as a vice-president of the Healthy and Artistic Dress Union, a short-lived organization promoting dress reform during the 1890s and early 1900s.

---

2. Clara Erskine Clement, *Women in the Fine Arts from the Seventh Century B.C. to the Twentieth Century A.D.*, Charleston, SC, BiblioBazaar LLC, 2007; p. 177.

3. Elise Lawton, *Evelyn Pickering De Morgan and the Allegorical Body*, Madison, NJ, Fairleigh Dickinson University Press, 2002; p. 35.

MANCHESTER PUBS

The Old Nag's Head, 19 Jackson's Row

Just off Deansgate. A true nostalgia-fest with décor reminiscent of the Manchester glory days, especially of Manchester and George Best. In the 1960s it was a policeman's drinking pub. Four thousand pictures and other images on the wall tell the whole story revealingly well. CAMRA says:

> 'A classic Victorian pub interior with plenty of wood panelling, many photos and posters and a fine island bar and staircase. Access from both Jackson's Row and Lloyd Street. First floor provides pool room with four pool tables and function room with a second bar. Second floor has roof garden'.

The George Best chimney is stunning.

The Circus Tavern

Small is beautiful. You can find the Circus Tavern on the corner of Portland and Princess Streets. This is the smallest pub in Manchester. The bar counter may well be the smallest in Europe — it measures only a few feet across and is not much longer in length. All in all, the property measures no more than 500 square feet with a maximum capacity somewhere around 30 people. If that worries you, don't, because staff bring your drinks to you. Built in about 1790, it qualifies as one of the oldest pubs in Manchester, although it only became a pub in about 1840 when a brewery was built there.

The Temple Bar, 100 Great Bridgewater St

This occupies a former underground public toilets on Great Bridgewater Street. The Bar Review website says this about The Temple:

> 'The Temple (formerly The Temple of Convenience) is a Manchester institution! A converted public toilet (yes, that's right!!!), it's one of Manchester's smallest bars and is very popular due to it's amazing array of foreign bottled beers and a great jukebox packed with Manchester bands (many of whom drink regularly here)'.

> And from the ubiquitous Mr/Ms Anonymous… 'I had heard of the Temple after hearing Elbow's Guy Garvey sing (literally) its praises and what a cracking wee bar it is!'

The Marble Arch, 73 Rochdale Rd

The Marble Brewery is a microbrewery which brews cask ale from organic and vegetarian ingredients. The pub was built in 1888 in Ancoats with some exceptional features that survive today: a façade of polished red granite, a high, glazed ceiling, ceramic walls and a bar that slopes down the hill. CAMRA says:

> take a moment to look up to appreciate its impressively stacked roof and ornate chimneys. Then enjoy the grandeur of the eponymous front entrance…It was built in 1888 on the site of a previous 1829 pub as a show house pub for McKenna's Brewery and had electric lighting installed from the start. The fine barrel vaulted ceramic tiled ceiling and decorative frieze…were revealed again in the early 1980's…the mosaic sloping floor leading you inexorably to the bar and the glazed tile walls add to the splendour of the pub.

Sam's Chop House, Back Pool Fold/Chapel Walks

Who is that man at the bar? The informative website knows exactly who he is…

> If you have visited Sam's in the past 9 years, you will have seen a bloke at the bar. A very large, still kind of a bloke. He wears a hat, has a prominent nose and a weary expression. It's probably all the drinkers bumping into him. One finger rests on his chin as he seems to ponder the selection of whisky and brandy on the back bar.

A former proprietor, A.H. Knowles, relocated Sam's from Market Street to its current home; he was an art school friend of Lowry's. Taking his inspiration from the statue of Ernest Hemingway at El Floridita in Cuba, a later owner approached Preston-based sculptor Peter Hodgkinson who got to work to produce the Lowry you see at the bar today.

Albert's Schloss, Peter Street

A little bit of the Alps in Manchester, and a convincing, atmospheric Bavarian *bier-keller* experience. Originally built in 1910 as a multi-purpose hall for the Manchester and Salford Wesleyan Mission, the Albert Memorial Hall was designed by William James Morley (1847–1930).

FURTHER READING

Alexis-Martin, Becky, 'Radium', in Paul Dobraszczyk, *Manchester: Something Rich and Strange* pp. 238ff, Manchester 2020

Ang JL, Collis S, Dhillon B, Cackett P. *The Eye in Forensic Medicine: A Narrative Review*. Asia Pac J Ophthalmol (Phila). 2021 Sep 14;10(5):486–494

Antonovic, Janis (April 2021). "John Leigh, Lydia Becker and their shared botanical interests". *Archives of Natural History*. 48 (1): 62–76.

Antrobus, Helen, (2019) *First In The Fight: 20 Women Who Made Manchester, iNostalgia*

Atreya A, Ateriya N, Menezes RG. *The eye in forensic practice: In the dead*. Med Leg J. 2024 May 1

Blackburn, Helen. *Women's Suffrage: A Record of the Women's Suffrage Movement In The British Isles*, with biographical sketches of Miss Becker. Charleston: Nabu Press, 2013. (originally published 1902 by Williams & Norgate.)

Bondeson, Jan (1997), *A Cabinet of Medical Curiosities*, I. B. Taurus,

Bondeson, Jan (2001), *Buried Alive: the Terrifying History of our Most Primal Fear*, W. W. Norton & Company

Brazendale, David (2005), *Lancashire's Historic Halls*, Carnegie Publishing

Chrystal, Paul *The Pubs of Manchester* (in press)

Chrystal, Paul, *Bramhall Through Time*

Chrystal, Paul, *Old Fallowfield*

Chrystal, Paul, *Old Didsbury*

Chrystal, Paul, (2021) *A History of Britain in 100 Objects*

Chrystal, Paul, (2023) *Factory Girls and Climbing Boys: Women and Children at Work*, Barnsley

Chrystal, Paul, (2025) *The Book in the Ancient World: How the Wisdom of the Ages was Preserved*

Chrystal, Paul, (2021) *A History of the World in 100 Pandemics, Plagues & Epidemics*

Chrystal, Paul, (2024) *150 World-Changing Women*

Chrystal, Paul, (2019) *The Romans in the North of England*, Destinworld

Cooper, Glynis (2007) *Manchester's Suburbs*, Breedon Books

Cooper, Glynis (2005) *Salford: An Illustrated History*, Breedon Books Publishing

Dobson, Jessie (1953), "Some Eighteenth Century Experiments in Embalming", *Journal of the History of Medicine and Allied Sciences 8* (4): 431–441

Fox, Brian, W. (196) Christie's: Christie Hospital and Holt Radium Institute, *A Brief History of a World Famous Cancer Hospital*, Christie Hospital NHS Trust, Manchester

Gaydos J. *History of Wound Care: A Solution to Sepsis: The Carrel-Dakin Method*. Today's Wound Clinic. 2017;11:2 .

Gerstmeyer, K. et al. *The Last Image. on the History of Optography*, European Society of Cataract and Refractive Surgeons.

Herbert, Michael (2012). *Up Then Brave Women: Manchester's Radical Women* 1819 – 1918. North West Labour History Society, 2012.

Holton, Sandra Stanley (1996). *Suffrage Days: Stories from the Women's Suffrage Movement*. London

Keen W.W. *Treatment of War Wounds*. Philadelphia, 1918

King, Ray (2006), *Detonation: Rebirth of a City*, Clear Publications

Lesley-Dixon, Kenneth (2018), Northern Ireland: *The Troubles from the Provos to the Det* 1968–1998, Barnsley

Liddington, Jill (1978). *One Hand Tied Behind Us: The Rise of the Women's Suffrage Movement*. London

Ogbourne, Derek: *Optography and Optograms*, The College of Optometrists.

Ogbourne, Derek (2008). Encyclopedia of Optography. Muswell Press.

Parker J.E. (2001). "Lydia Becker's "School for Science": a challenge to domesticity". *Women's History Review*

Phillips, Melanie (2004). *The Ascent of Woman: A History of the Suffragette Movement and the Ideas Behind It*. London

Pye, Denis, "Fellowship Is Life: the Bolton Clarion Cycling Club and the Clarion Movement 1896–1914", *North West Labour History Journal* 10

Pye, Denis, *"Charlie Reekie's Dream, the story of the Manchester Clarion Clubhouses 1897–1951"*, North West Labour History Journal 17

Pye, Denis, *Socialism, Fellowship and Food, the Manchester Clarion Café* 1908–1936, North West Labour History Journal 21

Roberts, Richard Julian (1990). *"Preface"*. John Dee's Library Catalogue. London: The Bibliographical Society.

Roberts, Richard Julian ed. (2005). *"A John Dee Chronology, 1509–1609"*. Renaissance Man: The Reconstructed Libraries of European Scholars: 1450–1700 Series One: The Books and Manuscripts of John Dee, 1527–1608. Adam Matthew Publications.

Robinson, John Martin (1986), T*he Architecture of Northern England*, Macmillan

Sanctuary from the Trenches: *The Stamford Hospital at Dunham Massey*, National Trust, 2014

Sutton, Charles William (1901). "Becker, Lydia Ernestine". In Lee, Sidney (ed.). *Dictionary of National Biography (1st supplement)*. London

Whitfield, Roy (1988) *Frederick Engels in Manchester: The Search For A Shadow*, Manchester, Working Class Movement Library

Williams, Gwyndaf (2003), *The enterprising city centre: Manchester's development challenge*, Spon

Wright, Maureen (2011) *Elizabeth Wolstenholme Elmy and the Victorian Feminist Movement – The biography of an insurgent woman*. Manchester

APPENDIX 1:
Report on the Relief of the Manchester Sufferers

In April 2019 Janette Martin produced an article covering the above report for History Workshop; the report has massive significance in the social history of Manchester, indeed the social history of the nation. *https://www. historyworkshop.org.uk/violence/radical-object-report-on-the-relief-of-the-manchester-sufferers/*

She introduces it as follows:
'a poignant and powerful alphabetical list of injuries received by people attending a political meeting in 1819. It is a shocking record of violence inflicted by the state on its own people… The report's authors, the Metropolitan Committee… on 5 November 1819 sent a deputation to Manchester which operated alongside the local committee to coordinate the best distribution of aid. In an era before the welfare state, this fund offered vital support, saving many of those hurt in the massacre and their families from complete destitution'.

Martin adds that in addition to this printed volume, the Library holds a manuscript relief book recognised by UNESCO as having world history significance. The Peterloo Relief Fund Account Book records the names of 350 people who received payments from the fund. As with the Metropolitan Committee Report it gives descriptions of their injuries and the circumstances in which they were hurt. While information is duplicated between the printed and manuscript volumes, they are tantalisingly different. Take, for example, Mary Fildes, a leading figure in the Manchester Female Reform Group. In the printed list she is described as: 'Beat about the head and face by Constables when escaping from the hustings'. The manuscript states that she 'was much beat by Constables & leaped off the Hustings when Mr Hunt was taken, was obliged to absent herself a fortnight to avoid imprisonment'. This would suggest that, while the respective relief committees shared information, they each made their own investigations into the injuries and personal circumstances of those injured at St Peter's Field.

Janette Martin concludes that
Two hundred years on, this slim pamphlet (and its chunkier manuscript companion) exposes the lies of Manchester magistrates and authorities who carefully downplayed the number of dead and injured and tried to pass off the event as a riot. Not only does it reinforce the scale of the massacre, the printed list of 'the Manchester Sufferers' humanises the story of Peterloo. It moves our thoughts away from numbers to actual people and, in doing so, gives voice to the victims.

Some extracts:

MARY FILDE CORNET STREET BESWICK: WAS MUCH BEAT BY CONSTABLES AND LEAPT OFF THE HUSTINGS...40/- (£91.60)

MARGARET BOOTH 126 ANCOATS LANE: MUCH TRAMPLED ON . 9 WEEKS CONFINED, BACK AND SIDES STILL SORE...20/- (£45.80)

SAMUEL ACKERLEY, 3 GRIGSON STREET DEANSGATE: A SABRE CUT ON HIS LEFT LEG, KNOCKED DOWN AND TEAMPLED ON ...11 YEARS OF AGE...20/-

JAMES BELL ANCOATS LANE: A WEAVER, CRUSHED AND THROWN DOWN, DISABLED A MONTH, HIS LOINS STILL PAINFUL...20/-

WILLIAM BARNES ANCOATS STREET: CRUSHED IN THE BREAST AND TRAMPLED BY THE CROWD, A VERY POOR AND WRETCHED OLD MAN OF 60...20/-

NANCY JACKSON: HER ELBOW BROKE, WAS TAKEN TO THE INFIRMARY, A WEAVER WITH FOUR CHILDREN, VERY POOR...20/-

EDWARD JOHNSON 67 HENRY STREET: TROD ON BY THE CAVALRY AND 2 RIBS FRACTURED, A WEAVER 50 YEARS OF AGE...20/-

RICH WILDE 9 COOP STREET, SWAN STREET: A BOY CUT ON THE BACK OF THE HEAD SEVERELY...20/-

JOHN RHODES 3 PITTS HOPWOOD: SABRE CUTS ON THE HEAD BY WHICH HE LOST MUCH BLOOD...A WOMAN SHAVED THE HAIR AND PUT ON A PLASTER... HE WAS DREADFULLY BRUISED INTERNALLY , SO THAT HE HAS NOT SINCE HELD UP HIS HEAD... AND DIED ABOUT THE 18TH NOVEMBER...TO HIS FSTHER 66/- (£151.14)

APPENDIX 2:
Shelley and the Masque of Anarchy

This famous poem written soon after the Peterloo atrocity has been called 'the first modern statement of the principle of nonviolent resistance'.

Stand ye calm and resolute,
Like a forest close and mute,
With folded arms and looks which are
Weapons of unvanquished war.

And if then the tyrants dare,
Let them ride among you there;
Slash, and stab, and maim and hew;
What they like, that let them do.

With folded arms and steady eyes,
And little fear, and less surprise,
Look upon them as they slay,
Till their rage has died away:

Then they will return with shame,
To the place from which they came,
And the blood thus shed will speak
In hot blushes on their cheek:

Rise, like lions after slumber
In unvanquishable number!
Shake your chains to earth like dew
Which in sleep had fallen on you:
Ye are many—they are few!

A version was adopted by Gandhi in his doctrine of Satyagraha. Gandhi, in pursuit of his own non-violent passive resistance was influenced and inspired by Shelley's nonviolence in protest and political action so much so that he would often quote *The Masque of Anarchy* to huge audiences during the campaign for an independent India.

Authors like Richard Holmes and Paul Foot consider it "the greatest political poem ever written in English".[1]

---

1. *Holmes, Richard (2003) Shelley: The Pursuit. New York Review of Books. p. 532. Foot, Paul (March–April 2006). "Shelley: Trumpet of Prophecy". International Socialist Review (46)*

Also available from the author

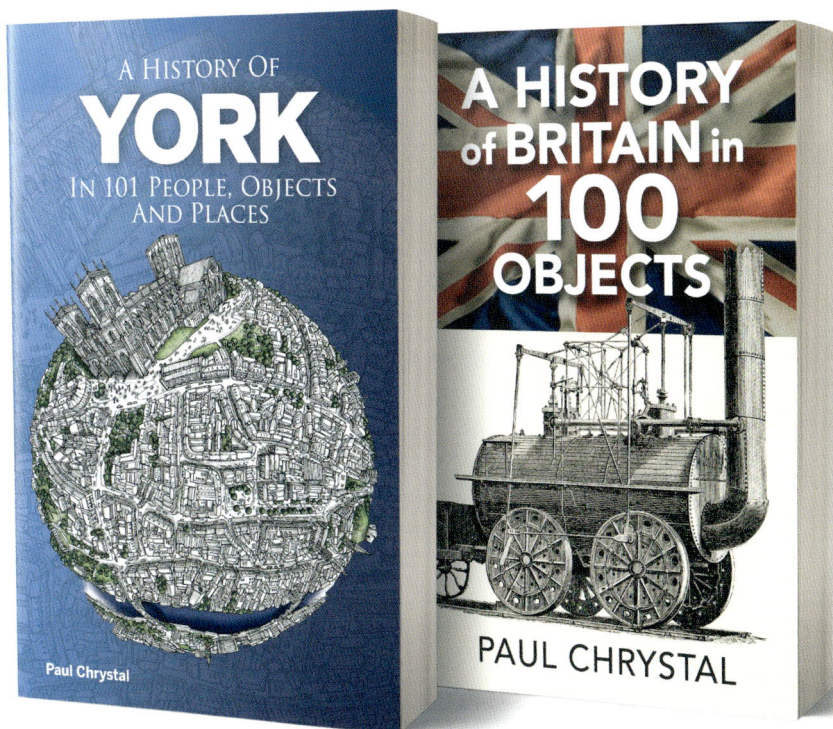

A History of York in 101 People, Objects & Places'

The History of Britain in 100 Objects